The Society for the Humanities

Cornell University

Studies in the Humanities
Edited by Max Black

IN SEARCH OF LITERARY THEORY

Studies in the Humanities

Edited by Max Black

The Morality of Scholarship
By Northrop Frye, Stuart Hampshire, and Conor Cruise O'Brien
Edited by Max Black

The Stubborn Structure: Essays on Criticism and Society
By Northrop Frye

*From the Many to the One: A Study of Personality and Views of
 Human Nature in the Context of Ancient Greek Society,
 Values, and Beliefs*
By A. W. H. Adkins

In Search of Literary Theory
By M. H. Abrams, E. D. Hirsch, Jr., Morton W. Bloomfield,
 Northrop Frye, Geoffrey Hartman, and Paul de Man
Edited by Morton W. Bloomfield

In Search of
Literary Theory

by M. H. ABRAMS
E. D. HIRSCH, JR.
MORTON W. BLOOMFIELD
NORTHROP FRYE
GEOFFREY HARTMAN
PAUL DE MAN

EDITED BY

Morton W. Bloomfield

Cornell University Press
Ithaca and London

International Standard Book Number 0-8014-0714-1
Library of Congress Catalog Card Number 70-38119

PRINTED IN THE UNITED STATES OF AMERICA

Librarians: Library of Congress cataloging information appears on the last page of the book.

Contents

Preface   vii
    by Morton W. Bloomfield

What's the Use of Theorizing about the Arts?   1
    by M. H. Abrams

Value and Knowledge in the Humanities   55
    by E. D. Hirsch, Jr.

The Two Cognitive Dimensions of the Humanities   73
    by Morton W. Bloomfield

The Critical Path: An Essay on the Social Context
    of Literary Criticism   91
    by Northrop Frye

Toward Literary History   195
    by Geoffrey Hartman

Literary History and Literary Modernity   237
    by Paul de Man

The Authors   269

Index   271

Preface

This book consists of a group of essays theorizing on the nature of literary study. The first essay deals with generalization in literary theory, the second with value in literary studies, the third with the dichotomy between "scientific" and "phenomenological" approaches to literature, the fourth with concern and involvement, and the last two with the historical approach as it relates to the study of literature. All the essays deal responsibly with issues basic to literary study, in a way that will provoke further discussion. Certainly much work remains before we can feel that we have a firm theoretical base for dealing with literature. It is hoped that this book will help to provide such a base.

The idea for the book originated in La Jolla, California, in the late fall of 1967, when Roy Harvey Pearce and I discussed the possibility of an issue of *Daedalus* devoted to the subject of theory in, and the various approaches to, the humanities. With the support of the Editor of *Daedalus*, Stephen Graubard, the American Academy of Arts and Sciences, and the Ford Foundation, Professor Pearce convened a conference in the spring of 1968 at La Jolla, under the auspices of the Uni-

versity of California at San Diego, to discuss the subject and
its many ramifications. Matters were pursued further at a
second conference, in September 1969, at the Villa Serbelloni,
Lake Como, Italy, which had generously been made available
by the Rockefeller Foundation. From the two conferences,
after exchanges of discussion and criticism, eleven papers were
prepared for publication in the Spring 1970 issue of *Daedalus*.
A twelfth essay, by M. H. Abrams, written in conjunction
with the conferences, was not ready in time to appear in the
spring. The obvious importance of the Abrams essay, when it
was completed, encouraged me to include it in the present
volume with five closely related essays from *Daedalus*—my
own and those by Paul de Man, Northrop Frye, Geoffrey
Hartman, and E. D. Hirsch, Jr. Readers concerned with questions relating to the theory and methods of literary studies
will now find the essays bearing on these matters gathered
together here, in compact and permanent form.

I wish to thank all those, especially the participants not
represented in this collection of essays, who helped to make
the book possible. Above all, I wish to thank Roy Harvey
Pearce, who, if not the "onlie begetter" of the volume, certainly was a major force in its creation.

MORTON W. BLOOMFIELD

Cambridge, Massachusetts

M. H. ABRAMS

What's the Use of Theorizing about the Arts?

T H E derogation or dismissal of theory in the criticism of art has a long history and has been manifested even by writers who have themselves engaged in both criticism and theory. In the last two or three decades, however, a number of philosophers have mounted an attack against critical theory, whether applied to a particular genre or to art in general, on grounds which, if they can survive scrutiny, are wholly devastating. For the claim is that, although the criticism of particular works of art is a valid activity, a valid critical or aesthetic theory is a logical impossibility.

These inquirers write in the philosophical climate of linguistic analysis which has been pervasive in England and America since the major writings of Bertrand Russell and G. E. Moore, and they deploy especially concepts derived from the later thought of Ludwig Wittgenstein, as represented in his *Philosophical Investigations* (1953). A number of earlier essays in this mode have been collected in *Aesthetics and Language*, edited by William Elton;[1] others have appeared at intervals in philosophic and aesthetic journals; but this ap-

---

[1] *Aesthetics and Language* (New York, 1954).

proach to the problems and procedures of critics and theorists of art has been most persistently sustained, and most fully developed, by Morris Weitz, first in a series of essays and then in a substantial book, *Hamlet and the Philosophy of Literary Criticism* (1964).

These philosophers treat criticism exclusively as a mode of language, and their analysis of criticism consists in identifying and describing the use of the distinctive terms, and in validating or invalidating the distinctive arguments, in critical discourse. In this aspect analytic metacriticism (the criticism of criticism) participates in the reigning intellectual tendency of our age, in and out of philosophy, to reduce all modes and subjects of inquiry to linguistic terms. The analytic approach to the language of criticism, however, takes its cues primarily from Wittgenstein's subtle exploration of his guiding concept that to determine the meaning of a word or expression we must look, not to the things it names or refers to, but to its use; naming is only one kind of use of some kinds of words in some contexts. The uses of a word or expression (or of the concept that it verbalizes) are the roles or functions that it performs or is capable of performing in actual utterances, and in performing these roles, it is governed by unstated rules that are observed by persons who know how to use the language. Discourse, then, is describable, metaphorically, as a diversity of language-games, and its rules of usage (though implicit and flexible) are comparable to the rules (though these are explicit and rigid) that govern the possible moves of a piece in a game of chess. The conventions that constitute the role or function of an expression in accordance with its implicit rules Wittgenstein calls its "grammar," or sometimes its "logical grammar," or "logical syntax." Unwittingly to violate the logical grammar of the way expressions function in everyday

4

language is to run the risk of philosophical muddle, paradox, and error.

Applying such insights to critical discourse about the arts, a number of philosophical analysts discriminate a variety of typical linguistic usages, each with its distinctive logical form. As Morris Weitz puts the enterprise, a problem of "the philosophy of art" is "the description of the actual functioning of the basic terms and kinds of argument of criticism"; in other words, "to get clear about the logic of critical talk about art."[2] All critics, and most philosophers, he claims, assume that the questions raised in criticism are of a single logical type, "namely, factual ones . . . to which true (or false) answers can be given," by reference to objectively existing facts in the work of art, or in the world. Weitz instead specifies four distinct procedures in critical discourse which, since they "function differently," "do different critical jobs," "play different roles," are logically "irreducible."[3] Three of these logical enterprises (description, explanation or interpretation, and evaluation) are legitimate, but a fourth (poetics or theory) is not. Though other analysts are not so systematic or detailed in their inventory, what they say indicates similar distinctions and paradigms of use, and a similar opposition between criticism and critical theory. Thus:

(1) Descriptions consist of true or false assertions about a work (for example, assertions about the words in the text, about the characters and their actions, or about the sequence of events in the plot), which are, in principle, verifiable by reference to "données," or "facts," about which there can

---

[2] "The Philosophy of Criticism," *Proceedings of the Third International Congress on Aesthetics*, Venice, Sept. 3–5, 1956.

[3] *Hamlet and the Philosophy of Literary Criticism* (Chicago and London, 1964), pp. ix–x, 213, 217, 285.

be no doubt or reasonable dispute. If assertions of this type remain doubtfully true or false, that is because, though they are verifiable in principle, the available evidence is inadequate to resolve the doubt.[4]

(2) Explanation and interpretation undertake to clarify a work by answering such questions as why a character acts as he does, what the proper meaning is of a passage or of the work as a whole, which of the elements in a work are central or primary, how the details of a work relate to each other. Interpretations cannot be proved to be true, but they can be "supported" by "reasons." C. L. Stevenson conceives an interpretation to be ultimately normative, or quasi-imperative, and claims that the reasons are not logically related to an interpretative judgment, but serve only to "guide" a critic's decision, as well as the decision of the reader to whom the critic addresses himself, by causal (that is, psychological) influence.[5] Morris Weitz, however, views interpretations as functioning "logically," in that they are explanatory "hypotheses" which can be "confirmed" by reasons that appeal to the factual elements, and the order of these elements, in the work that is being interpreted. As a hypothesis, however, an interpretation cannot be confirmed in the sense of being proved true, or uniquely correct, since counterhypotheses remain logically possible. An interpretation can only be confirmed by showing it to be "adequate," to the extent that it is clear, self-consistent, and serves to account for the data of a text without obvious omissions or distortions.[6]

(3) When a critic says that a work is good or bad, great or trivial, he does not assert or describe a property of the

[4] *Ibid.*, chap. 14.

[5] "Interpretation and Evaluation in Aesthetics," in Max Black, ed., *Philosophical Analysis* (Ithaca, N.Y., 1950), pp. 341–383.

[6] "The Philosophy of Criticism," pp. 207–216; *Hamlet*, chap. 15.

work; instead, he utters a judgment, or verdict, or assessment, which he supports by reasons, some of which are good reasons. Reasons for an evaluation involve criteria of value, or "criterion-characters," which are shown to be realized in the properties of the work of art.[7] Since the criteria of artistic merit depend on the kind of work being discussed, and also differ from age to age, from artistic school to school, and from critic to critic, disagreements about criteria (hence disagreements in evaluation) are perennial, and cannot be finally resolved. All a critic can do, when his criteria of value are challenged, is to justify them by further reasons which may win assent, but cannot be probative. Weitz, unlike other analysts, puts forward at this point the claim that some reasons for an evaluation are good reasons because they employ criteria of value—examples are "subtlety," "integration," and "freshness"—which are unchallengeable; that is, "the question, 'But what have these to do with . . . greatness?' cannot be intelligibly asked since no answer to it can be given."[8]

(4) Theory (or "poetics," "aesthetics") is a fourth, logically distinct linguistic activity which is engaged in by traditional philosophers and aestheticians, and also by practicing critics in a philosophical humor. Theory is defined as the attempt to answer, and to support the answers to, questions taking the form, "What is X?"—"What is tragedy?" "What is poetry?" "What is art?" But unlike the questions about particular works raised by practicing critics, these are bogus questions, and the answers to them are fallacies. Criticism (description, interpre-

---

[7] See, e.g., Helen Knight, "The Use of 'Good' in Aesthetic Judgments," in Elton, ed.; Paul Ziff, "Reasons in Art Criticism," in Joseph Margolis, ed., *Philosophy Looks at the Arts* (New York, 1962); Weitz, "Reasons in Criticism," *Journal of Aesthetics and Art Criticism*, 20 (1962), 429–437; Weitz, *Hamlet*, chap. 16.

[8] "Reasons in Criticism," pp. 436–437; *Hamlet*, pp. 276–284.

tation, evaluation) is a legitimate linguistic activity, but critical theorizing is not.

Analysts of critical discourse share Wittgenstein's distrust of what he calls "our craving for generality" which "is the resultant of a number of tendencies connected with particular philosophical confusions," and their critique of theory rests heavily upon his associated remarks about "family resemblances": Don't assume, for example, that the many proceedings we call "games" must have one thing in common, else they would not be called "games"; instead, *"look and see."* And when we look, we see nothing that is common to all things so called, but only "a complicated network of similarities overlapping and criss-crossing," like "the various resemblances between members of a family: build, features, colour of eyes. . . . And I shall say: 'games' form a family."[9]

This remarkably seminal analogy, which Wittgenstein used to show that we use some terms for things which share no single property, has been worked by some analytic philosophers into the view that a valid critical and aesthetic theory is a logical impossibility. Their claim is that such theory consists solely, or at least primarily, in the assertion and the systematic attempt to prove or support a true and essential definition of art, or of some type of art. "Traditional aesthetics," says William E. Kennick, "searches for the nature of Art or Beauty and finds it by definition," on the assumption that "all works of art must possess some common nature . . . a set of necessary and sufficient conditions for their being works of art at all."[10] The "main avowed concern" of aesthetic

[9] *The Blue and Brown Books* (New York, 1965), p. 17; *Philosophical Investigations,* trans. G. E. M. Anscombe (Oxford, 1953), secs. 65–67.

[10] "Does Traditional Aesthetics Rest on a Mistake?" *Mind,* 67 (1958), 318–319.

theory, according to Morris Weitz, is "the determination of the nature of art which can be formulated into a definition of it. It construes definition as the statement of the necessary and sufficient properties of what is being defined, where the statement purports to be a true or false claim about the essence of art." Similarly, the narrower theory called "poetics" consists of the attempt to answer a question about the nature of "one or other of the arts, or species of them" such as literature, painting, music, poetry, drama, or tragedy. "To each question, a poetics is a purportedly true answer in the form of a theory of the essential, defining, or necessary and sufficient, properties of the art in question."[11]

The characteristic procedure is then to show that this undertaking exemplifies the "essentialist fallacy," or the false assumption of "*unum nomen; unum nominatum*," hence "radically misconstrues the logic of the concept of art." For these general terms in fact have a great diversity of uses in ordinary and critical language, in which they are applied to works that possess no common property, but at most a varying pattern of family resemblances, among which none can qualify as a set of either necessary or sufficient conditions for the correct use of the term.[12] To this widespread argument Weitz adds another. Terms such as "art," "painting," "tragedy" are "open concepts," in that historical usage has assigned to them the task

[11] "The Role of Theory in Aesthetics," *Journal of Aesthetics and Art Criticism*, 15 (1956), 27; *Hamlet*, p. 286.

[12] See, e.g., in addition to Weitz and Kennick: John Wisdom, "Things and Persons," in *Philosophy and Psycho-analysis* (New York, 1969), pp. 222–226; W. B. Gallie, "The Function of Philosophical Aesthetics," in Elton, ed.; Paul Ziff, "The Task of Defining a Work of Art," *Philosophical Review*, 62 (1953), 57–78; Teddy Brunius, "The Uses of Works of Art," *Journal of Aesthetics and Art Criticism*, 22 (1963), 123–133; Marshall Cohen, "Aesthetic Essence," in Max Black, ed., *Philosophy in America* (Ithaca, N.Y., 1965).

of allowing for application to new and unforeseen cases. Thus "the very expansive, adventurous character of art, its ever-present changes and novel creations, makes it logically impossible to ensure any set of defining properties," for to close the open concept by specifying the necessary and sufficient conditions for its application "is to foreclose upon the use of the concept which is, at least in part, to accommodate itself to these new conditions."[13]

The conclusion is that aesthetic and poetic theory, as Kennick says, "rests on a mistake"; or as Weitz puts it, "aesthetic theory—all of it—is wrong in principle," "logically misbegotten," "logically impossible"; similarly, "poetics, unlike description, explanation, and evaluation, is an illegitimate procedure of criticism in that it tries to define what is indefinable."[14] Oddly, however, such apparently disabling pronouncements are often conjoined, in aesthetic analysts, with the acknowledgment that aesthetic theory has made valuable contributions—Weitz says "supremely valuable" contributions —to our understanding of particular works of art. For, mistakenly thinking that he is defining artistic essence, the theorist has inadvertently accomplished something else that is useful. Weitz explains this anomaly by adapting Charles Stevenson's concept of "persuasive definitions." "Every theory of art, like every poetics, is neither true nor false, but an honorific redefinition of 'art.'" For the terms "art," "poetry," "tragedy" in critical discourse convey an element of praise, and what are presented as definitions of the necessary and sufficient conditions for the use of such terms in fact function as a disguised, and thereby all the more effective, way of

[13] "The Role of Theory," pp. 31–33; *Hamlet*, pp. 307–308. Compare Ziff, "The Task of Defining a Work of Art," pp. 67–71, and Brunius, p. 125.

[14] "The Role of Theory," pp. 27–28; *Hamlet*, p. 311.

recommending these conditions as criteria of excellence in particular works of art, and thus serve to direct our attention to features of a work that may hitherto have been overlooked or distorted. Aesthetic theory, as definition, is "logically doomed to failure," but if looked upon as the use of "the definitional form, almost epigrammatically, to pin-point a crucial recommendation" to concentrate "on certain criteria of excellence," it serves to teach us "what to look for and how to look at it in art." Or as Kennick puts a similar point of view: "The mistake of the aestheticians can be turned to advantage." "The quest for essences" has "a by-product," in which the definition performs real work—not, however, "the work which the philosophers assign it, but a work of teaching people a new way of looking at pictures."[15]

I. Some Uses of Definitions in Theory

Even a stripped-down précis indicates the capacities of this metacriticism, and its great advantages over its immediate predecessor in analytic philosophy. Logical positivism had tended to apportion all uses of language into one of two categories: verifiable or falsifiable empirical assertions (systematized according to the rules of logic) and nonverifiable expressions, scientific language and emotive language, knowledge and pseudo knowledge, sense and nonsense. One great advance of this current analysis is that it recognizes a variety of linguistic procedures in criticism, in addition to verifiable descriptions of fact, which, while not demonstrably and ex-

[15] Weitz, "The Role of Theory," pp. 34–35; Weitz, *Hamlet*, pp. 309, 314–315; Kennick, pp. 323–325. See also Wisdom's brief but influential statement, *Philosophy and Psycho-analysis*, p. 225. On "persuasive definitions," see C. L. Stevenson, "Persuasive Definitions," in *Facts and Values* (New Haven and London, 1963), and "On 'What Is a Poem?'" *Philosophical Review*, 66 (1957).

clusively true, are nonetheless in their diverse ways rational, valid, and profitable human pursuits.

Still, some aspects and results of this procedure seem on the face of it questionable, and especially the easy way in which it disposes of all critical theory. The claim is that, for more than two thousand years, beginning with Aristotle, some of the most acute minds on record, in theorizing about the arts, have committed the same grammatico-logical blunders in stubborn pursuit of the same logically impossible goal—*enfin Wittgenstein vint*. The further claim is that the admittedly valuable consequences of critical theory are an unintended by-product, a spin-off from an inevitably abortive undertaking. Now, there is nothing inherently impossible in these assertions, and the advances in some areas of knowledge provide examples of long-standing errors that seem in some ways comparable. Nonetheless, before we accept this paradox of private errors–public benefits, it seems prudent to inquire whether the fault may lie, in at least some instances, not in the critical theories that are analyzed but in the analysis itself.

I should like to pursue such an inquiry, and to do so in accordance with what seem to me to be some important implications of Wittgenstein's own procedures in elucidating the uses of language. Wittgenstein's later writings are often cryptic, and like the insights of all philosophers of genius, they may be applied in opposite ways, one inhibiting and the other liberating. One of Wittgenstein's liberating insights is that the validity of language consists in the way it is in fact used to some purpose, rather than in its accordance with logical models of how it should be used; and another is his view that meanings do not consist in what expressions name and describe but in how they are used. The uses of language, he points out, are very many, and operate consonantly to a great diversity of implicit rules or conventions; to discover the actual use of language, we must be careful not to stop at the isolated expression or sentence, and not to insist that each stage of a discourse must be a picture corresponding to the facts. Instead, we must look to the "surroundings" of each expression, and these surroundings involve not only the immediate verbal context, and not simply a consideration of that particular one of many possible language-games the speaker or writer is playing. Also (and ultimately) we must look to the "form of life" of which each language-game is inherently a part—including the kind of human purposes, interests, and values that a particular language-game has evolved to realize. This is the liberating aspect of Wittgenstein's thought because it affirms that the role of philosophy is not to proscribe or limit, but to clarify and authenticate the powers that language, in its long development as part of man's "natural history," has shown that it in fact possesses in effecting man's needs.[16]

What, in fact, have critical and aesthetic theorists been up to? In answering this question, it behooves us to follow Wittgenstein's excellent advice: Don't say they *must* have done one thing or another, but *"look and see.* . . . Don't think, but look!"[17] It soon appears, however, that what we find when we look depends upon what theorist we look at, where in his writings we look, and with what expectations, categories, and aims.

The analysts I have been discussing cite, with striking unanimity, Clive Bell's theory as representative of aesthetic theory in general. If we look at Bell's influential little book we find that he sets out, as the title informs us, to answer the question *What Is Art?* He says that his answer will be an attempt at "a complete theory of visual art," and assumes that

[16] E.g., *Philosophical Investigations*, secs. 19–27, and pp. 223e–226e.
[17] *Philosophical Investigations*, sec. 66.

"either all works of visual art have some common quality, or when we speak of 'works of art' we gibber." He claims that to the question, what quality is common to all works of visual art? "only one answer seems possible—significant form," hence that although "the representative element in a work of art may not be harmful, always it is irrelevant." He then applies this discovery to the discussion both of postimpressionist and of earlier examples of visual art.[18] It does not seem unduly omissive nor distortive to say about Bell's theory, as the analysts do, that it consists of the proposal, elucidation, and attempted proof of a definition of visual art that purports to specify the necessary and sufficient conditions for the correct use of the term, that this attempt failed, but that in its failure it achieved something of great value to our appreciation of the arts. It achieved this end because, at a time (1914) when Edwardian amateurs were preoccupied with the representational elements of painting, Bell's theory taught them—by its actual function as persuasive rhetoric under the logical disguise of essential definition—how to look at the new nonrepresentational painting, and also how to discriminate and enjoy features in earlier representational painting that connoisseurs had hitherto minimized or overlooked.

But is Bell's little book in fact paradigmatic? Do all theories of art consist solely or primarily of the attempt to posit and prove an essential definition of art, or of a type of art? And does the validity of the over-all theoretical enterprise depend on the logical possibility of an essential definition of these general terms?

In this respect it is instructive to note that the philosophical critics of critical theory, although united in their rejection of the validity of general statements about what art is, do not

[18] *What Is Art?* (London, 1928), pp. v, 7–8, 25, and *passim.*

themselves hesitate to make unqualified assertions about "art," "painting," "criticism," "aesthetics," "aesthetic theory." And sometimes they use these general terms as the subjects of sentences that look very much like definitions.

Take for example the major book of Morris Weitz, the most thorough, and in many ways the most illuminating, of the metacritical analysts. His *Hamlet and the Philosophy of Literary Criticism* begins with the following paragraph:

Criticism is a form of studied discourse about works of art. It is a use of language primarily designed to facilitate and enrich the understanding of art. Involved in its practice are highly developed sets of vocabularies, various sorts of procedures and arguments, broad assumptions, and a vast diversity of specific goals and purposes.

This is surely a statement that, in logical as well as ordinary grammatical discourse, we would call a "definition of criticism." Its first sentence has the "X is a b c" form, in which "X" is the term to be defined and "a b c" specifies the meaning of X in the classical manner, *per genus et differentiam,* employing terms which the succeeding sentences go on to specify and expand. Weitz also asserts later that "the question, What is criticism?" is "the major concern of this book" (p. 133); so that one has grounds to claim, if one is inclined to be contentious, that Weitz's book, no less than Bell's, is a theory, in that the whole is designed to pose, elucidate, and prove a definition of the general term that names his subject, with the difference that the subject of Bell's theory is "art" and the subject of Weitz's is "criticism."

But is the "logical function" of Weitz's *definiens* to specify the essential, or the necessary and sufficient, conditions for the use of the word "criticism"? Weitz himself claims that it is not, for on the page following this definition he rejects "the persistent logical motivation of traditional philosophy of

15

criticism that a definitive and univocal answer is forthcoming to the question, What is criticism?" But such evidence for the function of his own definition is immediately undermined by his salutary advice, in the next sentence, that "we actually 'look and see' (to borrow a phrase from Wittgenstein), i.e., [that] we examine what critics do in their essays of criticism instead of what they *say* they do" (p. viii).

If what Weitz says that he is doing isn't adequate evidence, then how are we to find out what is the actual role (hence, "logic") of his opening definition? No amount of looking at the isolated definition—considered as a fixed and self-identifying logical form, outside its verbal surroundings—will serve to settle the matter. The role of this definition can only be determined by examining what it in fact does when it is put to work in the rest of the book. Only after we have done this are we able to say with assurance that Weitz's initial statement does not function as an essential definition—that is, as a closed concept of "criticism" whose claim at complete generality is made plausible only by ignoring or steam-rollering over counterevidence. Instead we find that it is used, not as a ruling definition, but as a working definition: it serves, in a preliminary way, to block out the area of his inquiry, and also to introduce some categories that he will use to organize his inquiry into that area. For example, by delimiting his use of "criticism" to "studied discourse," Weitz rules out of his cognizance the use of "criticism" for what Anatole France called the narration of "the adventures of [the critic's] soul among masterpieces," and by delimiting it to discourse about "works of art," he rules out a large part of the area covered by the term in such a standard work as Matthew Arnold's "The Function of Criticism at the Present Time." Furthermore, by predicating that criticism is "a use of language" involving a variety of "procedures and arguments" adapted to "a vast diversity of specific goals," Weitz posits the main exploratory categories—as against the many alternative categories used by other metacritics—which are characteristic of the current philosophy of linguistic analysis, and which in his book demonstrate their usefulness by producing the profitable, if not entirely satisfactory, discoveries that I have already outlined.

In short, Weitz does what any inquirer must do, whatever his subject, and however he eschews *a priorism* and the craving for generalization: he indicates what he proposes to talk about, and how and to what end he undertakes to talk about it. And the more diverse the family of objects to which a general term is applied in common discourse, the more important it becomes, if we are to talk to some effect, that we specify and limit our own use of the term. For this purpose a formal definition is not indispensable (some inquirers, including a number of philosophical analysts, prefer to leave the what and how of their inquiry to be inferred from their practical and piecemeal operations), but it is certainly a very handy, economical, and widely used linguistic device, whether it is presented, as Weitz and most other writers present it, at or near the beginning of their work, or whether it is allowed to emerge by a seeming induction in the middle, or even at the end.

The question, then, is not whether critical theorists define art, or even whether they claim the definition to be an essential one, but whether all of them in fact use the definition in the way that Weitz and other philosophical analysts say they do, rather than in the way that Weitz uses his definition of criticism. The only way to find out is to look and see, and then only on condition that we adopt an inquiring rather than a contentious posture and set ourselves to see what is going on, rather than what we are certain in advance must be going on, and only if we avoid the analysts' mistake of stopping too soon at the isolated definition, instead of observing how it functions in its total surroundings. We are also more apt to be enlightened if, instead of looking at the theory of a polemicist like Clive Bell (who was the effective champion of an important revolution in taste, but a bit short on philosophical acumen), we look at the work of nonprogrammatic theorists who, by wide consent, have made the most important contributions to our knowledge. A good example of this sort is the writer whose treatise made "poetics" a standard term for the theory of an art.

Aristotle's *De Poetica,* after a brief announcement of its main topics, begins:

Epic poetry and tragedy, as also Comedy, Dithyrambic poetry, and most flute-playing and lyre-playing, are all, viewed as a whole, modes of imitation. But at the same time they differ from one another in three ways, either by a difference of kind in their means, or by differences in the objects, or in the manner of their imitations.

In his *Topics,* I. 5, Aristotle declared that "a 'definition' is a phrase signifying a thing's essence." Now let us assume, although he doesn't say so, that he offers the sentences I have quoted from the *Poetics* as a definition of the essence of the arts (including, as he soon makes clear, painting and dancing, as well as poetry and music), and let us assume also that he would consent to the maneuver whereby philosophical analysts equate an essential definition with a statement of necessary and sufficient conditions. Still, what matters is the actual role that his definition plays in his over-all inquiry, and this role, it soon becomes evident, is not legislative but exploratory, and in a very enlightening way.

Take the key predicate, "imitation." Aristotle adopted the word "*mimesis*" from ordinary language, but instead of feel-

ing committed to its ordinary usages, he specialized it to suit
the purposes of his inquiry—no less legitimately than physicists
in later centuries specialized the ordinary meanings of words
like "mass," "acceleration," "energy" for their own, very
different purposes. Plato, for example, had employed "*mimesis*" to include the work of the artisan, the statesman, and the
moralist, as well as the poet and artist. That usage suited the
purpose of his inquiry, in which the prime issue, as he says
in his discussion of poetry in the *Republic,* is "whether a man
is to be good or bad"; and the basic terms of his theory are
devised to make it impossible to consider poetry otherwise
than in rivalry with all other human products and institutions, although at a farther remove from the ultimate criterion
of all reality and value, the realm of Ideas. Thus as Plato's
lawmaker, in politely rejecting poets from his state, explains:
"Our whole state is an imitation of the best and noblest
life. . . . You are poets and we are poets . . . rivals and
antagonists in the noblest of dramas."[19] Aristotle, as the course
of the *Poetics* makes clear, establishes for "*mimesis*" a very
different role, as a term specific to both rudimentary and
developed forms of poetry and the arts, as distinct from all
other human activities and products, and he thereby sets up
a new language-game. For this game, by severing poetry from
rivalry with other human pursuits, makes it possible to consider poetry as poetry and not another thing, according to its
distinctive criteria and artistic reasons for being.

By employing his supplementary distinctions between the
objects of human experience that are imitated, the artistic
medium of the imitation, and the manner (such as narrative or
dramatic) in which the imitation is rendered, Aristotle is also

---

[19] *Laws* vii. 817.

able to differentiate poetry from the other arts, and then to establish classes of poems, such as epic, comedy, and tragedy, each with its distinctive features and appropriate criteria. Focusing his attention on tragedy, he defines this genre in its turn as an imitation of an action that is serious and complete, in appropriate language and in the dramatic manner, then adds an identification of its distinctive emotional power: "arousing pity and fear, wherewith to accomplish its catharsis of such emotions." Applying the total theoretical tools now available, Aristotle goes on to discriminate within a tragedy such elements as plot, characters, diction, thought, and to consider both the relative importance and the interrelations of these elements. He then analyzes the features and construction of each element, from the point of view of what best serves the artistic purpose of tragedy by maximizing the distinctively "tragic pleasure," or "tragic fear and pity." Hence, for example, his criteria for the most effective tragic plots: the need for a unified plot, representing a single action that constitutes a complete whole; the need to reshape any materials provided by history into a plot by substituting artistic determinants for historical contingency; the effectiveness of the use of peripety and discovery to mark the shift from complication to denouement, in the turning point at which the hero of the tragedy, greater and nobler than the normal person, through his tragic error falls from happiness to misery; and so on, through all the diverse observations of this terse and original little treatise.

Some observations are in order about what Aristotle does, as against what a number of analysts assume that, as a critical theorist, he must be doing:

(1) The whole of the *Poetics*, according to the criteria of the analysts, counts as theory and not as applied criticism, for its basic statements are all generalizations about the arts, or

about a class of art such as poetry, or about a species of poetry such as tragedy and its typical elements, organization, and effects; Aristotle refers to particular works only to exemplify or clarify such general statements. Of this theory, however, definitions certainly do not constitute a major part, but are used only briefly and passingly, as a way of introducing one or another area of investigation. And the body of the theory does not consist of an attempt—whether vain or successful—to support and "prove" the definition. It consists instead of putting to work the terms, distinctions, and categories proposed in the initial definition (which are supplemented, in a way consistent with this definition, as the need arises) in the analysis of the distinctive elements, organization, and characteristic powers of various kinds of poetic art.

(2) This theory makes a valid contribution to knowledge. It provides, among other things, knowledge how to experience and enjoy works of art—not only tragedies as a class but also a particular tragedy—by providing terms and analytic devices which enable us to experience them in a discriminating rather than a crude way, by directing our attention to their important features and the ways these features are ordered according to distinctively artistic reasons for order. This contribution to our ability to see works of art with new eyes is not an inadvertent by-product of Aristotle's attempt at a logical impossibility; it is the result of his deliberate undertaking, as he asserts in his opening statement, "to speak not only of the art [of poetry] in general but also of its species and their respective capacities; of the structure of plot required for a good poem; of the number and nature of the constituent parts of a poem; and likewise of any other matters in the same line of inquiry." The degree to which we are indebted to Aristotle's theory for concepts that make possible a discriminating and organized appreciation of literary art is obscured by the

extent to which his terms and distinctions long ago became the common vocabulary of discourse about works of narrative and dramatic literature.

This is the primary service of a good critical theory, for in bringing us, with new insights and powers of discrimination, to individual works of art in their immediacy, it enhances our appreciation of the only places where artistic values are in fact realized. But as inquisitive men we are interested not only in knowing *how* to enhance our direct experience of these values, but also in knowing *about* the works in which such values have their residence, including their relations to each other and to other human pursuits. In a number of brief but pregnant passages Aristotle also contributes to our knowledge about art as it is diversely related to, yet distinguishable from, other human activities and achievements such as history, philosophy, and politics—and here, too, in a systematic and coherent way that follows from the extended application of his initial definition and analytic categories.

(3) Although Aristotle's theory is grounded, inescapably, on the Greek dramas then available to his inquiry, there is nothing in the logical nature of the theory itself to make it function as a closed definition that forecloses the possibility of encompassing dramatic creativity and novelty. It is true that a number of later critics, especially in the Renaissance, used the *Poetics* as though it were a legislative and regulative rather than an open and empirical theory, with the result that they condemned innovative forms of serious drama, or else distorted their features by describing them in forced accordance with Aristotle's commentary. But, if employed in his own spirit of inquiry, Aristotle's method and distinctions enable us to recognize, and to specify the novel characteristics of, non-Aristotelian forms of tragic drama and tragic plots. For example, Shakespeare's *Macbeth* and Arthur Miller's

Death of a Salesman, different as they are from Sophocles' *Oedipus* and from each other, both "imitate" actions that have seriousness, dimension, integrity, and end in a catastrophe for the protagonist, so that we may, with good reason, decide to extend to these plays the term "tragedy." But the very distinctions introduced in the *Poetics* enable us to identify those important differences in the protagonists, plot, language, and effects that distinguish these tragedies from Aristotelian tragedy and from each other as well. Furthermore, Aristotle's general method for differentiating literary types and for establishing their distinctive criteria by the systematic investigation of their multiple "causes" (in other words, of their diverse artistic reasons) is itself an open method, which can be adapted to the analysis of any literary form, including those, such as the novel or cinema, which were not invented until long after the *Poetics* had been written.[20]

II. The Uses of Diversity

We are faced with the fact, however, that Aristotle is only one of many theorists, and that in the predicates of their definitions of art other theorists replace Aristotle's operative term, "imitation," by terms and expressions with patently different meanings: a work of art is a means to the end of teaching, or pleasing, or both; or an expression of feelings; or a product of the creative imagination; or a distinctive form of communication; or a world of its own autonomous kind; or a variant form of an archetypal myth; and so on. Philosophical analysts have used such discrepant assertions to add plausibility to their claim that an essential definition of a work of

[20] Recent and impressive examples of the expansion of the method and distinctions of Aristotle's *Poetics* to a variety of literary forms is the collection of essays in R. S. Crane, ed., *Critics and Criticism* (Chicago, 1952).

art is logically impossible; for if it were possible, how do we explain that no one has yet located a common feature of objects denoted by the general term "art" that will satisfy more than a fraction of people who profess to be experts on the subject?

Some theorists, like Clive Bell, have indeed claimed to have discovered the essence of art, and many more have felt that, in order to justify their own definitions, they had to attack the definitions of other theorists. Yet upon investigation we find that all those who, in the course of time, emerge with the reputation of major theorists of art have in fact contributed important new knowledge—both knowledge how to look at and appreciate art, and knowledge about art in its diverse circumstances and relations—and they have succeeded in doing so not despite their basic discrepancies, but as a direct result of these discrepancies.

The actual use of an expression can only be determined (in Wittgenstein's term) within its surroundings. If now we enlarge our view from the surroundings of a definition within a particular theory to its surroundings in all the other definitions that it was intended to counter or qualify or supplant, I think we can make out a use, and accordingly, a "logical character," both of a definition and of the total theory within which the definition occurs, that we have hitherto overlooked; for this is a use that is relative to alternative manners of proceeding. It now appears that to propose a definition of art, or of a form of art, though it is couched in a grammatical form indistinguishable from that of a universal assertion, is much like taking a stand. The theorist takes his stand on that one of many possible vantage points that will provide what strikes him as the most revealing perspective on the area of his interest. Or to use a different visual analogy adopted from Coleridge (who was critic, theorist, and metacritic, and especially interested in the role of alternative theories in observation), the use of a critical theory is not to reflect the given artistic facts, but to serve as a "speculative instrument" that will arm one's critical vision. As Coleridge put it, observation is to meditation (by which he means theory) only "as eyes, for which [meditation] has pre-determined their field of vision, and to which, as to *its* organ, it communicates a microscopic power." And again: "The razor's edge becomes a saw to the armed vision."[21] Whatever analogue we adopt needs to bring out the fact that critical definitions and theories may be discrepant without conflict, and mutually supplementary instead of mutually exclusive, since each delimits and structures its field in its own way. The test of the validity of a theory is what it proves capable of doing when it is put to work. And each good (that is, serviceable) theory, as the history of critical theory amply demonstrates, is capable of providing insights into hitherto overlooked or neglected features and structural relations of works of art, of grouping works of art in new and interesting ways, and also of revealing new distinctions and relations between things that (from its special point of view) are art and things that are not art. One way to estimate their diverse contributions is to imagine the impoverishment to criticism if we did not possess the theoretical writings of, say, Aristotle, Horace, Longinus, Kant, Coleridge, Eliot—or Clive Bell. No theory is adequate to tell the whole story, for each one has limits correlative with its powers. As a speculative instrument, it has its particular angle and focus of vision, and what for one speculative instrument is an indistinct or blank area requires an alternative speculative instrument if it is to be brought into sharp focus for inspection.

[21] *Biographia Literaria*, ed. John Shawcross (2 vols.; Oxford, 1907), II, 64; I, 81.

Better to bring out one other point, let me return from optical metaphors to Wittgenstein's favorite analogue of a game. Each critical theorist, it can be said, pursuing his particular interests and purposes, selects and specializes his operative and categorical terms, and in consequence sets up a distinctive language-game whose playing field overlaps but doesn't coincide with that of other critical language-games and which is played according to grammatico-logical rules in some degree special to itself. The aims, fields, and rules of various critical language-games are sufficiently similar, however, so that some of their assertions are conflicting rather than alternative; but to determine which assertions these are, and how to decide the conflict between them, is a difficult exercise in the comparative grammar of language-games.

To lend plausibility to these sweeping claims beyond that provided by the prior experience of each reader, I have space for only a single example; so I shall choose Coleridge, both because his critical theory is as different as it could be from that of Aristotle, and also because it represents a type that is treated with particular severity by philosophical analysts. As Morris Weitz remarks:

Throughout [Coleridge's] writings there is a steady concern for philosophy, for essences, and fundamental principles, and a pervasive conviction that philosophy, psychology, art, and criticism are interrelated. Indeed, Coleridge's most ostensible characteristic, even as a practicing critic, is this recurrent reference to fundamental principles. . . .

It would be a fascinating task, even if devastating to Coleridge, I believe, to subject his doctrines to a more adequate philosophical scrutiny than he would have tolerated.[22]

Coleridge as critic dismays the analyst not simply because he is an inveterate theorist, but because his type of theory

[22] *Hamlet*, p. 166.

violates so many current caveats. Under the compulsion to be inclusive and coherent in his thinking, Coleridge derives his generalizations about art from metaphysical generalizations about the total universe. He insists that the only criticism that is "fair and philosophical" is one based on "principles, which [the critic] holds for the foundation of poetry in general," and he chooses to base his own criticism on "the component faculties of the human mind itself, and their comparative dignity and importance." As a consequence his operative terms and categories are hopelessly "mentalistic," and also are deliberately contrived to conflate description and evaluation, for "according to the faculty . . . from which the pleasure given by any poem or passage was derived, I estimated [its] merit."[23] Unembarrassedly setting himself the question, "What is poetry?" Coleridge proceeds to answer it in terms of the nature of the "poetic genius itself," which involves above all the activity of "that synthetic and magical power, to which we have exclusively appropriated the name of imagination," and which "reveals itself in the balance or reconciliation of opposite or discordant qualities."[24] And he defines the imagination, in turn, as a creative power which operates as an organic process to effect an organic product. The resulting theory would seem to be a hopeless tangle of categorical confusions. On the one hand, Coleridge finds imagination manifested not only in poetry, but also in many nonartistic human processes and products. And on the other hand, he represents imaginative creativity as analogous to all modes of creativity—that is, to all processes of the bringing-into-being of anything really new, including the universe itself; and he often describes such creative process and its products in organic terms—that is, in terms that are literal for

[23] *Biographia Literaria*, II, 85; I, 14.
[24] *Ibid.*, II, 12.

a growing plant, but metaphorical for artistic invention and a work of art. For example: "Could a rule be given from *without*, poetry would cease to be poetry, and sink into mechanical art. . . . The *rules* of IMAGINATION are themselves the very powers of growth and production." As opposed to "mechanic" form, "organic form," such as we find manifested in Shakespeare's plays, "is innate; it shapes as it develops itself from within, and the fullness of its development is one and the same with the perfection of its outer form."[25]

Weitz, citing this and other passages, remarks in understatement that Coleridge's doctrine of poetic drama "implies a metaphysical theory about nature that is certainly disputable." Oddly, however, although he finds Coleridge's critical principles untenable and his arguments "inconsistent," Weitz gives Coleridge's applied criticism the very highest marks. His criticism "is magnificent in its fullness and concreteness," his apologia for Shakespeare "stands in evaluative criticism as a model," and his analysis of the opening scene in *Hamlet* is "one of the great examples of descriptive criticism anywhere," "a marvel of pointed reading such that one can never read or see that first scene except through his eyes."[26]

Are we to take it, then, that Coleridge's criticism is a happy escape from his unfortunate metaphysical theory, or achieved in spite of it? If we look and see, all the indications are otherwise. The major insights of Coleridge's critical analyses, interpretations, and evaluations, including the passages on Shakespeare that Weitz most praises, are integral with his metaphysical and critical theory, in that they put to work the terms and categories developed within the theory. For example, Coleridge declared that in Shakespeare we find "*growth*

[25] *Ibid.*, II, 65; *Coleridge's Shakespearean Criticism*, ed. T. M. Raysor (2 vols.; Cambridge, Mass., 1930), I, 224.
[26] Weitz, *Hamlet*, pp. 174, 187, 233.

as in a plant. No ready cut and dried [structure]." "All is growth, evolution, *genesis*—each line, each work almost, begets the following."[27] The reigning neoclassic theory had viewed art as artisanry: the artist selects parts and puts them together according to the rules of "decorum," or fittingness, to achieve a preconceived design and appropriate effects. A cardinal aspect both of Coleridge's metaphysics and his aesthetic theory was the replacement of the model of the artisan by that of the genesis and growth of a plant, and such resulting critical concepts as generation from a seed-idea or element, evolution according to inherent principles or "laws," and the assimilation of disparates into an organic unity in which the elements alter their identities as parts in an organized whole, are what enabled him to discriminate features and relations of literary works which had been inconceivable to earlier critics, in the literal sense that they lacked the general concepts through which to see them.

If we accept the view that the meaning and justification of a way of speaking is the purpose it serves in its surroundings, we ought also to accept the difficult conclusion that once a concept or assertion is adopted as the basis of a critical theory, its origin and truth-claim, whether empirical or metaphysical, cease to matter, for its validity in this context is to be determined by its power of illumination when brought to bear in the scrutiny of works of art. An organic theory of art served Coleridge as a primary, although not exclusive, speculative instrument, and the value of the discoveries it made possible is attested not only by the virtues of his own criticism, but also by the extent to which the use of organic language in applied criticism has, in various ways, been adopted by other critics ever since it was established and developed in the

[27] *Coleridge's Shakespearean Criticism*, I, 233; *Coleridge's Miscellaneous Criticism*, ed. T. M. Raysor (Cambridge, Mass., 1936), p. 89.

theories of Coleridge and his German contemporaries. But of course it is difficult to measure the contribution of innovative terms whose very success has brought them into the public domain of aesthetic discourse.

III. Logical Grammar and Fluid Critical Discourse

I want to return briefly to the procedure of Weitz and other philosophical analysts of distinguishing the procedures of critics into diverse logical types, because it seems to me that the way they apply these distinctions has concealed the pervasive and varied role of theory in applied criticism. The formulation of logical models is validly based on inherent demands or necessities in the ways we use critical concepts and support critical judgments—necessities which we all sense, but which traditional logic leaves largely out of account—and such paradigms can be used to clarify the implicit structure of aesthetic reasoning. We want to be sure, however, that they are applied only in a way that is appropriate to the language-game as it is in fact played. The models, for example, are fixed, delimited in their sphere of operation, and explicit in their rules. But when we look at the actual goings-on in this or that critical essay, we find everything quite otherwise: the discourse is fluid, the concepts and associated modes of reasoning are complex and mixed, and the inherent demands, or "rules," of usage are implicit, variable, tenuous, and elusive. Only in his own paradigms of artifice are Weitz's four modes of critical usage, as he claims, "irreducible." In the fluid movement of a sustained critical discourse they are indistinct, interinvolved, and in a quasi-systematic fashion, interdependent. Wittgenstein asks us "to compare the multiplicity of the tools in language and of the ways they are used . . . with what logicians have said about the structure of language. (Including the author of the *Tractatus Logico-Philosophicus.*)"[28] In applying Wittgenstein's own comments on logical grammar in order to enlarge the number of logical formulas, we must beware the risk of distorting and hampering the flow of profitable discourse by a reductive logical "calculus" which is merely a different form of the calculus that Wittgenstein had undertaken to develop in his *Tractatus,* and against which his later philosophy is a sustained warning, through the presentation of counterexamples.

Take, as an instance, the logical form that Weitz in his analysis of *Hamlet* criticism calls "description," which he identifies as true-or-false assertions of "data or *données* that cannot be denied." The critical questions capable of answers that approximate this ideal are very limited; for example: How many words are there in a particular speech, or in the whole play? Which speeches are in verse and which in prose? Does Hamlet in his soliloquy utter the speech-sounds "too, too solid flesh" or "too, too sullied flesh"? But when we move from words to the meanings of a speech or passage, we are in another realm, for meanings need to be construed, and whatever is construed in a work of literature tends to depart from the logical paradigm. Weitz lists as examples the questions, is Hamlet "athletic, fearless, vulnerable, dilatory, adoring of his father . . . mad . . . ambitious . . . melancholic"? Questions of this order do not meet Weitz's own criteria of being capable of answers that are "true or false, verifiable and logically independent of explanation and evaluation."[29] For the answers require interpretation, and in accordance not only with linguistic but also with *artistic* criteria, in that the interpretation of Hamlet's character is inter-involved with the interpretation of the play in which he plays a central role.

[28] *Philosophical Investigations*, sec. 23.
[29] *Hamlet*, pp. 230, 238–239, 244.

Such answers are, therefore, rationally contestable and have in fact been persistently contested.

And what critical utterances fit the logical paradigm by which "interpretations," in their turn, are strictly divided from "evaluations"? Among Weitz's examples of pure interpretation we find the statements that a work is "poignant," "vivacious," "serene," "profound."[30] That such predications involve—give us to know—not only how a critic sees or interprets features of a work, but also that he sees these features as invested with value, becomes clear if we imagine what it would be like if a critic, after asserting that a work is serene and profound, should go on to the verdict that it is valueless, or a bad work of art. Such a sequence would not constitute a logical fallacy, but it would be a linguistic surprise, because the implicit rules for the ordinary critical use of such terms lead us to assume the critic's approval and esteem. A critic would need in some way to establish a special context of usage in order to be able to say that he finds a work serene and profound, yet artistically worthless, without giving the effect of incoherence or indecisiveness. In most criticism, in fact, evaluation is continuously effected in the process of describing and interpreting, through the use of the hundreds of available expressions such as subtlety, vividness, economy, precision, coherence, sincerity, maturity, unified sensibility, tightly organized, complexly ironic. . . . When we find an assertion that matches Weitz's evaluative paradigm, "X is good, great, excellent, mediocre," or "X is good . . . because P," it is apt to be in a polemical context, or to be used to assess a work for the buying public, or to clinch a case already implicitly made, or to enhance the persuasiveness of a critique by a show of intellectual rigor.

[30] "The Philosophy of Criticism," pp. 207–209.

My main caveat against a rigid use of logical models, however, is that they take no account of the obvious character of any instance of sustained critical discourse—that it is not only fluid, but that it has a source, that (despite eddies and side runnels) it is flowing somewhere, and that it flows in response to forces which are to some extent inherent in the kind of critical discourse it is. Let me drop this hydrodynamic analogue at the point where it becomes an inconvenience. The potential facts, or features, of a work of art or literature—whether long like *Hamlet*, or of middle length like "Lycidas," or short like "A Spirit Did My Slumber Seal"—are numberless, and some of them only come into view from a particular theoretical perspective. For many of what count as artistic or literary facts are in part constructed, and they are constructed by the act of being construed. As Coleridge, who was interested in this as in all aspects of the role of theory, put it: "Facts, you know, are not truths; they are not conclusions; they are not premisses, but in the nature and parts of premisses."[31] The theoretical principles, categories, distinctions, and manner of proceeding built into a critic's elected mode of discourse—his language-game—cooperate with whatever constitutes the *données* of a work so as both to shape the facts and to identify which are the significant facts, and also to foster the kinds of hypotheses the critic will bring to the interpretation of particular passages and of the work as a whole, as well as the kinds of criteria which enable him both to discover and to assess the values in the work. These activities are not performed separately or sequentially, but in a continuous and interdependent process, in a discourse that is kept coherent and directional toward the ends in view by the pervasive but often implicit influence of the critic's theoretical premises and orientation.

[31] *The Table Talk and Omniana* (London, 1917), p. 165.

Sometimes a shift in the theoretical vantage effects a spectacular transformation in the description as well as the interpretation and evaluation of works of art. As an example, for centuries it was entirely obvious to all critics of Shakespeare, however divergent their perspectives, that the salient features of his plays were the kind that Aristotle had identified —that is, characters who perform the actions and speak the language constituting the text. Then less than a half-century ago a number of able critics took the theoretical stand that a poetic drama, like all genuine literature, is essentially a mode of language which is antithetical to the language of science; hence that, since the language of science is literal, simple in its reference, logical in its method, and has verifiable truth as its aim, the antithetic language of poetry is inherently figurative or symbolic, ambiguous in its meaning, ironic, paradoxical, and in other ways "counterlogical" in its method, and organized so as to explore a "theme" rather than to assert a truth. In the criticism of writers such as Wilson Knight, Philip Wheelwright, Cleanth Brooks, and Robert Heilman, the salient features of Shakespeare's plays, when examined from this perspective, were not characters, but patterns of words and images, and the central action turned out to be an ironic and paradoxical "symbolic action," of which the dynamic element is an evolving theme. The evaluation of Shakespeare from this point of view equaled the earlier high estimation of his artistic standing, although on very different grounds and criteria. The same perspective, however, when applied to writers such as Donne, Blake, Wordsworth, Shelley, Tennyson, resulted in a drastic reordering of their traditional rankings in the hierarchy of the English poets. And though he may himself prefer to take his stand on the premise that literature is primarily about people rather than constituted by patterns of thematic imagery, the candid reader will not deny the value of some of the insights made possible by a criticism based on the alternative possibility.

IV. Does Criticism Presuppose Theory?

But a number of philosophical analysts claim that some criticism is entirely theory-free and carries on its proper work of analysis and assessment unimpeded by general presuppositions. William Kennick, for example, says that a second mistake of traditional aesthetics, coordinate with the mistake of thinking that a theory of art is logically possible, is the "assumption: Criticism presupposes Aesthetic Theory"—an assumption he translates as "the view that responsible criticism is impossible without standards or criteria universally applicable to all works of art." "Criticism," according to Morris Weitz, "need not state, imply, or presuppose a true poetics . . . or an aesthetics of art in order to render intelligible or to justify its utterances" about a particular work. Stuart Hampshire is even more insistent: "Neither an artist nor a critical spectator unavoidably needs an aesthetic; and when in Aesthetics one moves from the particular to the general, one is travelling in the wrong direction." There is here a craving for aesthetic particularity no less extreme than the traditional craving for generality against which Hampshire is reacting. The critic, he asserts, "is a mere spectator: . . . it is only required that he should see the object exactly as it is," and as a "unique object . . . individual and unrepeatable." "The peculiar features of particular objects, with their own originality of arrangement, remain constant and unaffected by the spectator's choices and priorities."[32]

Hampshire's comments suggest a conceptual model of the

[32] Kennick, p. 325, also p. 334; Weitz, *Hamlet*, p. 318; Stuart Hampshire, "Logic and Appreciation," in Elton, ed., pp. 169, 165.

critical encounter which, I think, lurks also behind the insistence by other analysts that the ultimate use of criticism, and the by-product which makes even bogus definitions inadvertently profitable, is to demonstrate by example "what to look for and how to look at it in art." The ideal is one in which an intelligent and sensitive observer, undistracted by any theoretical presuppositions about the nature of art or of a kind of art, engages with a unique work, which comes endowed with aesthetic features that are simply (though more or less obviously or obscurely) there, and proceeds to register those features that he is acute enough to discover. This model of a pure critical confrontation, of course, does not even remotely approximate the conditions of our actual dealings with a work of art. Should that anomaly, a cultivated and intelligent man whose mind was unviolated by general aesthetic preconceptions, encounter a work of art, he would have nothing to say that we should account artistic criticism.

Does all criticism presuppose theory? Not if by "presuppose" we mean a logical relation, such that a given theory strictly entails a particular critique, or that from a given critique we can infer its precise theoretical antecedents. The inter-related elements of an explicit theory—including definitions, categories, distinctions, criteria, and method of proceeding—are not related to their specific application to a particular work, or class of works, in this strictly logical way, nor merely in a simple causal way, as the conditions that effect particular aesthetic judgments. Instead, they are related in the curious way, compounded of quasi-logical and causal relations, that we indicate by terms such as "foster," "generate," "suggest," "bring out," or even "control" and "inform."

Granted the use of "presuppose" to include relations of this sort, we can say with assurance that yes, all criticism presupposes theory, and in at least two ways. First, any discourse about works of art that is sufficiently sustained and ordered to count as criticism has attributes—for example, the kinds of features in the work it discriminates or ignores, the kinds of terms it uses or fails to use, the relations it specifies, the literal or analogical mode of reasoning it exhibits—which serve as indices of the type of theoretical perspective to which the critic is committed, whether explicitly or implicitly, and whether deliberately or as a matter of habit. Second, any sustained critical discourse is likely to use some terms that have been invented for their own purposes by earlier aesthetic theorists, and will inescapably use other terms, taken from ordinary language, but applied in accordance with specialized rules of usage which, historical investigation shows, have been developed by earlier aesthetic theorists. These terms and modes of usage have become part of the linguistic and cultural tradition that all educated men inherit, so that the discourse of any individual critic presupposes theory, in the sense that at least some elements in the language-game he elects to play, although open to modification, have in the first instance come to him ready-made from the history of critical theory.

Here is a simple example from Matthew Arnold, whom I choose because, more than almost all major critics, he seems to approach Hampshire's ideal—that the critic "should see the object exactly as it is"—by deliberately undertaking to eschew general theory and, in his words, "to see the object as in itself it really is." In "The Study of Poetry," Arnold briefly surveys important English poets in the endeavor to detect in each

the degree in which a high poetic quality is present or wanting there. Critics give themselves great labour to draw out what in the abstract constitutes the character of a high quality of poetry. It is much better simply to have recourse to concrete examples . . . and to say: The characters of a high quality of poetry are what is expressed *there.*

Coming to Chaucer, he cites two passages spoken by the Prioress in *The Canterbury Tales*, then comments that, great though Chaucer's poetry is, it falls short in an essential aspect of the poetic quality of the greatest writers such as Homer, Dante, and Shakespeare: "The substance of Chaucer's poetry, his view of things and his criticism of life, has largeness, freedom, shrewdness, benignity; but it has not this high seriousness."[33]

From evidences in this one sentence we can infer some important presuppositions which, had Arnold been an inveterate theorizer like Coleridge, he might have asserted in an express theory of poetry. For example, since he employs terms such as "freedom," "benignity," "high seriousness" as criteria for high poetic quality, and since the use of such terms involves a moral aspect, we know that Arnold did not, like some of his contemporaries, view poetry from the vantage of art for art's sake, but instead was committed to an alternative theoretical position, that poetic qualities and values are not exclusive of, nor even discriminable from, moral qualities and values. Furthermore, Arnold's terms for poetic qualities are of a special kind: they signify, literally, aspects of human character that involve a man's general attitudes to life. Undertaking to look directly at Chaucer's poetry and to describe simply what he finds there, Arnold discovers its most prominent and important features to be qualities of character that many critics of Chaucer do not mention, and others expressly reject as an instance of the "personal heresy," hence aesthetically irrelevant.

It is clear that Arnold's discovery of these features presupposes the view that there is a detectable authorial presence behind all the fictitious characters in a narrative poem like *The Canterbury Tales*, and that the moral aspects and atti-

[33] In *Essays in Criticism, Second Series* (London, 1891), pp. 20, 32–33.

tudes manifested by that presence are the primary features of a work which determine both the kind and excellence of its poetic quality. Arnold was able to presuppose that view because it was an element in the diverse critical languages that he had inherited—an element which had in the first instance been the product of a specific theory. We find it in Aristotle—not in his *Poetics* but in his *Rhetoric*—in the claim that a public speaker inescapably projects an ethos, a personal character which may be different from his actual self but serves as an important means of persuading the audience to give credence to him and his arguments. The Greek critic Longinus expanded the use of this concept from rhetoric to literature, by asserting that the supreme stylistic quality he calls "the sublime" reflects the character of its author: "Sublimity is the echo of a great soul." This way of dealing with literature, by the time it was inherited by Arnold, had been greatly extended and subtilized, especially by those romantic critics who based their criticism on the theoretical premise that literature is the expression of its author's character and feelings. And though, during the three or four decades that have just passed, the predominance of the New Criticism, based on the alternative premise that a poem is an autonomous object, blocked out as poetically irrelevant "the personal heresy" or "the biographical fallacy," current critics are adopting a stance from which, with some excitement, they are rediscovering characterological features that are "objective" properties of a work of art—although they now attach these properties to a projected and pervasive presence in a work that they call, not "ethos," nor "Chaucer," but "voice."

V. Does Metacriticism Presuppose Theory?

Are those philosophical analysts who deny the logical possibility of aesthetic theory themselves theory-free? As soon as we examine what these philosophers, in analyzing critical discourse, find it relevant or irrelevant to talk about and how they elect to talk about it—as soon as we do meta-metacriticism—it becomes clear that they have privately known all along the extension of the general term "art," and the criteria by which this extension is at least loosely specified. Their claim of ignorance about the proper meaning of "art" has in fact functioned as a pretense, like Socrates' guise of ignorance, in the service of pursuing a special kind of philosophical inquiry in a special way. Furthermore, this meaning does not coincide with any use of the term in "ordinary language." Instead, the criteria of "art" presupposed by the analysts are highly specialized, are employed exclusively by a class of intellectuals who share a current climate of opinion, and are a heritage from quite recent developments in aesthetic theory.

Sometimes the evidences for these prepossessions are quite explicit. Stuart Hampshire raises the possibility that "perhaps there is no subject-matter" of aesthetics, and as we know, he regards any movement in criticism from the particular to the general as retrograde. Yet he hangs his argument on the assertion that "a work of art is gratuitous"—not some works, or some class of works, but "a work of art" in the universal sense. "The canons of . . . perfection and imperfection," he says, are thus "internal to the work itself." On this ground Hampshire differentiates sharply between "aesthetic judgments" and moral judgments, and forbids any intrusion into criticism of the "common vocabulary" which, since it was "created for practical purposes, obstructs any disinterested perception of things." For "in so far as the perfection of the work is assessed by some external criterion, it is not being assessed as a work of art." "Nothing but holding an object still in attention, by itself and for its own sake, would count as having an aesthetic interest in it."[34] Kennick agrees with

[34] Hampshire, pp. 161–167.

Hampshire that "a work of art is gratuitous," and generalizes that "art has no function or purpose . . . and this is an insight to be gained from the 'art for art's sake' position." Paul Ziff, although equally suspicious of aesthetic generalization, asserts: "Nothing can be a reason why [a] painting is good unless it is a reason why the painting is worth contemplating. (One can add: for its own sake, but that is redundant.)"[35]

In Morris Weitz the indications are less direct, but point to a similar preconception about what is and is not aesthetic. Evaluations of works of art, he says, apply criteria which are supported by reasons, and the good reasons are unchallengeable reasons. Criteria such as "truthful" or "moral" cannot be supported by good or convincing reasons "since it is always possible to dissociate artistic greatness from truth or morality"; indeed, all criteria are challengeable which have to do with "the *effects* of art," as well as with "the *relation* between art and the world." But the case is entirely different for such statements as "X is great because it is subtle, integrated, fresh." Criteria such as these are "aesthetic, where by aesthetic I mean some criterion which cannot be challenged," for to ask what such criteria have to do with artistic greatness "makes no sense," because nothing can possibly serve as an answer.[36] Now, by "unchallengeable" Weitz cannot mean that such criteria have not been challenged, for they certainly have been. "Freshness," for example: "You praise a thing for being 'fresh,' " T. E. Hulme remarked, implying that "it is good because it is fresh. Now this is certainly wrong, there is nothing particularly desirable about freshness *per se*. Works

[35] Kennick, pp. 331, 329; Ziff, "Appreciation and Evaluation," in Joseph Margolis, ed., *Philosophy Looks at the Arts* (New York, 1962), p. 161.
[36] "The Philosophy of Criticism," pp. 215–216; see also *Hamlet*, pp. 276–282.

of art aren't eggs."[37] By an "unchallengeable," hence an "aesthetic criterion," Weitz means that, unlike criteria of artistic greatness that involve moral or veridical or psychological claims, it does not relate the work to something outside itself, but terminates in the work *qua* work. "In aesthetic validation," he declares, "this is where we must all stop for there is no further place to go."

Note that the claim that a work of art is "gratuitous"—serving no purpose beyond the work itself—does not accord with the claims of the artists who made these works, until about a hundred or so years ago. Dante declared to Can Grande that the purpose of his *Divine Comedy* was "to remove those living in this life from a state of misery and to lead them to a state of happiness"; Milton wrote *Paradise Lost* "to justify the ways of God to men"; Wordsworth said that each of his poems "has a worthy *purpose*," and that he wished "either to be considered as a Teacher, or as nothing"; while for many Christian centuries painters undertook to represent and enforce religious truths and musicians composed for the greater glory of God. Also, for fifteen hundred years and more it occurred to no critic to use the terms of the modern analysts, in assertions that the criteria of a work of art are "internal to itself," or that the proper perception of a work is "disinterested," a mode of contemplation "for its own sake," or that aesthetic judgments are to be sharply distinguished from moral and practical judgments, in that they assess the work of art "as a work of art"—that is, as the locus and terminus of aesthetic qualities and values, without reference to "external" relationships.

This critical vocabulary had its specific origins in the eighteenth century, in a particular social and intellectual milieu, and as part of a newly emerging mode of life. In

[37] *Speculations*, ed. Herbert Read (London, 1936), p. 135.

western Europe, at a time of expanding wealth and a rapidly growing middle class, there was an immense spread of a leisure-time pursuit hitherto confined to the life style of some members of the aristocracy. This pursuit was connoisseurship, the development of "taste" in a variety of experiences that were pursued primarily for pleasure. The market for poetry and "belles-lettres" expanded; there developed great public collections of paintings and sculpture; the audiences for theatre, concerts, opera grew apace; tours were organized to visit and admire architectural monuments, including the great private mansions and their landscaped settings. A consequence of this social phenomenon was the natural assumption that these objects—literature, painting, sculpture, music, landscape-gardening, architecture—despite their patent differences in media and other features, have something in common that makes them eligible for the common experience of connoisseurship.[38] Another consequence was a theoretical interest in a mode of activity that was patently not moral or utilitarian, since it was an escape, a holiday from everyday moral and utilitarian concerns; with this was often associated a demand for practical guidance in developing a "good taste" that would serve not only to enhance the pleasures of connoisseurship, but also as a sign of social status. All these concerns are writ large in the essays of Joseph Addison, whose acute *Spectator* papers on such subjects, especially the group on "The Pleasures of the Imagination," served to found an amateur's science of aesthetics, which Alexander Baumgarten later in the century named, professionalized, and elevated to philosophical respectability.

[38] For the emergence of the modern classification of "the fine arts" in the eighteenth century, see Paul Oskar Kristeller, "The Modern System of the Arts: A Study in the History of Aesthetics," *Journal of the History of Ideas*, 12 (1951), 496–527, and 13 (1952), 17–46.

The new aesthetic theory developed in two separate but parallel modes, both adumbrated in Addison, Shaftesbury, and other amateur theorists before they were adopted and elaborated by professional philosophers, and both (it is of interest to note) reliant on the importation into the field of art of terms and concepts which had earlier been developed in metaphysics and theology. In one line of thought, the root concept was that the artist possesses a creative faculty called the "imagination," that his act of bringing-into-being a work of art is like that of God in creating the universe, and that his artistic product is therefore a "second nature," or "second world," different from the natural world, whose sole responsibility is to its own internal laws and whose sole end is simply to exist. Viewing the poet's creative act on the model of Leibnitz's cosmogony—according to which God's creation of the world necessarily accorded with the laws of noncontradiction and "compossibility"—Baumgarten, inventor of the term "aesthetics," effected the artistic theory that, because it is produced by a poet who is "like a maker or a creator . . . the poem ought to be a sort of world." But since the poetic world is "heterocosmic," it is not subject to the criterion of truth to the world we live in, but only to the criterion of "heterocosmic truth"—that is, self-consistency and internal coherence. The "aesthetic end" thus has no reference to ordinary morality and ordinary truth, but is simply "the perfection of sensuous cognition . . . that is, beauty." Or as Karl Philipp Moritz wrote in 1788, a work of art is its own microcosm whose beauty "has no need to be useful." For beauty "needs no end, no purpose for its presence outside itself, but has its entire value, and the end of its existence in itself. . . . [The energy of the artist] creates for itself its own world, in which nothing isolated has a place, but everything is after its own fashion a self-sufficient whole."[39]

[39] See Baumgarten, *Meditationes philosophicae* (1735), secs. 51–69;

The other line of thought took as its starting point the experience, not of the maker, but of the connoisseur of the arts, and defined the common element in such experience as a special attitude and a special kind of judgment. The basic concept was, in this instance, imported from theological and ethical views of the attitude appropriate to God's moral perfection. Combating post-Hobbesian theories of egoistic ethics and a utilitarian religion, Shaftesbury had defined as the proper religious attitude "the disinterested love of God" for his own sake, because of "the excellence of the object," as against the service of God "for interest merely." In Shaftesbury and various followers, the disinterested concern with God for His internal rather than instrumental excellence became the model for describing both the "moral sense" and artistic "taste"— that is, both the cultivated man's attitude to moral virtue or moral beauty, and the connoisseur's attitude to artistic virtue or sensuous beauty. Later, however, "disinterestedness" came to be used to differentiate specifically aesthetic attitudes and judgments from moral as well as practical and utilitarian concerns.[40] By 1790, when Kant formulated the classic definition of aesthetic perception and judgment, it had come to a conclusion parallel with the definition of art by reference to aesthetic creation and the mode of being of a work of art. "Taste," according to Kant, is the faculty of judging "by means of delight or aversion *apart from any interest*. The object of such delight is called *beautiful*"; and the judgment of beauty is differentiated from judgments of truth and of

---

Aesthetica (1750), secs. 14, 441, 511–518, 585; K. P. Moritz, *Ueber die bildende Nachahmung des Schönen*, in *Deutsche Litteraturdenkmale des 18. und 19. Jahrhunderts*, XXXI, pp. 10–12, 16.

[40] Shaftesbury, *Characteristics*, ed. J. M. Robertson (2 vols.; London, 1900), II, 54–56. See Jerome Stolnitz, "On the Origins of 'Aesthetic Disinterestedness,'" *Journal of Aesthetics and Art Criticism*, 20 (1961–62), 131–143.

moral goodness in that it is "simply *contemplative*," "disinterested," indifferent to the reality of the object, and free of "utility" or reference to any end "external" to the perfection of the object itself.[41]

The basic aesthetic terms and concepts in a number of analytic metacritics, it is apparent, emerged only some two centuries ago, were imported from metaphysical, theological, and ethical doctrines, and were developed by the very thinkers who established the field of art as a separate philosophical discipline, for which they coined the name "aesthetics" and within which they undertook to frame a theory of the utmost generality in a vocabulary that would enable them to talk about all the arts at once. The question arises, why should some analytic philosophers think that just these presuppositions about the nature of art and aesthetic experience are so obviously true as to require no defense, and so free of theory, essential definitions, and aesthetic generalizations that they can serve as the ground of arguments against the validity of all such theory, definitions, and generalizations?

There are, I think, two plausible reasons for this anomaly. For one thing, to assert about the work of art that it is gratuitous, to be enjoyed as an end in itself, and to be appraised by criteria internal to itself, is to generalize in terms of function, purpose, attitudes, in a way that might seem to be free of the "*unum nomen; unum nominatum*" fallacy and the family-resemblance mistake—though only on the naïve view which, taking Wittgenstein's behest to "look and see" entirely literally, assumes that nothing is to be accounted a common element if it is not a visible feature of the objects denoted by a general term.[42] More important, however, is the fact that

[41] *Critique of Aesthetic Judgment*, trans. J. C. Meredith (Oxford, 1911), pp. 48–50, 69.

[42] For a critique of this view see Maurice Mandelbaum, "Family

the success of these terms in dealing with certain problems of the arts have made them in the course of the last century the current coin of aesthetic interchange. The expressions, with their implicit rules of specialized use, have become so much a part of the common language both of literate amateurs and professional philosophers of art—or what comes to the same thing, they have become so much a part of the modern intellectual climate—that they seem to be simply given in common experience, and so serve as what Aristotle in his *Rhetoric* called "commonplaces": concepts from which we argue, but for which we feel no need to argue.

Is the theory of art employing these commonplaces as primary categories a valid theory? Surely it is, for it has served as the great enabling act of modern criticism in that it has made it possible for us to talk about art for what it distinctively is, in differentiation from all other human products and all moral and practical activities—to talk about art as art, a poem as a poem, and an individual work of art as a unique entity, to be described and judged by criteria most appropriate to itself and not another kind of thing. It is not the sole language that has been developed for such a purpose: Aristotle's theory, as we saw earlier, provided quite different terms which nonetheless enabled him to talk about some artistic products in a way appropriate to their own distinctive features, causes, modes of organization, and criteria; but our eighteenth-century heritage of the view of art-as-such, and especially its new emphasis on the experience of the connoisseur, has better suited modern interests and proclivities. But is this theory in itself adequate to deal with all the important human concerns with art? We need only to bring ourselves down from the high and radically simplifying vantage point

Resemblances and Generalizations Concerning the Arts," *American Philosophical Quarterly*, 2 (1965), 1–10.

of current aesthetic discourse into the clutter and tangle of the total "surroundings" of an actual encounter with *King Lear*, or the "St. Matthew's Passion," or *Guernica*, to see how inadequate such a theory is to account for the way these works engage our total consciousness and call insistently upon our sympathies and antipathies, our range of knowledge, our common humanity, our sense of what life and the world are really like and how people really act, our deep moral convictions and even religious beliefs (or lack of them).

But how are we to do theoretical justice to the full range of our experience of a work of art? Only by dropping the useful but limited way of talking about art *qua* art and developing an alternative language, or much more likely, by adapting one of the existing languages, such as Plato's, or Johnson's, or Arnold's, or Lionel Trilling's, which were developed to deal with a work of art in some of the many ways in which it is deeply involved with other human activities, values, and concerns. But can't we devise a single critical language that will do all of these useful and valuable things? I believe not, for no one set of premises and coherent mode of discourse suffices to say everything important, but only the kind of things, relative to selected human purposes, toward which that discourse is oriented.

If I am right in asserting that what we account as critical theory is diverse in its composition and function and inescapable in extended critical discourse, and also that a diversity of theories are valid, in the variety of their usefulness for a comprehensive understanding and appreciation of art, then we are in a position to judge the assertion by some philosophical analysts with which we began. The claim was that all critical and aesthetic theory consists solely, or primarily, in the assertion and attempted proof of an essential definition of art and thus is an extended logical mistake. About this claim we can now say that (1) it is itself the attempt to assert and prove an essential definition of the term "critical theory," (2) it is a mistake which forecloses investigation of what able theorists have in fact done, and (3) it actually functions as a persuasive redefinition of "critical theory," in that it delimits the common uses of the term by setting up a preferred criterion for its application that serves to discredit what it purports to define.

VI. Certainty, Rationality, and Critical Knowledge

The inadequacy of their views of the role of critical theory has not prevented these philosophers from saying many important things about criticism itself. An especially important service, I earlier remarked, has been their insistence that a variety of critical arguments are rational even though they can achieve certainty only in the limited area in which the arguments concern artistic facts. I have argued, indeed, that even this in some ways claims too much—that the analytic paradigms for each type of critical argument are often inapplicable to fluid critical discourse, and that not only interpretations and evaluations, but even what count as significant artistic facts, are to some extent relative to a theoretical frame of discourse which has been elected by the individual critic. And this raises a question which has been recurrent in the conference that led to the essays in this volume: Is no certainty possible in critical discourse? And if not, how can we claim that critical discourse yields valid knowledge?

Put in this way, the question is, I think, misleading, because "certainty" is a loaded term: it gives the impression that it is a universal criterion for knowledge, yet tends in philosophical discourse to be tied to certain highly specialized models of reasoning. In the seventeenth century, when the model for achieving certainty (outside of divine revelation) was logic, defenders of the emerging "new science" tried to validate its claim to certain knowledge by concepts, such as the "principle of sufficient reason," which seemed to bridge the gap between the necessary truths of logic and assertions of empirical facts and laws. Later, when the physical sciences had triumphantly established their own claim to cognitive validity, the methods of scientific verification tended to assume a status, on a peer with that of logic, as the sole model for achieving knowledge in all empirical inquiries. Such was the assumption, in the nineteenth century, of the philosophy of positivism, and in the twentieth, of the philosophy of logical positivism. And even in our post-positivist climate many of us still feel uneasy about claiming validity for knowledge which cannot be certified by some plausible simulacrum of the model of formal logic, or of "scientific method," or both together. But we will get clear about what we are really doing in artistic criticism, and in various related areas of inquiry, only if we face up to the full consequences of the realization that these pursuits are neither logic nor science, but their own kinds of discourse, adapted to their own kinds of problems, having their own criteria of rationality, and yielding their own kinds of knowledge, to which the term "certainty" does not apply. But if this knowledge is not "certain," neither is it, strictly speaking, "uncertain"; both terms, insofar as they are tied to alien models of discourse, are misleading.

In this respect, one must be wary about the attempt by E. D. Hirsch, in this volume, to renew our "confidence in the scientific side" of criticism and related studies by claiming that they share with the sciences a "universal logic of inquiry" which results in a body of knowledge that "is scientific in precisely the same sense that geology or physics is scientific," differing only in degree of "exactitude." Hirsch identifies the logic of inquiry common to criticism and the physical sciences as that described by Karl Popper and other philosophers of science: it is the method of positing, testing, and falsifying alternative hypotheses by the principle of "evidence and logic," with the result of achieving an ever higher degree of tenability for the hypothesis that survives the ordeal.

I concur with the general tenor of Hirsch's argument for the rationality of literary study and am dismayed, as he is, by the irrationality and irresponsibility of much that passes for criticism. And one can, like Hirsch in his various writings, refer to the hypothetico-deductive model in order to say enlightening things about the procedures, such as interpretation, that are involved in literary and aesthetic criticism. But to look at the procedures of a physical scientist and of a critic in their over-all surroundings is to see how radical are the differences in problems, aims, and activities which are obscured by asserting that both enterprises accord with a single logical model.

For example: the physicist tacitly shares with other physicists a perspective which sharply limits what shall count as facts; he poses questions which rule out all normative or evaluative terms; he tries to formulate hypotheses which are capable of being indubitably falsified by specific experimental observations; and his over-all aim, by a drastic exclusion of individual differences, is to achieve an ever-greater generality in knowledge, in a procedure so controlled by rigid rules as to approximate certainty (in the sense of universal agreement by other competent observers) at every step of the way. In dealing with complex literary texts, on the other hand, a critic employs one of many available perspectives to conduct a fluid and largely uncodified discourse, in which some facts have the property of being altered by the hypothesis which appeals to them for support; his questions typically involve normative and evaluative elements; there is no clear line at which his interpretative hypothesis is falsified; a central aim, at the extreme from maximum generality, is to establish the knowledge of individual objects in their distinctive, concrete, and value-full particularity; and although he may claim that his interpretation is uniquely true, he is not really surprised to find that other intelligent and able critics disagree. E. D. Hirsch does well to remind us that the progressiveness of literary studies depends on its status as a collaborative enterprise in which diverse practitioners consent to the criteria of rationality. We must remember, however, that this progress consists in part in the accumulation of alternative and complementary critical theories and procedures, in a fashion very different from the progress of the science of physics toward ever-greater generality. The difference is indicated in Whitehead's dictum that a science that hesitates to forget its founders is lost. A humane study that forgets its founders is impoverished; a great critic is subject to correction and supplementation, but is never entirely outmoded; and progress in fact depends on our maintaining the perspectives and the insights of the past as live options, lest we fall into a contemporary narrowness of view, or be doomed to repeat old errors and laboriously to rediscover ancient insights.

Rather than to exaggerate the commonalty of method in science and criticism, it would be more profitable to say that while criticism involves the use of logic and scientific method, it must go far beyond their capacities if it is to do its proper job. Though responsible to the formal rules of reasoning, and though in its own way empirical, criticism must initiate its chief functions in an area where these simplified calculi stop, for the models of logic and of scientific method achieve their extraordinary efficacy and their diverse modes of certainty by the device of systematically excluding just those features of experience that, humanly speaking, matter most. Inevitably, therefore, when critical discourse engages with its objects, it is controlled in considerable part by norms that we call good sense, sagacity, tact, sensibility, taste. These are terms by which we indicate that, though we are operating in a region where the rules are uncodified and elusive and there is room for the play of irreducible temperamental differences, yet decisions and judgments are not arbitrary, but are subject to broad criteria such as coherent-incoherent, adequate-omissive, penetrating-silly, just-distorting, revealing-obfuscatory, disinterested-partisan, better-worse. Although such a mode of discourse is rarely capable of rigidly conclusive arguments, it possesses just the kind of rationality it needs to achieve its own purposes; and although its knowledge is not, judged by an alien criterion, certain, it must satisfy an equivalent criterion in its own realm of discourse, for which, in lieu of a specialized term, we use a word like valid, or sound.

A ·pertinent comment is that of Wittgenstein, in discussing the difference between mathematical and other modes of certainty: "We remain unconscious of the prodigious diversity of all the everyday language-games," and "the kind of certainty is the kind of language-game." He goes on to remind us also that in these matters language is not the ultimate reference, for "what has to be accepted, the given, is—so one could say—*forms of life.*"[43] Let us imagine a critical language-game, and the form of life that it inescapably involves, which would in fact achieve the goal of certainty that one is tempted to hold up as the ideal of all rational discourse. There would be only one permissible theoretical stance, all the descriptive and normative terms would have fixed criteria of use, and reasoning would proceed entirely in accordance with established logical calculi. Such a language, if applied to a work

[43] *Philosophical Investigations*, 224e, 226e.

of literature by any intelligent and practiced critic, could indeed be expected to yield certainty, in the sense that the resulting interpretation and evaluation would be conclusive and would enforce the consent of all critics who follow the rules of that critical game. If, however, instead of holding up such certainty as an abstract ideal, we realize in imagination the form of life in which such critical discourse would be standard, we find it inhuman and repulsive; for it is an ideal that could be achieved only in a form of political, social, and artistic life like that which Aldous Huxley direly foreboded in *Brave New World* or George Orwell in *1984*.

Writing in the spirit of Wittgenstein, J. L. Austin remarked that our language is not an ideal form, but is designed for use "in the human predicament."[44] One way to describe criticism and related modes of inquiry is to say that they are a language-game—or a family of language-games—designed to cope in a rational way with those aspects of the human predicament in which valid knowledge and understanding are essential, but certainty is impossible. This is of course an extremely difficult undertaking, but as Wittgenstein remarks, what cannot be gainsaid is, "This language-game is played";[45] and what its great exponents have achieved shows how well and profitably the game can in fact be played. The name of this game is the humanities.

---

[44] *Philosophical Papers* (Oxford, 1961), p. 100.
[45] *Philosophical Investigations*, sec. 654.

E. D. HIRSCH, JR.

Value and Knowledge
in the Humanities

I WAS asked to write about some of the theoretical problems surrounding the concept of value in humane studies, a technical and theoretical subject that I have wrestled with before in print. But the pressing questions about value in the humanities are not technical, theoretical questions. Values are what people value—individually and in groups; values belong to the history of opinion, to anthropology, psychology, and sociology. Of course, there is need for theoretical analysis, especially in sorting out some of the confusions that arise when values are understood as having autonomous existence, but I do not find such exercises very pertinent when the hidden questions are really: What *can* be the values of the humanities and what values *should* the humanities serve in the world? These, to my mind, are not abstract, theoretical questions. They are pleas for re-examination and self-justification at a time when humane studies are under attack for being "irrelevant," which is to say lacking in value.

I have observed three kinds of response to the basic question that our students are pressing us to ask. At one extreme, the question is repudiated as a self-defeating obstacle to freedom of inquiry—a Philistinic incomprehension of the inherent value in study for its own sake—a "barbarism of virtue." At the other extreme, we find professors accepting the accusation of irrelevance and joining their students to demand . . . well, "relevance," which is to say real value. The most striking example of the latter was the palace revolution in the Modern Language Association in 1968, in which the dissidents demanded, and in some part gained, ideological and political commitments from that elephantine association of scholars. But the most representative response has been sympathy for student concern and puzzlement about the ways in which humane study can and should be valuable. This condition of puzzlement I find the most honorable response of all not only because the problem *is* puzzling, but also because perplexity is more conducive to thinking out the problem than complacency on the one side or mindless moralism on the other.

The straightforward defense of things-as-they-are, of academic freedom, and of "the value of knowledge for its own sake" is an unsatisfactory response not only because it fails, in fact, to satisfy us or our students, but also because it cannot withstand the detached analysis that it commends. First of all, "knowledge for its own sake" is not and cannot be a value. Knowledge of any sort becomes a value when it is valuable to people. And, if the knowledge pursued by professors in the humanities is not something they can persuade their students to value, then a problem exists—whether or not we think it ought to exist. If we cannot persuade either our students or ourselves, then certainly the problem is acute. "Knowledge for its own sake" is a pathetic fallacy. Who is knowledge?

The second line of defense in the conservative argument is "academic freedom." Freedom of inquiry is not by itself a value that sufficiently justifies humane studies. Precisely because humanistic inquiry is free, it requires justification. For freedom of inquiry implies choice: choice of subject matter, of questions to be asked, of emphasis. But choice cannot be ethically neutral. While I am pursuing one sort of inquiry, I am excluding, for the moment, other sorts, and my freedom to practice this selectivity is consequently not all that I care about: I care about one sort of pursuit in preference to others. So, willy-nilly, value decisions come into play that go beyond the value decision in favor of freedom. On what bases do I make these further choices? No doubt I would need a depth psychologist to help me answer that, and I would also need a sage because I want to make a choice that is good, that is valuable. The implicit idea that an invisible hand assures the beneficial results of free inquiry is an evasion of responsibility.

The radical answer as expressed, for example, by the dissidents of the Modern Language Association is irresponsible in a different way. Where the conservative defender of academic freedom is naive to think that inquiry based upon choices can be ethically neutral, the radical activist is naive to suppose that inquiry as such can be bound to an ideology. Only the *choice* of a question is in the province of moral or ideological commitment. Once the choice is made, the results of inquiry are determined by evidence and by logic. It is an intellectual scandal to confuse relevance with inquiry by assuming that a particular social, moral, or political commitment must predetermine the results of an inquiry.

The fusion of ideology and inquiry is a sickness to which humane studies are peculiarly vulnerable. Historians had been composing Whig views of history long before Karl Mannheim made his troublesome generalizations about the sociology of knowledge. But this fusion of ideology and inquiry most scientists would, on good evidence, vigorously resist. There is no doubt that ideology *can* predetermine the results of inquiry and is more likely to do so if the inquirer assumes that the fusion is inevitable. But this assumption boils down to pure skepticism with regard to inquiry itself. If ideology predetermines the results of inquiry, then inquiry itself is a charade in the service of ideology. We are then left with nothing but ideology.

This is the kind of skepticism that I detect behind the vigorous political activism within the Modern Language Association. Many humanists (and this is emphatically true of many MLA members) have lost faith in the scientific side of their enterprise. While they rightly conceive the centrality of relevance and value, they have overreacted in a way that betrays an underlying skepticism with regard to inquiry itself. This overreaction also betrays something more laudable. It implies a recognition that our professional activity has become more and more self-absorbed, abstract, esoteric, and trivialized. Skepticism and decadence! If the professors sense it, the students sense it more acutely. But we can overcome decadence without giving way to skepticism, for decadence in the humanities is the foster child of skepticism.

This filial and incestuous relationship (like Milton's Sin and Death) is exemplified in the recent history of literary studies. Literary skepticism owes something, of course, to notions like Mannheim's that have pervaded the intellectual atmosphere, but the direct historical lineage can be traced to the victory about thirty years ago of interpretive (so-called "critical") study over external historical study. Now this victory meant a genuine renovation and invigoration of literary study. The new "relevance" then defeated the old, decadent, trivial, external study which searched out facts about Shakespeare in the Public Record Office instead of pondering the meaning of his plays. But this new revolution was also betrayed. When everyone began to ponder "the works themselves," a premium began to be placed on new "readings" instead of new facts, and the "readings" as they multiplied became more and more diversified, more and more remote, ingenious, abstract, and decadent. The fashion of close reading has now run its course. The excitement and relevance it carried at first has declined into mechanical exercises which engage students only a little less than their teachers. For naturally, if every reading of a standard text merely becomes a new addition to the growing list, one very probable consequence will be a sense of futility, relativism, and skepticism. The only thing to be looked for is a new "approach" or a "novel and interesting perspective." Why not turn to politics and social action?

That is the negative side of the renewed soul-searching in the humanities. But emphasis on renewal, on touching earth again, on forging a connection between our teaching, our writing, and the concerns of our students—these are also impulses toward health and recovery. One sees signs of recovery in the repudiation of esotericism and faddism even while one observes the continued dominance of these symptoms. The therapeutic virtue of dissent will be dissipated, however, unless the underlying skepticism about humanistic inquiry itself is also combatted and unless there is also a renewal of confidence in the scientific side of our enterprise.

I use the word "scientific." In the humanities it has been a red flag since the nineteenth century. In the earlier conflict between science and humanistic culture, "science" signified a dehumanizing positivism, and now it has become an even more disturbing term, signifying also the dehumanization of life by technology. My original title for this paper was "Value and *Science* in the Humanities," but since stock responses are not to be discounted, I have substituted the word "knowledge." It is time, however, to show my hand: "Science" *is* "knowledge," both in etymology and in fact. All serious inquiry, including humanistic inquiry, aims at knowledge and is consequently scientific. It is scientific in precisely the same sense that geology or physics is scientific. Nor is the proposition blunted or qualified by saying, "Yes, well then, call the humanities 'sciences,' but distinguish them from the 'exact' sciences." That merely avoids the issue since exactitude is a variable in all fields of inquiry. In fact, to concede that a result of inquiry may be only an uncertain approximation is, in itself, a way of achieving exactitude in results, a way of making knowledge exact.

The attempt to formulate a satisfactory theoretical distinction between the cognitive element in the humanities and in the natural sciences has an interesting and predominantly German history. Whether or not the debate (conducted mainly by Neo-Kantians toward the end of the nineteenth century) was influenced by the appropriate neutrality of the word *Wissenschaft* remains an unanswered question. (The closest English equivalent to *Wissenschaft* is the word "discipline," which is not close enough.) In any case, it became convenient to conduct the debate by distinguishing the *Geisteswissenschaften* or *Kulturwissenschaften* on the one side from the *Naturwissenschaften* on the other. And the purpose of the distinction was to defend the autonomous character of knowledge in the humanities against the intellectual imperialism of natural science. For if humane knowledge tried to compete with science on its own, positivistic grounds, then the humanities would belie their native character and turn into mere pseudo science.

In the first volume of his *Introduction to the Humane Sciences* (1883), Wilhelm Dilthey attempted to set forth coherent theoretical foundations for the *Geisteswissenschaften*, just as William Whewell had done for the natural sciences in his *History of the Inductive Sciences* (1837) and John Stuart Mill had done in his *System of [inductive] Logic* (1843). Dilthey's attempt, however, was strikingly influenced by these two books, and his epistemological models were dependent upon those of natural science. The main distinctions he drew between the two great domains pertained to their subject matter rather than their methodology.

This view was sharply challenged by Wilhelm Windelband eleven years later in his famous lecture on "History and Natural Science." He proposed that the division of knowledge into natural and humane sciences was justified not merely by their different subject matters, but also and more fundamentally "by the formal character of their different epistemological goals," for "the one seeks *general* laws, while the other seeks *particular* historical facts." Natural science, therefore, is "nomothetic" or legislative, while humane knowledge is "idiographic" or unique and individual. Subsumption under general laws in the natural sciences is *Erklären*, but the aim of humane studies is *Verstehen*, understanding the particular in its uniqueness.

The ensuing discussion comprised Dilthey's answer, *Naturwissenschaften und Geisteswissenschaften* (1895), and a book by Heinrich Rickert, *Kulturwissenschaften und Naturwissenschaften* (1899). The debate is still instructive, not for what it resolved, but for what it failed to resolve. In replying to Windelband, Dilthey was surely right to insist that generalizing and particularizing aims are common to both domains. But was Dilthey's distinction any more adequate or definitive —namely, the distinction between the internal and the external sciences? All the distinctions brought forward in the debate are useful as indications of preponderant tendencies; as adequate, subsumptive generalizations, they are total failures.

The debate about the nature of the humanities did not stop

with Dilthey and Windelband nor did the theory of science stop with Whewell and Mill, but I shall venture to suggest that at least one element of scientific theory is by now well established and is identical with the theory of cognitive inquiry in the humanities. The progress and consolidation of knowledge in both domains are governed by the critical testing of hypotheses with reference to evidence and logic. If we look at any field of inquiry, we discover that it can be described as a congeries of hypotheses, some of them well accepted and others in rivalry with alternative hypotheses. We also discover a large body of evidence relevant to those hypotheses and potentially relevant to others not yet conceived. Under this conception, all empirical inquiry is a process directed toward increasing the probability of learning the truth. This probability is, of course, increased whenever supportive evidence is increased. On the other hand, when hypotheses are called into doubt by the discovery of unfavorable evidence, then some adjustment is made, or some rival hypothesis accepted, or the whole issue is thrown into doubt. But in all these latter cases, the direction is still toward increased probability of truth, since the very instability imposed by unfavorable evidence reduces confidence in previously accepted hypotheses and to that extent reduces the probability of error. Knowledge in all empirical domains thus turns out to be a process rather than a static system, and the direction of the process is toward increased probability of learning the truth.

Now this is a very abstract and simplified model for inquiry, but it is the kind of model that every serious inquirer assumes. Furthermore, it is an accurate model to the extent that it *is* widely assumed. For I have referred not only to the logical relationship between evidence, hypothesis, and probability, but also to a communal enterprise that exists only to the extent that this logical relationship remains the thought-model (or ideology!) for the members of a community of inquirers. On the simplest level, the members of the community cannot even maintain an increasing body of evidence unless past evidence is stored and is brought to bear, when relevant, on hypotheses presently entertained. Nor can the model be accurate if unfavorable evidence is suppressed by a conspiracy of the inquiring community. Nor is the model descriptive if no one bothers to bring unfavorable evidence to bear upon a hypothesis to which it is relevant. Thus in a special sense, there is a sociology of knowledge on which inquiry depends, on which all science depends. And to the extent that this sense of the communal enterprise collapses, so does the discipline itself collapse as a discipline.

Now it is perfectly true that all the individual members in a discipline do not preserve a selfless devotion to the communal enterprise. The inspiriting description of such devotion in Max Weber's *"Wissenschaft als Beruf"* remains one of Weber's ideal types. The spirit of advocacy and the spirit of vanity are almost never completely absent in any individual endeavor. And this, no doubt, will complicate any accurate description of a discipline. But healthy and progressive disciplines do exist. Somehow, even if partly through counter-advocacy and counter-vanity, past evidence is borne upon present hypotheses, and unfavorable evidence is sought in order to test hypotheses. A sense of the community exists precisely because a sense of the discipline exists. The key factor is that the process of knowledge occurs *on the level of the discipline*. Despite individual eccentricities, brilliant guesses accompanied by brilliant perversities, the direction of knowledge goes forward at the level of the discipline. The probability of truth does in fact increase, so long as the sense of the inquiring community persists and inferences are drawn at the level of the discipline.

The communal aspect of knowledge insures that widespread skepticism will bring into existence the historical grounds for skepticism in a discipline. If there is a decline in commitment to the critical testing of hypotheses against all the known relevant evidence, and if the consolidation and discovery of evidence are neglected, then the process of knowledge ceases, and skepticism regarding the actuality of that process is entirely warranted. But the converse is also true: Commitment to the logic of inquiry and to the communal nature of a discipline guarantees an actual process of knowledge, and this holds for every subject of empirical inquiry, including every subject in the humanities.

The communal conception of a discipline is widely assumed in the humanities, but also widely undercut by the humanists' emphasis on rhetoric. Now obviously the consolidated knowledge within a discipline has nothing directly to do with rhetoric. On the other hand, the communal acceptance of hypotheses has much to do with persuasion, and persuasion in doubtful matters requires attention to rhetoric. Furthermore, the goals of humanists often comprise aims that go beyond the aim of knowledge, such as taking aesthetic pleasure in discourse or persuading readers to adopt value preferences that can be related to the cognition of a subject matter. Thus the perennial questions arise: Is Clio science or muse? Is literary criticism an art or a science? The importance of rhetoric makes these appear to be difficult questions in the humanities, but in fact they are not. Obviously, rhetoric can subserve knowledge as well as intellectual chicanery; rhetoric can make the worse reason appear the better. But when a discipline is viewed as a communal enterprise, the hypotheses it tests are not bound to any single expression of them. Hypotheses have to be communicated as well as tested, but *what* is communicated must be used, tested, and expressed by others in a different form. If this condition is not met, the hypothesis is not really subject to criticism at the level of the discipline and has nothing to do with knowledge. It is therefore essential to distinguish hypotheses and evidence from the rhetoric used to convey them. The *writing* of history is an art, or can be, but history is not an art; it is a discipline, which is to say a science. The same is true implicitly of literary studies, though one sometimes despairs that this concept can be widely accepted nowadays. When it is accepted, the discipline will regain its health.

What I have just said implies that I identify the health of the humanities with their scientific self-confidence. That is true, but it is only half the story. The health of a discipline as a discipline is entirely dependent upon the devoted allegiance of its members to the logic of inquiry. But the health of the humanities is also dependent upon their axiological self-confidence, their sense that they are pursuing *valuable* inquiry. It is just as important to distinguish these two kinds of health as it is to promote both. Indeed, I think we can have both only if we are capable of making this distinction. We humanists sometimes blur the distinction between value and knowledge just as we sometimes blur the one between rhetoric and knowledge. It is just as easy to know rigorously what is not worth knowing as it is to express with eloquent persuasiveness what is in fact nonsense. Some recent debates in literary theory have centered on whether the knowledge of a literary work can be separated from a judgment of its value, as though it were somehow not possible for two critics to understand a work with equal accuracy and yet esteem it quite differently. But, of course, they can do this. The humanist's urge

67

to conflate valuation and knowledge can be explained, but the explanation would be a digression from the issue at hand—which is the central importance of avoiding this confusion.

Why is it important? Without this confusion, we can redirect attention to the fact that a scientific or cognitive element inheres in every field of the humanities, that the logic of this scientific process is the same for all subject matters, and that this process of knowledge can be followed out on subjects of intense value or on subjects whose value will probably be very low, both now and in the future. The distinction is important, therefore, to protect the integrity of inquiry in the humanities so that inquiry itself is not repudiated simply because some of its subject matters may have become trivial. The distinction is important, too, because it encourages a choice of those subject matters that are not trivial and whose potential or actual value is high.

This has come to be well understood in the natural sciences, where decisions about the probable value of inquiry involve immense allocations of money and human talent, both of which are limited. Now it is perfectly true that the future value of any inquiry is an unknown, and this is the most powerful argument for total freedom of inquiry. On the other hand, if we were not able to make shrewd predictions about the future value of an inquiry, we could not award the few research grants available in the humanities. And surely, in a sense, each humanist awards himself his own research grant when he decides what professional projects he will pursue in the time available to him. The logical integrity of inquiry is a machine of fatalism, but the choice of inquiry is potentially free and should not be determined for us by a drift in the currents of intellectual fashion. This is why the present demand that humanists make an accounting is a potential source of axiological health for the humanities.

Of course, the demand could be barbaric—especially when made by barbarians. Clearly, many aspects, valuable aspects, of humanistic knowledge do not bear even indirectly on racism, social justice, or Vietnam. The demand for the *immediate* relevance of every aspect of humanistic inquiry is just as mindless and self-defeating as the demand for immediate applicability in the natural sciences. Yet surely the immediacy of problems does not disqualify them as subjects of inquiry; surely the concept of "pure" research is overrated if no one can predict how such research could possibly be valuable. If the prediction cannot be made, then the likelihood that the research will ever be valuable is clearly reduced, even though it may in fact turn out to be of great moment. No one will inhibit a humanist (since he does not need a big laboratory) from pursuing whatever happens to interest him. But if he cannot foresee potential value in his work, according to whatever value scheme he honors, then he should not be surprised if his work turns out to have small value.

Consequently, it is not really barbaric to question the ideal of purity in research by pointing to the ethical dimension—to the fact that choice of a subject for inquiry *is* a choice and therefore also an ethical problem. One way to resolve an ethical problem is to consider it consciously, to think out the probable consequences of the choice in comparison with the probable consequences of alternative choices. So many *ad hoc* factors will enter into such a consideration that it would be foolish to classify them abstractly. Nevertheless, one element in such a consideration by a humanist seems to me unavoidable. Humanistic inquiries are normally pursued in the universities, and humanists are normally university teachers. The question "What should I study?" is therefore normally asked by someone who must also ask himself "What shall I teach my students?" Certainly, the two questions are not the same.

But since an individual's energy is limited, just as are communal resources, the two questions are not totally unrelated.

Almost every university is rethinking its curriculum, while university departments, especially in the humanities, are asking themselves "What shall we teach our students?" One reason this is happening is that the various humanistic disciplines have undergone the kind of development I described as having occurred in literary studies—the kind of development that occurs in almost every field of inquiry. An inspiriting revolution takes place, an invigorating change of emphasis; this direction is pursued with enthusiasm until similar projects begin to multiply and then crowd upon one another—like thronged colonies of lemmings who must drown themselves in the sea. The inquiries have replicated themselves, have become trivial, abstract, disoriented, and decadent. At the same time, these inquiries form the basis for our teaching, and our students readily perceive the disconnection between our present forms of inquiry and the earlier enthusiasm that sponsored them. I am not aware of any university course in which a teacher's conviction of vitality and value in a subject has not infected a large portion of his students, particularly if he is able to say why the subject is vital and important.

This observation has two divergent implications for humanistic pursuits. One of them is that some of us may have to separate very decisively the questions "What shall I study?" and "What shall I teach?" If my students are looking for life wisdom in Shakespeare when I have a special fondness for the problem of how forest scenes were staged in the Elizabethan theater, and if I am giving *the* undergraduate course in Shakespeare, I will have to separate my two lives to some extent. Humanists do have a vocational obligation in our secularized world; the hungry mouths need to be fed as honestly as possible. This does not mean that I should not even mention the fascinating problem of Elizabethan staging. My students will be fascinated too, particularly if I disclose my awareness that there are far more important questions to be asked about Shakespeare. Sometimes this kind of separation is inevitable. Speaking personally, I have a powerful conviction of the value and importance of pursuing certain theoretical and technical problems. Most of my students are only mildly interested in these, and I have had to learn how to direct my teaching, without entirely abandoning my special interests, to problems that are somewhat more pressing to them than to me.

On the other hand, this separation of roles is not always an inevitable condition of the inquirer-teacher in the humanities. After all, the humanist is also a teacher of new values and new needs, which can replace some of those his students bring with them. But I am firmly persuaded that humanistic inquiry must seem vital to the teacher before it can seem so to his students. An ideal condition of health in the humanities exists when inquiry and teaching are not widely separated, when inquiry appears vital to teacher and student alike. This condition is usually met when a field of inquiry is itself renewed, when it touches earth again and becomes convinced of its own worth and of the brave new worlds it has to conquer. That means revolution—intellectual revolution. Such revolutions have always occurred and always will, and the one that is now going on should be welcomed for the temporary rejuvenation it can bring.

The rejuvenation of humanistic inquiry is not likely to occur, however, if the revolution is implicitly directed against inquiry itself. In this heterogeneous culture, humanists no longer share a guild ethic. They may or. may not agree that every historical inquiry is valuable because it "tells us something about man" or "broadens our horizons." And they will hardly agree about the relative importance of different inquiries or about which text belongs to "the best that is known and thought in the world." But the agreement of humanists with regard to inquiry itself is another matter. Humanists are such only because they belong to a community of inquirers. The humanities exist only because such a community exists, and that community cannot exist except by a shared allegiance to the universal logic of inquiry. Unexamined skepticism on this point is not a tough-minded virtue, but a vice that is fatal to any communal intellectual pursuit. There is a supra-individual and timeless contribution in the humanist's professional work that resides in its authentically scientific aspect. We humanists give up everything if we make this cognitive aspect a mere hostage to our ideological concern for relevance and value.

MORTON W. BLOOMFIELD

The Two Cognitive Dimensions
of the Humanities

"What is love?
One name for it is knowledge."

Robert Penn Warren
Audubon: A Vision

THE humanities and those aspects of the social sciences that are like the humanities stand in a unique relationship to their subject matter. The subject matter of the humanities has an interior, a subjective dimension that competes in some ways with the humanistic method itself as a mode of understanding. We can know things, Thomas Aquinas says, *per cognitionem* or *per connaturalitatem*.[1] The humanities know in this dual way—from the outside or from the inside. And this double path of knowing is perhaps the chief characteristic of the study of humanities. It leads to the question Kierkegaard raised: Can one be both Leporello and Don Juan simultaneously? Leporello lists the thousand and one conquests of his master, while Don Juan enjoys them. Experiencing as well as knowing is a way of understanding, and the humanities have to wrestle with both modes and at certain

[1] *St. Thomas* I:I, 6 and II:II, 452. Cf. "A knowledge of things involves two considerations, that is, form and nature. Form appears in the external deposition of a thing; nature in its interior quality" (Hugh of St. Victor, *De Sacramentis*, quoted in D. W. Robertson, Jr., *A Preface to Chaucer: Studies in Medieval Perspectives* [Princeton, 1962], p. 297).

75

reaches attempt some kind of synthesis or at least keep them in some kind of satisfying balance.

The scientific method does not face such a duality. Science can, unlike the humanities, keep a strict separation from its subject matter. Even when the observer is himself an inescapable part of his observations, the connection creates an epistemological problem about objective accuracy, not an alternative to its way of knowing. Science has no interest in the inner feel or experience of what it studies. In fact, its ideal is existentially indifferent statements. But the humanities have a very peculiar relationship to their subject matter, because the subject matter can offer an alternative to them. Georg Simmel said that "Philosophy is, so to speak, the first of its own problems."[2] One can just read a novel or contemplate a picture, give up the whole cognitive attempt, and still have a desirable experience. The subject matter of the humanities offers an existential supplement or even alternative to itself. As students of the humanities, we are asking the reader and student by our scientific or classifying work to take an extra slice of cake, perhaps drier, more stale, and even moldier than the first.

Part of the humanistic process is obviously analytic and scientific. It is often, by contrast with its subject matter, considered the dull part: setting up texts, writing biography, establishing facts, describing the historical and cultural background—the kind of material the older philological and humanistic journals specialize in. This "science of the humanities" treats the inner experience only as outer experience. If it is studying social facts and concepts, it adopts the "roles and games" approach in which nothing has any inward meaning except when it bears directly on the outer.

[2] Cf. Kurt H. Wolff, ed., *Georg Simmel, 1858–1918: A Collection of Essays with Translations and a Bibliography* (Columbus, O., 1959), p. 282.

Yet the full study of the humanities, especially in the field of the arts, offers something more. This extra quality was not understood by A. E. Housman when he raised the matter of literary study in his Cambridge Inaugural Lecture in May 1911.

Why is it that the scholar is the only man of science of whom it is ever demanded that he should display taste and feeling? Literature, subject of his science, is surely not alone among the subjects of science in possessing aesthetic qualities and in making appeal to the emotions. The botanist and the astronomer have for their provinces two worlds of beauty and magnificence not inferior in their way to literature; but no one expects the botanist to throw up his hands and say "how beautiful" nor the astronomer to fall down flat and say "how magnificent": no one would praise their taste if they did perform these ceremonies and no one calls them unappreciative pedants because they do not. Why should the scholar alone indulge in public ecstasy?[3]

Although Housman showed in his poetry that he knew what inward experience was, even if his was a very sentimental and self-indulgent knowledge, he does not seem to understand that the human sciences demand something more than the natural sciences nor that what he calls aesthetic qualities are partially forced into his experience by the very nature of scholarship, even when it is as austerely textual as his was. "Reality is different from, and more than, the totality of facts and events which anyhow is unascertainable," writes Hannah Arendt.[4] Or to put it the opposite way, as Gabriel Marcel writes, "I am not my life."[5]

[3] Quoted in the *Times* (London) *Literary Supplement* (May 9, 1968), p. 476.

[4] Hannah Arendt, "Truth and Politics," in Peter Laslett and W. G. Runciman, eds., *Philosophy, Politics and Society*, 3d series (New York, 1967), p. 131.

[5] "Position et approches concretes du mystere ontologique," *Philosophes contemporains, Textes et etudes* 3 (Louvain and Paris, 1949), p. 64, written in 1933.

External facts do not constitute the whole history of humanistic events and objects; they can be lived as well as understood. That external understanding may be important and fascinating I do not wish to deny. If we cannot say, as the Reverend David Scot said in 1827, that "we are in suspense whether the rabbit or coney be the Saphan of the Hebrew Bible,"[6] we can recognize the joy of factual discovery, the pleasure of a correct textual reading, and the delight of accuracy. Gaetan Picon writes, "L'oeuvre d'art—et singulièrement l'oeouvre litteraire—ne s'impose pas seulement à nous comme un objet de jouissance ou de connaissance; elle s'offre à l'esprit comme objet d'interrogation, d'enquête, de perplexité." (The work of art—and especially the literary work—does not impose itself on us as an object for enjoyment or for knowledge; it offers itself to the mind as an object of interrogation, of inquiry, of perplexity.)[7] This challenge to find out, to inquire, to solve is one that to some cannot be rejected. Yet there is more to the humanities than facts and answers to the questions they offer to the spirit; they must be enjoyed and yet not just enjoyed. The double pull of the humanities puts us at times into a dilemma.

The popular feeling that to analyze a beautiful poem or picture is somehow a desecration is not entirely ridiculous; it has some truth in it. Experience can always laugh at analysis; Don Juan can always be amused by his amanuensis Leporello. But it must be remembered that Leporello can also enjoy Don Juan. Classification as well as experience has its joys, and experience can create its own dilemmas for the inquiring mind.

Can we not, as some would suggest, throw over the attempt

[6] David Scot, quoted in Charles Coulston Gillispie, *Genesis and Geology*, Harvard Historical Studies, No. 58 (Cambridge, Mass., 1951).

[7] Gaetan Picon, *L'écrivain et son ombre* (Paris, 1953), p. 4.

to understand art and history and plunge into existentialistic reality? We can and indeed most people do. Can we not agree with St. Augustine that "Nemo nisi per amiticiam cogniscitur"? As scholars, it seems to me that we must do otherwise. There is something about events and human objects that only experience can give; no one but a black can understand certain aspects of the black experience. Yet there is something about the black experience that only someone who can get out of it and look at it from the outside can understand. Experience as such has a terrible incompleteness for the inquiring mind. Analysis is not enough, it is true, but it can satisfy in a very deep way when it is close to its objects. Although nothing is enough, informed enjoyment and a historical dimension to one's experience, a conviction of accuracy, have the power to answer nagging questions and demands and can civilize a man more than destroy him.

In these days when the whole enterprise of art and its historical study have become questionable to some people, it is right to look at the basic dilemma presented by this dualism. The pursuit of the humanities has become in some ways nightmarish. The knowledge explosion can destroy the humanities in a way that it cannot destroy the sciences. The human mind can no longer comprehend humanistic interpretations; there is no control to throw out erroneous theories, and of facts there can be no end. The criterion of corrigibility lacks in many aspects of humanistic study. Completeness as a humanistic goal is no longer possible. We must get back to basic questions: In what relation must experience stand to its understanding? How can we use intellectual analysis when we obtain understanding by experience? What is the relation of the subjective dimension of experience to its objective dimension?

These questions were basically raised by the Hegelian tradition in Germany in the nineteenth century. It is not my task here to go into the various answers proposed by Hegel himself, by Marx, by Wilhelm Dilthey and others. This has been and still is a continuing concern. I can only make a few tentative suggestions, so that we can perhaps see more clearly what English literature has to do with literature or the study of history with history.

This problem of outer and inner is related to the logical problem of the same and the different, a problem discussed at least since the twelfth century when Adelard of Bath wrote his *De eodem et diverso*[8] concerning minds that see similarities in things and those that see differences. We might call them "same-seers" and "difference-seers" respectively. Today we would say that the scientist attempts to see the sameness of things, attempts to put different things into the same category, whereas the humanist attempts to see the uniqueness of things, whereby one thing differs from all others. The Middle Ages viewed this relationship differently: The sciences saw the difference of things, the contemplator the samenesses. This perhaps is a measure of the differences between our outlook and the medieval qualitative outlook, but the general notion is useful even if in a logical rather than a psychological world of discourse. The problem has an abstract logical significance. Adelard knew, however, that reality was one and that it was all à matter of points of view (*respectus*) on the same universe.

Adelard could see the issue merely as a matter of *respectus*, but we cannot. We can agree that the reality is the same, but since nineteenth-century German philosophy came on the scene, and since the rise of modern existentialist philosophers,

8 Hans Willner, ed., *Des Adelard von Bath Trakat De eodem et diverso, Zum ersten Male herausgegeben und historischkritisch untersucht*, BGPMA4, 1 (Munster, 1903).

the division has come to nag at us in an especial kind of way. Both sides have enormous claims on us, and the question of reconciliation or balance has even more menacing implications.

Marxism has argued that in action we unite both the subjective and objective and overcome the alienation of the understanding process. By emphasizing as a goal of philosophy change and not understanding, Marx and Engels believed that knowing and experience become one. One trouble with this solution is that action may become the judge of truth. It may all end in vulgar ideology, and political expediency can become the criterion of truth (although this criterion is by no means limited to Marxist or so-called Marxist states).

Modern myth-and-symbol thinkers find the solution in their especial subject. The archetypes are at once the most subjective and the most objective of intellectual patterns. If we plunge deeply enough into our own self, we shall discover a nonself in the depths of our being, a nonself possessed of archetypical patterns common to all men. This Jungean solution to the problem of inner and outer has many adherents these days, but because it denies the surface and the living body of art, to my mind it fails to account for diversity. It is all finally the same or a few sames; nothing is different. The myth thinkers are same-seers. I do not deny that such patterns may well exist, but I do not think that they can provide us with our solution except at the level of mystical experience.

The scientific approach that looks at experience and events and objects from the outside is so pervasive today that little really needs to be done to describe it. When it approaches a work of art, it attempts to see the structural and inner relations from a cognitive point of view. When it accounts for the work's being, it attempts to recreate the historical circumstances of its creation and at times the psychology of the author. If it cannot take the text as established, to establish it is also one of its tasks.

Historically, the scientific or objective point of view arose in Greece. Greek philosophy was attuned by some development we do not understand to interpret the world in terms of samenesses, to develop laws to explain the various manifestations, immanent laws according to which nature moves. Whether it be water or opposites, air or reason, the Greeks sought to subsume phenomena under one or more general principles. At the same time Greece developed a great art, an art so overwhelming that even to this day there is no artistic experience so powerful and so all-encompassing as its greatest products. But the subjective dimension of art was always strictly separated from reason and truth. Much classic Greek art, if it was not parodic or satiric, was religious in nature, both in subject matter and in making possible the re-experience of divine or heroic events.

The Hebraic view emphasized experience and the subjective dimension. The objectivity of God was a revealing, an opening, a calling. The ancient Hebrews did not emphasize the unity of God by stating merely that He is one, but by stating "Hear O Israel the Lord your God is One." What one must know is not merely that God is one, but that God speaks to man that He is one. As Martin Buber wrote:

The great achievement of Israel is not so much that it has told mankind of the one, real God, the origin and goal of all that exists, but rather that it has taught men that they can address this God in very reality, that men can say Thou to Him, that we human beings can stand face to face with Him, that there is communion between God and man.[9]

The subjective approach has its roots in ancient Israel and

[9] Martin Buber, *Hasidism*, trans. Greta Hortete (New York, 1948), p. 96. Father Ong has pointed out to me that there is no vocative

in the Judaeo-Christian tradition. Its immediate goal is to seek the diversity and uniqueness of experience. Its method is to read closely, to see vividly, and to experience again the inner meaning of another being and, by extension, of an object.[10]

So far I have been chiefly writing as if the only task of humanistic endeavor is to account for works of art, but the humanities also embrace philosophy and history. Something should be said about these subjects, as their inner or subjective dimension is perhaps not immediately apparent. We can always experience a work of art. But how do we experience history or philosophy?

I think it must at once be admitted that the objective part of the humanistic enterprise certainly occupies a greater role in the disciplines of history and philosophy than in the study of literature and art and music.[11] It becomes a question as to what is the inner dimension of both subjects, whereas one has no question as to the inner experience of literature, art, or music since the inner part of these is like life itself. Just as "I" can be "he" in life, depending on the stance, so one can enjoy Hamlet as experience and at the same time speculate about his character.

The inner experience of philosophy is, I think, what has been known through the ages as wisdom. One experiences philosophy by living or by associating with traditional wisdom, preserved in the ancient forms of proverbs, didactic epigrams, teaching poems, apothegms, riddles, charms, and prayer. At first sight the relation between a disquisition on the

---

form of *Deus*. However, there are certainly Greek and Latin addresses to deities or the Supreme Deity.

[10] The common view, going back in Anglo-Saxon countries largely to Matthew Arnold, that Hebraism is mainly puritanical and morally earnest is only true to a minor extent.

[11] I shall omit discussion of linguistics, which is partly a humanist discipline, and those humanistic aspects of the social sciences, as posing special problems requiring special analyses.

meaning of the word "good" and the assumption of the role of a wise and moral man seems to be very much apart. But if one considers the final goal of morality and ethics to be action, and in a deep sense it must be thus, one can see the inner side of even a linguistic-philosophic discussion. Parts of philosophy, such as logic, are essentially methodological and cognitive sciences, just as are parts of literature, for example, textual work; but there are ethics and metaethics as well as logic in philosophy. Even enterprises like this paper, which attempts to understand the meaning of the humanistic enterprise, have a lived aspect—or at least can have one.

History also has an inner dimension that may come from psychological reconstruction of the past or, even more profoundly, from the contemporary historical awareness and self-awareness of the historian. The historian who sees himself as part of history is re-enacting the historical experience in himself. This historicization of the historian as he writes or works is the main way his subject itself becomes a work of knowing. Needless to say, the historical awareness of the historian is fraught with danger; but when successful, it increases the greatness of his history.

Literary and art criticism can also be either scientific or existential in approach; sometimes they are both. A certain type of criticism attempts to get at the inward "feel" of what is being analyzed. Other types are structural and scientific. Normally the best work tries to relate the pattern to the experience. This kind of humanistic exploration comes closest to balancing the demands of both ways: It gives us a way of overcoming the dualism that must dominate humanistic study most of the time.

Humanistic study has, then, this unique characteristic—that its own subject matter is in some way and in varying degree in competition with itself as a way of knowing. The humanities are a way of knowing dealing with an alternative way of knowing and are subject to all the restraints, contradictions, and ambiguities inherent in such a situation.

There is, of course, a slight inner dimension to the subject matter of some of the sciences, as Housman has indicated. It is, however, very slight—much less than the objective dimension of humanistic study. Even when, as in biology, the subject is life, it is not consciousness as an experience but its physical basis that biology or biological psychology is interested in. Furthermore, as we have already stated, certain social sciences or parts of them also have an inner dimension, usually their historical and anthropological aspects. It is to these aspects of the social sciences that the humanistic scholar feels closest.

Because of this double mode of knowing, humanistic study at its best must be humble, aware that its subject matter is a potential rival, and, finally, concerned with values. Its own enterprise must to some extent always be suspect and must create its own final justification not only by the Aristotelian dictum that "all men desire to know," but also by its contribution to the enrichment of another experience. Nor can humanistic study use the test of success and economy that science can use, except when in its most scientific phase. It must be torn between law and love and can never rest in one and forget the other.

The final end of scientific investigation in the humanities is to know everything; the final end of inner experience is to face the demonic. When both get out of hand, we have chaos indeed. The great novel of this struggle is *Moby Dick* and its hero is Ishmael. As Beongcheon Yu writes: "Moby Dick becomes a masterpiece through its precarious balance, achieved by Melville's sure artistic instinct to subordinate Ahab to Ishmael."[12]

[12] Beongcheon Yu, "Ishmael's Equal Eye: The Source of Balance in *Moby Dick*," *ELH*, 32 (1965), 125. The dual aspect of human

Ahab is demonic man; Ishmael is analytic man. Ishmael needs Ahab more than Ahab needs Ishmael, but humanity must have Ishmael to observe and control Ahab in order to be able to exist at all. The demonic ends only in destruction and anarchy; the analytic ends in the inhuman and the mechanical. But Ishmael is in the end victorious. The destruction of the *Pequod* creates a "vital center" from which a coffin life buoy shoots up to save Ishmael. Alienation can ultimately find healing, and the act that ironically heals is the telling of the novel itself.[13]

Moby Dick begins with an etymology and names and then, like the encyclopedia it is, presents extracts about whales, thereby apeing completeness. Out of external knowledge of "whale" comes a story told by Ishmael who intersperses more information. The names and the extracts give us clues to the meaning of the novel. I wish merely to pause a moment at the names, for the "science" of names can provide us with the kind of bridge I think we are looking for.

In spite of Aquinas' comment that wise people do not worry about names,[14] one must say that Kabbalistic speculation about the names of God or the listing of the ninety-nine names of Allah that we find in Islam was a matter of the greatest import in overcoming the opposition between knowledge and experience in medieval times. There was then no problem about God, but there was a problem about naming Him.[15] In his *On the Divine Names*, the Pseudo-Dionysius in

experience as lived and as understood was a continual source of fascination to Melville. J. Hillis Miller has privately pointed out to me this dual cognition in *Benito Cereno*, for example.

[13] Cf. Odysseus' weeping when he hears the minstrel at the court of King Alcinous tell the story of the attack on Troy and of his own part in it (Book 8, end). I am indebted to Eric Weil for recalling this episode to me.

[14] See St. Thomas, II *Sent.* 3, 1, 1.

[15] See Luis Martinez Gomez, "From the Names of God to the

the sixth century posed for Christianity the problem that also faced Judaism and was later to confront the Moslem world.[16] If God is to listen to us, if He is to turn toward us, He must be called by His right name. Since a man will not turn to us if we call him by a wrong name, why then should God do so?

Naming is a very complex procedure and proper naming is even more puzzling. The whole process at some stage belongs to the vocative and deictic world, whether present or in mind.[17] Names are important essentially to the humanist, and in a way the goal of humanistic endeavor is to find correct names so that the world may respond to us. Priore Blanco, the arch-scientist, asks young Fabrizio in Stendhal's *The Charterhouse of Parma*, "What more do I know about a horse when I am told that in Latin it is called *equus?*" The "more" is what the humanities is finally all about.

Like most elements in life, and perhaps life itself, the humanistic endeavor at its highest moments must be a balance between antithetical forces. One of the outstanding characteristics of life is its inside-outside dichotomy. Merleau-Ponty says somewhere that the mind is in the body, but the body is also in the mind. In this respect, the humanities at their most ideal level imitate life itself, so that outside may become in-

Name of God: Nicholas of Cusa," trans. Aloysius C. Owen, *International Philosophical Quarterly*, 5 (1965), 80–102. Nicholas of Cusa was fascinatingly concerned with the names of God, especially in his *De Docta Ignorantia*.

[16] The concern with names in the Pseudo-Dionysius probably echoes Neoplatonic interests. I have not been able to pursue this matter very far, but see the discussion of divine names in Iamblichus, *De mysteriis Aegyptiorum*, VII, 4–5.

[17] Cf. John Holloway, *Language and Intelligence* (London, 1951), p. 21. "The relation of naming is in fact both complex and puzzling; it is far from possessing such complete and convenient simplicity. . . . Indeed, it is doubtful if the relation between a proper name, and that object which it names, is really a relation of meaning at all."

side and inside, outside. At its highest, work in the humanities is akin to life itself.

Moby Dick presents the classical dilemma of pure exteriority versus pure interiority in the figures of Ishmael and Ahab, and this dichotomy is reflected in the original title of *The White Whale or Moby Dick*. One can regard the whale as white whale or one can chase Moby Dick. Moby Dick will ultimately destroy a man; the whale will ultimately be completely known and classified. But analytic man, when he experiences the vital center, can unite both species and name to return to tell a tale that begins "Call me Ishmael." The teller has learned that names are important and must come first. The White Whale *or* Moby Dick becomes The White Whale *and* Moby Dick. Ahab must, however, always go down to destruction so that Ishmael can learn and so that he may be preserved to tell a story—the very story, in fact, that tells us of Ahab and Ishmael.

I do not believe that a bridge must always be thrown across the two cognitive dimensions of the humanities. We need both classification and experience. At times Bitzer's definition of a horse is required: "Quadruped. Graminivorous. Forty teeth . . ." and so on.[18] Sissy Jupe may really know more about horses than the egregious Bitzer, but we need him for a certain kind of understanding. At other times, "There are some enterprises in which a careful disorderliness [like life] is the true method."[19] On those occasions, we must plunge into the disorderliness of life. It is characteristic of the humanities to be balanced between the two. I would argue that the essence of the humanities is finally, then, a cognitive matter— a knowing about another knowing. But at times a link between the two must be built, and names both proper and common

---

[18] Charles Dickens, *Hard Times,* chap. 2.
[19] Herman Melville, *Moby Dick,* chap. 81.

provide us with a way of doing this—possible through the art of literary criticism in its broadest sense. We must know the right names so that things and beings may respond to us. We must know what the names are. If we cannot at times be satisfied in both cognitive ways, we are doomed to an eternal split and to wandering in the night.

Finally, we must say again that the dichotomous nature of the humanities is a given that is desirable to overcome only at times. It is never possible to blend the two forever; they must remain two different modes, two different *respectus*. They finally *are*, and Don Juan and Leporello cannot become Don Leporello. The tension can never be finally relieved. However, moments of bridging can exist and each side can open to the other. One can be great as a humanistic "scientist," and one can be great as a phenomenological thinker or creator, and finally one can be great in both at once.[20] Perhaps in the last are the greatest achievements of all.

[20] The experience of the humanities that stands in opposition to the "science" of the humanities is itself double in aspect. Literary and phenomenological criticism can attempt through consciousness to attain the verbal experience of living, which is not the same as living itself. In other words, there are really three sides here: scientific or exterior cognition, phenomenological and lived cognition, the latter two of which are closely related as varieties of interior cognition. A phenomenological study of *Hamlet* is not the same as the viewing or reading of *Hamlet*, but it is closer to it than a scholarly study. I have not attempted to develop here this dual aspect of interior cognition.

Many of the distinctions frequently given to characterize the humanities as a separate discipline do not seem valid to me. It is true, for example, that there is a large, playful, and aesthetic element in the humanities, as when documents or things are studied for their own sake. But these characteristics can be found in all scientific study, even if perhaps not to quite the same extent. Even the test of the practical or useful will not apply, for the humanities can also be very practical —in some forms of society more so than the physical sciences.

I wish to thank my good friend Roy Harvey Pearce for some suggestions that I have used here.

89

NORTHROP FRYE

The Critical Path: An Essay on the Social Context of Literary Criticism[1]

[1] A lengthier and more developed version of this essay has been published as a separate book by Indiana University Press.

I

T HE phrase "The Critical Path" is, I understand, a term in business administration, and was one that I
began hearing extensively used during the preparations for the
Montreal Expo in 1967. It associated itself in my mind with the
closing sentences of Kant's *Critique of Pure Reason*, where he
says that dogmatism and skepticism have both had it as tenable
philosophical positions, and that "the critical path is alone
open." It also associated itself with a turning point in my own
development. About twenty-five years ago, when still in middle life, I lost my way in the dark wood of Blake's prophecies,
and looked around for some path that would get me out of
there. There were many paths, some well trodden and
equipped with signposts, but all pointing in what for me was
the wrong direction. They directed me to the social conditions of Blake's time, to the history of the occult tradition,
to psychological factors in Blake's mind, and other subjects
quite valid in themselves. But my task was the specific problem of trying to crack Blake's symbolic code, and I had a feeling that the way to that led directly through literature itself.
The critical path I wanted, therefore, was a theory of criticism
which would, first, account for the major phenomena of liter-

ary experience, and, second, would lead to some view of the place of literature in civilization as a whole.

Following the bent that Blake had given me, I became particularly interested in two questions. One was: What is the total subject of study of which criticism forms a part? I rejected the easy answer: "Criticism is a subdivision of literature," because it seemed obvious to me that literature is not a subject of study at all apart from some aspect of criticism. There seemed to me two possible larger contexts of criticism: one, the unified criticism of all the arts, which did not (and does not yet) exist; the other, some larger study of verbal expression which had not yet been defined. The latter seemed more immediately promising: the former was the area of aesthetics, in which (at least at that time) relatively few technically competent literary critics appeared to be much interested. But there was a strong centrifugal drift from criticism toward social, philosophical, or religious interests, which had set in at least as early as Coleridge. I viewed this with some suspicion, because it seemed to me that an unjustified sense of claustrophobia underlay it. A critic devoting himself wholly to literature is often tempted to feel that he can never be anything more than a second-class writer or thinker, because his work is based on the work of what almost by definition are greater men. I felt, then, that a theory of criticism was needed which would set the critic's activity in its proper light, and that once we had that, a critic's other interests would represent an expansion of criticism rather than an escape from it.

The other question was: How do we arrive at poetic meaning? This question was closely related to the other question of context. When I first began to write on critical theory, I was startled to realize how general was the agreement that criticism had no presuppositions of its own, but had to be "grounded" on some other subject. The disagreements were not over that, but over the question of what the proper subjects were that criticism ought to depend on. The older European philological basis, a very sound one, had already been discarded, in most North American universities, for a mixture of history and philosophy, evidently on the assumption that every work of literature is what Sir Walter Raleigh said *Paradise Lost* was, a monument to dead ideas. I myself was soon identified as one of the critics who took their assumptions from anthropology and psychology, then still widely regarded as the wrong subjects. I have always insisted that criticism cannot take presuppositions from elsewhere, which always means wrenching them out of their real context, and must work out its own. But mental habits are hard to break, especially bad habits, and, because I found the term "archetype" a useful one, I am still often called a Jungian critic, and classified with Miss Maud Bodkin, whose book I have read with interest, but whom, on the evidence of that book, I resemble about as closely as I resemble the late Sarah Bernhardt.

In the last generation, of which I am now speaking, the accepted critical procedure was to take a work of literature, let us say a poem for short, and treat it as a document to be related to some context outside literature. One of the most obvious of these documentary approaches was the biographical one, where the poem is taken to be a document illustrating something in the poet's life. The golden age of this approach was the nineteenth century, and its strongest proponent was Carlyle, for whom great poetry could only be the personal rhetoric of a great man. The model great man was Goethe, who, for Carlyle, was to be admired not so much for the quality of his poetry as for the number of things he had been able to do besides writing poetry. Of course no one denies the relevance of the poet's life to his work: doubts arise only when the sense of that relevance is carried to uncritical extremes. In the first place, there are variations in the degree of its relevance: it is more important for Byron than for Wordsworth, more important for D. H. Lawrence than for T. S. Eliot. Secondly, when we have no real knowledge of a poet's life at all, it is better to leave it alone than to invent a biography out of fancied allusions in the poetry, as nineteenth-century critics so often did with Shakespeare, and as many are still doing with the sonnets.

In these days, a biographical approach is likely to move from the manifest to the latent personal content of the poem, and from a biographical approach properly speaking to a psychological one, which at present means very largely a Freudian one. All documentary approaches to literature are allegorical approaches, and this fact becomes even more obvious when poems are taken to be allegories of Freudian repressions, unresolved conflicts or tensions between ego and id, or, for another school, of the Jungian process of individuation. A considerable amount of determinism enters at this stage. It still seems unquestionable to many critics that literature has its origin in psychological processes, and that it can be explained only in terms that are ultimately psychological terms. But what is true of allegorical poetry is equally true of allegorical criticism: in both fields allegory is a technique that calls for tact. When the whiteness of Moby Dick is explained as a Lockian *tabula rasa*, or Alice in Wonderland discussed in terms of her hypothetical toilet training, or Arnold's "Where ignorant armies clash by night" taken as a covert reference to the copulation of his parents, one is reminded of the exempla from natural history made by medieval preachers. The bee carries earth in its feet to ballast itself when it flies, and thereby reminds us of the Incarnation, when God took up an earthly form. The example is ingenious and entertaining, and only unsatisfying if one happens to be interested in bees. Naturally such practices have produced a reaction from critics who see the futility of trying to base their professional scholarly competence on an amateur enthusiasm for something else. But I do not think it helps any merely to write cautionary treatises urging critics that they should be careful not to do too much various things that they are not effectively doing at all.

In any case, there will always be critics, probably the great majority, for whom the ultimate source of a poem is not the individual poet at all, but rather the social situation from which the poet springs, and of which he is the spokesman and the medium. This takes us into the area of historical criticism. Here again no one can or should deny the relevance of literature to history, but here again the relation is an indirect one, more relevant to some poets than to others. The historical subculture known as the history of ideas is more consistently rewarding, for ideas, like poems, cannot exist until they are verbalized. Here the allegorizing tendency in all such criticism shows up very clearly.

Once more, some historical critics, like the biographical ones, will want to go from manifest to latent social content, from the historical context of the poem to its context in some unified overview of history. Of these enlarged historical perspectives, Marxism is today the most widely adopted, and perhaps inherently the most serious. Here again, as with psychological criticism, the determinism in the approach, which includes a determination to find the ultimate meaning of literature in something that is not literature, is unmistakable. At the time of which I am speaking, there was also a conservative Catholic determinism, strongly influenced by Eliot, which adopted, as the summit of Western cultural values, the medieval synthesis of the period of St. Thomas Aquinas, and looked down benignantly on everything that followed it as a kind of toboggan slide, rushing through nominalism, Protestantism, liberalism, subjective idealism, and so on to the solipsism in which the critic's non-Thomist contemporaries were assumed to be enclosed.

All these documentary approaches, even when correctly handled, are subject to at least three limitations, which every experienced scholar interested in them has to reckon with. In the first place, they do not account for the literary form of what they are discussing. Identifying Edward King and documenting Milton's attitude to the Church of England will throw no light on *Lycidas* as a pastoral elegy with specific classical and Italian lines of ancestry. Secondly, they do not account for the poetic and metaphorical language of the literary work. Documentary criticism in general is based on the assumption that the literal or real meaning of a poem is not what it says as a poem, but is something to be expressed by a prose paraphrase derived from the poem. Thirdly, they do not account for the fact that the unique quality of a poet is often in a quite negative relation to the chosen context. To understand fully Blake's *Milton* and *Jerusalem* one needs to know something of his quarrel with Hayley and his sedition trial, but one also needs to be aware of the vast disproportion between these very minor events in a very quiet life and their apocalyptic transformation in the poems. Similarly, one may write a whole shelf of books about the life of Milton studied in connection with the history of his time, and still fail to notice that Milton's greatness as a poet has a good deal to do with his profound and perverse misunderstanding of the history of his time.

By the time I began writing criticism, the so-called "new criticism" had established itself as a technique of explication. This was a rhetorical form of criticism, and from the beginning rhetoric has meant two things: the figuration of language and the persuasive powers of an orator. New criticism dealt with rhetoric in the former sense, and established a counterweight to the biographical approach which treated poetry as a personal rhetoric. The great merit of explicatory criticism was that it accepted poetic language as the basis for poetic meaning. On this basis, it built up a resistance to all "background" criticism that explained the literary in terms of the nonliterary. At the same time, it deprived itself of the great strength of documentary criticism: the sense of context. It simply explicated one work after another, paying little attention to any larger structural principles connecting the different works explicated. The limitations of this approach soon became obvious, and most of the new critics sooner or later fell back on one of the established documentary contexts, generally the historical one, although they were regarded at first as antihistorical. One or two have even been Marxists, but in general the movement, at least in America, was anti-Marxist. Marxists had previously condemned a somewhat similar tendency in Russian criticism as "formalism," because they realized that if they began by conceding literary form as the basis for literary significance, the assumptions on which Marxist bureaucracies rationalized their censorship of the arts would be greatly weakened. They would logically have to end, in fact, in giving poets and novelists the same kind of freedom that they had reluctantly been compelled to grant to the physical scientists. More recently, my Toronto colleague Marshall McLuhan has placed an extreme and somewhat paradoxical formalism, expressed in the phrase "the medium is the message," within the context of a neo-Marxist determinism in which communications media play the same role that instruments of production do in more orthodox Marxism. In him the centrifugal tendency in criticism which I spoke of a moment ago has expanded into a new mosaic code. Professor McLuhan formed his views under the influence of the conservative wing of the new critical movement, and many traces of an earlier Thomist determinism can be found in *The Gutenberg Galaxy*.

It seemed to me that, after accepting the poetic form of a poem as its literal meaning, the next step was to look for some context for it within literature itself. And of course the most obvious context for a poem is the entire output of its author. Just as explication, by stressing the more objective aspect of rhetoric, had formed a corrective to the excesses of biographical criticism, so a study of a poet's whole work might form the basis of a kind of "psychological" criticism that would operate within literature, and so provide some balance for the kind that ends in the bosom of Freud. Poetry is, after all, a technique of communication: it engages the conscious part of the mind as well as the murkier areas, and what a poet succeeds in communicating to others is at least as important as what he fails to resolve for himself. One soon becomes aware that every poet has his own distinctive structure of imagery, which usually emerges even in his earliest work, and which does not and cannot essentially change. This larger context of the poem within its author's entire "mental landscape" (to use a phrase often employed in a different connection) is assumed in all the best explication—Spitzer's, for example. I became aware of its importance myself, when working on Blake, as soon as I realized that Blake's special symbolic names and the like did form a genuine structure of poetic imagery and not, despite his use of the word, a "system," to which he was bound like an administrator to a computer. I got another lead here from Yeats's early essay on the philosophy of Shelley's poetry, for by "philosophy" Yeats really meant structure of imagery.

100

There was another difficulty with new criticism which was only a technical one, but still pointed to the necessity for a sense of context. Whenever we read anything there are two mental operations we perform, which succeed one another in time. First we follow the narrative movement in the act of reading, turning over the pages to get to the end. Afterwards, we can look at the work as a simultaneous unity and study its structure. This latter act is the critical response properly speaking: the ordinary reader seldom needs to bother with it. The chief material of rhetorical analysis consists of a study of the poetic "texture," and such a study plunges one into a complicated labyrinth of ambiguities, multiple meanings, recurring images, and echoes of both sound and sense. A full explication of a long and complex work which was based on the reading process could well become much longer, and more difficult to read, than the work itself. Such linear explications have some advantages as a teaching technique, but for publishing purposes it is more practicable to start with the second stage. This involves attaching the rhetorical analysis to a deductive framework derived from a study of the structure, and the context of that structure shows us where we should begin to look for our central images and ambiguities. The difficulty in transferring explication from the reading process to the study of structure has left some curious traces in new critical theory. One of them is again in McLuhan, who makes it the basis for a distinction between the "linear" demands of the printed media and the "simultaneous" impact of the electronic ones.

I was still not satisfied: I wanted a historical approach to literature, but an approach that would be or include a genuine history of literature, and not the assimilating of literature to some other kind of history. It was at this point that the immense importance of certain structural elements in the literary tradition, such as conventions, genres, and the recurring use of certain images or image-clusters, which I came to call archetypes, forced itself on me. T. S. Eliot had already spoken of tradition as a creative and informing power operating on the poet specifically as a craftsman, and not generally as a cultivated person. But neither he nor anyone else seemed to get to the point of identifying the factors of that tradition, of what it is that makes possible the creation of new works of literature out of earlier ones.

And yet convention, within literature, seemed to be a force even stronger than history. The difference between medieval poets using courtly love conventions in the London of Richard II and Cavalier poets using the same conventions in the London of Charles II is far less than the difference in social conditions between the two ages. I began to suspect that a poet's relation to poetry was much more like a scientist's relation to his science than was generally thought. Literature and science, of course, differ profoundly in the way in which science is able to absorb the work of predecessors in a steadily growing body of knowledge, whereas literature shows no such progressive tendencies. We shall perhaps understand this fact more clearly as we go on. Apart from that, the psychological processes involved seem much the same. The scientist cannot become a scientist until he immerses himself in his science, until he attaches his own thinking to the body of what is thought in his day about that science, until he becomes less a man thinking about his science than a kind of incarnation of that science thinking through him. What is true of science is true of all academic disciplines. No scholar, *qua* scholar, can think for himself or think at random: he can only expand an organic body of thought, add something logically related to what he or someone else has already thought. But this is precisely the way that poets have always talked about their relation to poetry: from Homer to Rimbaud, poets have invariably insisted that they were simply places where something new in literature was able to take its own shape. The new critics had resisted the background approach to criticism, but they had not destroyed the oratorical conception of poetry as a personal rhetoric.

From here it is clear that one has to take a final step. Criticism must develop a sense of history within literature to complement the historical criticism that relates literature to a historical background. Similarly, it must develop its own form of historical overview, on the basis of what is inside literature rather than outside it. Instead of fitting literature deterministically into a prefabricated scheme of history, the critic should see literature as, like a science, a unified, coherent, and autonomous created form, historically conditioned but shaping its own history, not determined by any external historical process. This total body of literature can be studied through its larger structural principles, which I have just described as conventions, genres, and recurring image-groups, or archetypes. When criticism develops a proper sense of the history of literature, the history of what is not literature does not cease to exist or to be relevant to the critic. Similarly, seeing literature as a single created form does not withdraw it from a social context: on the contrary, it becomes far easier to see what its place in civilization is. Criticism will always have two aspects, one turned toward the structure of literature as a whole and one turned toward the other cultural phenomena that form its environment. Together, they balance each other; when one is worked on to the exclusion of the other, the critical perspective goes out of focus. If criticism is in proper balance, the "centrifugal" tendency of critics to move from critical to larger social issues becomes more intelligible. Such a movement need not, and should not, be due to a dissatisfaction with the narrowness of criticism as a discipline, but should be simply the result of a sense of social context, a sense present in all critics from whom one is in the least likely to learn anything.

II

The conventions, genres, and archetypes of literature do not simply appear: they must develop historically from origins, or perhaps from a common origin. In pursuing this line of thought, I have turned repeatedly to Giambattista Vico, one of the very few thinkers to understand anything of the historical role of the poetic impulse in civilization as a whole. Vico describes how a society, in its earliest phase, sets up a framework of mythology, out of which all its verbal culture grows, including its literature. Vico's main interest is in the history of law, but it is not difficult to apply his principles to other verbal disciplines. Primitive verbal culture consists of, among other things, a group of stories. Some of these stories take on a central and canonical importance: they are believed to have really happened, or else to explain or recount something that is centrally important for a society's history, religion, or social structure. These canonical stories are the ones we call myths: they are similar in literary form to folk tales and legends, but have a more specialized social function. Because of this function, myths tend to take root in a specific culture and to stick together to form a mythology, whereas folk tales lead a more nomadic existence, traveling over the world interchanging themes and motifs. This distinction is a fateful one for the critic, because the whole historical dimension of the study of literature is bound up in it. If the critic attends only to the similarity in form between myth and folk tale, he embarks on an oversimplified structuralism in which there is no real historical perspective at all. Once a mythology is formed, a temenos or magic circle is drawn around a culture, and literature develops historically within a limited orbit of language, reference, allusion, beliefs, transmitted and shared tradition.

As a culture develops, its mythology tends to become encyclopedic, expanding into a total myth covering a society's view of its past, present, and future, its relation to its gods and its neighbors, its traditions, its social and religious duties, and its ultimate destiny. We naturally think of a mythology as a human cultural product, but few societies think of their mythologies at the beginning as something that they have themselves created. They think of them rather as a revelation given them from the gods, or their remote ancestors, or a period before time began. It is particularly law and religious ritual that are most frequently thought of as divinely revealed. A fully developed or encyclopedic myth comprises everything that it most concerns its society to know, and I shall therefore speak of it as the myth of concern.

The myth of concern exists to hold society together, so far as words can help to do this. For it, truth and reality are not directly connected with reasoning or evidence, but are socially established. What is true, for concern, is what society does and believes in response to authority, and a belief, so far as a belief is verbalized, is a statement of willingness to participate in a myth of concern. The language of concern is, therefore, an expression of belief. In origin, a myth of concern is largely undifferentiated: it has its roots in religion, but religion has also at that stage the function of *religio*, the binding together of the community in common acts and assumptions. It is only later that the myth of concern tends to limit itself to a more specific religious area as other aspects of culture become more secularized. In this later stage it becomes more exclusively a myth of what Paul Tillich calls ultimate concern, the myth of man's relation to other worlds, other beings, other lives, other dimensions of time and space. The myth of concern which European and American culture has inherited is, of course, the Judaeo-Christian myth as set out in the Bible, and as taught in the form of doctrine by the Christian Church. The encyclopedic form of the Bible, stretching from creation to apocalypse, makes it particularly well fitted to provide a mythical framework for a culture, though supplemented in our literature by an extensive development of classical mythology, which also takes on something of an encyclopedic shape in Ovid's *Metamorphoses* and elsewhere.

Vico was also the first, so far as I know, to indicate something of the crucial importance of a distinction which has been vigorously pursued by some scholars quite recently. This is the distinction between the oral or preliterate culture in which the myth of concern normally begins, and the writing culture which succeeds it. An oral culture depends on memory, and consequently it also depends mainly on verse, the simplest and most memorable way of conventionalizing the rhythm of speech. In oral culture, mythology and literature are almost coterminous: the teachers of the myth are poets, or people with skills akin to the poetic, who survive in legend or history as bards, prophets, religious teachers, or culture heroes of various kinds. With a writing culture, prose develops, and the continuity of prose enables philosophy to take form, as a mode of thought articulated by logic and dialectic. Similarly, history detaches itself from epic, and gradually becomes the study of what actually occurred. Further, as a writing culture is usually a counting and measuring culture as well, scientific and mathematical procedures form part of the same change in mental attitude.

The mental habits brought in by a writing and measuring

culture are very different from those of concern. Here, the driving forces binding society together have relaxed somewhat, and man may think of himself, not only as forming part of a community, but also as confronting an objective world or order of nature. Truth in this context becomes truth of correspondence, the alignment of a structure of words or numbers with a body of external phenomena. Such ideas as knowledge for its own sake, or Aristotle's axiom that all men by nature desire to know, are luxuries depending on the existence of written documents. It is clear that this approach to truth and reality tends to individualize a culture, to make the philosopher, the scientist, the poet, individually masters of a specialized craft. The normal tendency of truth of correspondence is nonmythical, appealing not directly to concern but to impersonal evidence and verification. The mental attitudes it develops, however, which include objectivity, suspension of judgment, tolerance, and respect for the individual, become social attitudes as well, and consolidate around a central relationship to society. The verbal expression of concern for these attitudes I shall call the myth of freedom. The myth of freedom is a part of the myth of concern, but is a part that stresses the importance of the nonmythical elements in culture, of the truths and realities that are studied rather than created, provided by nature rather than by human desire. It thus refers to the safeguarding of certain social values not directly connected with the myth of concern, such as the tolerance of opinion which dissents from it. It constitutes the "liberal" element in society, as the myth of concern constitutes the conservative one, and those who hold it are unlikely to form a much larger group than an educated minority. To form the community as a whole is not the function of the myth of freedom: it has to find its place in, and come to terms

107

with, the society of which it forms part. Its relation to that society is symbiotic, though sometimes regarded, in times of deep conflict, as simply parasitic.

In the ancient world, Greek culture made the transition to writing, and to the mental habits of writing, with fair completeness, as far as its minority of cultural leaders was concerned. The expulsion of poets from Plato's republic was the sign that Greek culture was no longer to be confined by the idioms of the poets. The result is that the scientific, philosophical, mathematical, and historical presuppositions of Western culture come mainly from the Greeks. Our whole liberal tradition in education, as the etymology of the word "academic" shows, is essentially of Greek origin. A parallel shift to writing and prose took place in Hebrew culture around the time of the Deuteronomic reform, which transformed a mass of legends and oracles into a sacred book written mainly in prose. But the prose of the Old Testament maintains a much closer link with the oral tradition. Philosophy, within the Biblical canon, still retains its primitive connection with proverb and oracle: Biblical history is at no time clearly separable from legend or historical reminiscence. Whatever secular Hebrew culture developed did so outside the canon. The specific contribution of Hebrew and Biblical mythology to our own culture was in its concentration on a central myth of concern, and the rigorous subordination of all other cultural factors to it.

For Judaism, what is true and real is what God says and does; for Christianity, truth is ultimately truth of personality, specifically the personality of Christ. Within Christianity there has always been a feeling that whatever in one's faith is true owes its truth to being in the Bible, or to being taught by the Church on the basis of the Bible. In the First Epistle of John there is a verse setting forth the doctrine of the Trinity which New Testament scholars generally recognize to be a late insertion. The insertion is not simply a pious fraud: if one believes the doctrine of the Trinity, then, from the point of view of the myth of concern, the way to make it true is to get it into the Bible. Nor is the procedure any different from what had gone on in the holy book for centuries: we cannot trace any part of the Bible back to a time when it was not being edited, redacted, conflated, glossed, and expurgated.

When we ask what impelled Hebrew culture to develop its unique conception of a definitive sacred book, one of the answers clearly has to do with the fact that Israel was a defeated and subjected nation, with few intervals of military success and a long memory for them. Monotheism is an idea that seems to be suggested by the conception of a world empire: the first monotheist on record was an Egyptian pharaoh, and among the most devout monotheists of the ancient world were the world-conquering Persians. The monotheism of the Hebrews, by contrast, was bound up with the conception of the one God as their God, united in a contract of blood with them, whose will would eventually re-establish their kingdom and overthrow the great empires of the earth. The Jewish conception of a "Day of Jehovah," which was adopted into Christianity as the Last Judgment, points to something very different from imperial monotheism. Hebrew monotheism differed from all similar creeds in being a socially and politically revolutionary belief, and this revolutionary quality was inherited by Christianity.

It is hard to overstate the importance for today of the fact that the Western myth of concern is in origin a revolutionary myth. I said that a religious myth of concern tends increasingly as it goes on to specialize in another world, and in proportion as it does so a more secular and political myth of concern arises to supplement it. This situation reached a crucial stage around the close of the eighteenth century, when the Christian monopoly of the Western myth of concern began to give way to a more pluralistic situation in which a number of new revolutionary political myths of concern shared the field with it. Of these, the most important were the myth of democracy and the revolutionary working-class myth centered on Marxism. The former, which drew from both classical and Christian sources, was a myth of concern which attempted to incorporate a myth of freedom within itself; the latter was a more direct descendant of the original Judaeo-Christian revolutionary attitude. The link of continuity between Christianity and the revolutionary movements of our own time is much less obvious than the Greek ancestry of our academic and liberal attitudes, as every revolution forms itself in opposition to its predecessor. But the link is there: it is not easy to break out of the mental habits formed by a mythical framework, or what is often called tradition, and even if it is possible we must first know what that tradition is. Naturally, in the nineteenth century, and even earlier, there were many who insisted that the true myth of concern could only be found in a revived Christianity, and the production of such manifestoes has been a cultural heavy industry ever since. But not many of these—not even those of Kierkegaard, who was more aware of the kind of implications we are considering here than most—have been able or willing to recognize the revolutionary characteristics of the Christian myth.

One of these characteristics is the belief in a unique historical revelation. This belief, which gives so many liberals so much difficulty with Christianity, is an essential part of a revolutionary attitude: a revolution starts then and there, not all over the place at different times. It begins with Jesus and not with the Pharisees or Essenes; with Marx and not with Owen or the Saint-Simonians. Along with the uniqueness goes the conception of a canon of essential and approved texts, and a clear drawing of lines against even the most neighborly of heresies. In fact, the attack on the heresy helps to define a revolutionary doctrine in a way that an attack on total opposition does not. Christianity defined itself, not by attacking unbelievers, but by attacking Arians or Gnostics and calling them unbelievers; Marxism defines itself, not by attacking capitalist imperialism, but by attacking Trotsky or Liu Shao-Chi and calling them agents of capitalist imperialism. Another characteristic is the resistance to any kind of "revisionism," or incorporating of other cultural elements into the thought of the revolutionary leadership. The revolutions within Christianity, notably the Protestant ones, usually professed to be a return to the pure gospel of their founder, and this must also be the professed aim of new Marxist party lines. There is even an ultra-Puritan movement in Marxism back to the early alienation essays of Marx, before social and institutional Marxism began. The antirevisionist tendency is normally an antiliberal tendency. Revolutions, naturally, are directed against some power-holding ascendancy, and liberals, from "enervate Origen," as Eliot calls him, to Erasmus, and from Erasmus to the politic liberals of our own day, are regularly taken by revolutionaries to be, consciously or unconsciously, spokesmen for the opposed establishment.

The conservative reaction to early Christianity was typical of conservative reactions to revolutionary movements. The earliest external reference to Christians, in Tacitus' *Annals,* speaks of them with a blistering contempt which is highly significant, coming as it does from a by no means weak or hysterical writer. Much later, the Emperor Marcus Aurelius

111

complained that he had tried to get rid of the Christians by persecution, but had been unable to make much impression on them because of their *parataxis*, their military discipline. Even he did not recognize that the Christian Church had been duplicating the Roman authority within a power-structure which could go underground in time of persecution until the time came for it to emerge and take over. Eventually that time came, and then, of course, the cyclical movement which is inherent in the very word "revolution" began to operate.

In every structured society the ascendant class attempts to take over the myth of concern and make it, or an essential part of it, a rationalization of its ascendancy. In proportion as Christianity gained secular authority, its myth of concern tended to associate itself with the myths of the various ascendant classes as they succeeded one another. In the Middle Ages, the conception of a structure of authority, requiring protection from above and obedience from below, found its way into the religious myth as well as the social system. The connection between Protestantism and the rise of the bourgeoisie has been considerably overlabored by historians and social scientists, but still in the nineteenth century Matthew Arnold was able, with some plausibility, to associate the "Hebraic" or Judaeo-Christian tradition with the mores of the Victorian middle class. Certainly the association of Christianity with the middle class did a good deal to popularize the Marxist conception of a proletarian or excluded-class myth of concern. Yet Christianity has always remained a revolutionary myth, never completely merging with any ascendant-class myth in the way that, apparently, Hinduism and Confucianism did in the Far East.

In the earlier Christian centuries, the dethroned "pagan" tradition began slowly to form a liberal opposition, modifying, relaxing, and expanding the revolutionary narrowness of the

112

Christian myth of concern. Some of this was reflected in literature: we shall return to this later. Christianity, like most revolutionary movements, required from its most dedicated followers the extra energy that comes from sexual sublimation. The poets developed, mainly from Ovid, a convention of love poetry, which also often ended in sublimation, or even frustration, but also often did not, and in any case made it imaginatively clear that Eros was a mighty force to be reckoned with. Again, the Christian myth, by remaining so close to the oral tradition, had thrown a strong emphasis on the ear, on the hearing of the word, on the receptivity to authority that binds a society together. In the word "idolatry," and in its recurring iconoclasm, Christianity expressed its antagonism to the hypnotizing power of the external visible world. It was, again, a more liberal expansion of Christian culture that developed the visual arts, including the arts of the theatre, so much disliked by the more rigorous Christians, including Pascal and many of the Puritans. The growing realism and direct observation of experience and nature in Western art also helped to relax the Christian preoccupation with unifying society in a common bond of belief. The Christian teaching that there were no gods and nothing numinous in nature, that nature was a fellow creature of man, and that the gods men had previously discovered in nature were all devils, reflects a certain fear of turning away from social concern to natural objects: the development of modern science, on the other hand, much as it owes to Christianity, also, from Copernicus onward, drew heavily from Platonic and other classical world views.

The central question of concern, what must we do to be saved? is much the same in all ages, but naturally the conceptions of salvation differ. There are two worlds for man: one is the environment of nature and existing society, which is presented to man as a datum and is first of all to be studied; and the other is the world he wants to live in, the civilization that he accepts as an ideal and tries to realize. For traditional Christianity, God alone is creative, and the creative power in man must follow divine models. God built the first city and planted the first garden; God in creating nature was the first artist; God designed the primary laws of mankind and revealed to him the true religion. For most radical myths of concern in our day, the only creative power in the situation comes from man himself, hence its truth or reality is connected with human desire, with what we want to see exist, and with human practical skill, with what we are able to make exist. Marx did not, so far as I know, speak of this created reality as myth: that association for revolutionary thought was made later, chiefly by Georges Sorel. But the tendency of the radical outlook was certainly to associate the reality of desire and practical energy with human will and creative power, not with the acceptance of external or revealed authority. Philosophers, said Marx, have studied the world but not changed it, and for him it was time for the philosophical myth of freedom to be subordinated again to a new but wholly human and secular myth of concern.

III

In trying to see where the poet belongs in this dialectic of concern and freedom, I should like to turn to the two great "defenses" of poetry in English literature, those by Sidney and Shelley. Both works are familiar, but in the present context they may show less familiar aspects. It is obvious that a defense of poetry, whoever writes it, contributes, at least potentially, to a critic's confession of faith. Defense implies attack: Sidney's essay is usually contrasted with the kind of antipoetic statement often called "Puritan," such as Stephen

Gosson's *Schoole of Abuse* (although technically Gosson was not a Puritan and Sidney was), and Shelley takes off from his friend Thomas Love Peacock's satire, *The Four Ages of Poetry*.

In most Elizabethan criticism we find some reference to the poet as having been dispossessed from a greater heritage. Sidney stresses this theme less than many of his contemporaries, but still it is there, attached to the common Renaissance assumption that in all human achievements the greatest are the earliest. In a distant past, even before Homer, a period associated with such legendary names as Musaeus, Linus, and Orpheus, along with Zoroaster in religion and Hermes Trismegistus in philosophy, the poet, we are told, was the lawgiver of society, the founder of civilization. This refers, as noted above, to the conditions of an oral or preliterate culture, in which the professional poet is, if not exactly the lawgiver, at least the educator, the man who knows. That is, he is the man who remembers, and consequently knows the traditional and proper formulas of knowledge. He knows the names of the gods, their genealogy, and their dealings with men; the names of the kings and the tribal legends, the stories of battles won and enemies conquered, the popular wisdom of proverbs and the esoteric wisdom of oracles, the calendar and the seasons, the lucky and unlucky days and the phases of the moon, charms and spells, the right methods of sacrifice, appropriate prayers, and formulas for greeting strangers. In short, he knows the kind of thing that we can still see in the poetry of Homer and Hesiod, in the heroic poetry of the North, in the popular ballads and folk epics still to be found in Slavic countries and in Central Asia.

The characteristics of oral poetry are familiar, the most familiar being the formulaic unit, the stock epithets, and the metrical phrases that can be moved around at will in a poetic process which is always close to improvisation. An oral culture is necessarily a highly ritualized one, and oral poetry has strong affinities with magic. There is magic in the great roll calls of names, like the Greek ships in Homer or the elemental spirits in Hesiod, in the carefully stereotyped descriptions of ritual and councils of war, in the oblique and riddling epithets like the Anglo-Saxon kenning, in the sententious reflections that express the inevitable reactions to certain recurring human situations. Magic means secret wisdom, the keys to all knowledge, as becomes more obvious when the poet's repertory of legend expands into a vast interlocking epic cycle, which begins in turn to suggest the outlines of an encyclopedic myth of concern. The Elizabethan critics (Sidney less than, for instance, Chapman) sensed a kind of encyclopedic synthesis in Homer, and they had the same kind of sentimental admiration for it that many people in our day have had for the cultural synthesis of the Middle Ages. The ideal of universal knowledge achieved in and through poetry has continued to haunt poets and critics ever since.

Oral formulaic poetry has a driving power behind it that is very hard to recapture in individually conceived and written poetry. The sinewy strength of Homer is the despair of imitators and translators alike: the style is neither lofty nor familiar, neither naive nor ingenious, but passes beyond all such distinctions. We can get a clearer idea of the effect of such poetry, perhaps, from another formulaic art, the music of the high baroque. In an intensely formulaic composer, such as Vivaldi, the same scale and chord passages, the same harmonic and melodic progressions, the same cadences, appear over and over again, yet the effect is not monotony but the release of a self-propelled energy. One of the keenest sources of pleasure in listening to poetry or music is the fulfilling of a *general* expectation, of a sort that is possible only in highly conventionalized art. If a particular expectation is being fulfilled, when we know exactly what is going to be said, as in listening to something very familiar, our attention is relaxed, and what we are participating in tends to become either a ritual or a bore, or possibly both. If we have no idea what is coming next, our attention is tense and subject to fatigue. The intermediate area, where we do not know what Pope will say but do know that he will say it in a beautifully turned couplet, where we do not know in a detective story who murdered X but do know that somebody did, is the area of closest unity between poet and audience.

So far as it is a technique, Homer's energy can be matched by the later poets of a writing culture, but the kind of general expectation he raises is based on something that hardly can be. This is the total empathy between poet and audience which arises when the poet is neither the teacher of his audience nor a spokesman for them, but both at once. Such a poet needs to make no moral judgments, for the standards implied are already shared. We cannot even call him a conservative, for that is still a partisan term, and in every judgment or reflective statement he does make he is formulating his hearer's thought as well as his own.

In oral culture the continuity of verse forms an odd contrast to the discontinuity of prose. Continuous prose is based, not on the physical pulsation of verse, but on a conceptual or semantic rhythm which is much more difficult and sophisticated. The primitive prose of concern, easily illustrated from the Bible, expresses itself in a discontinuous sequence of aphorisms, like the proverbs which are the vehicle of popular philosophy, or oracular sayings of "wise men," the commandments of authoritative teachers of the myth of concern, or the brief narratives in the lives of such teachers that lead up to some crucial saying or action. The effect of the discontinuity is to suggest that the statements are existential, and have to be absorbed into the consciousness one at a time, instead of being linked with each other by argument. Oracular prose writers from Heraclitus to Marshall McLuhan have exploited the sense of extra profundity that comes from leaving more time and space and less sequential connection at the end of a sentence. In Sidney's day Bacon was experimenting, in his essays, with a form of oracular concerned prose derived from the study of rhetoric and designed to "come home to men's business and bosoms," as he put it. In the earliest essays particularly, each sentence is really a paragraph in itself. In contrast, such metaphors as "the pursuit of truth wherever it may lead" show how closely associated the truth of correspondence is with the technique of continuous prose writing.

Of course by Sidney's time the mental habits of a writing culture were in the ascendant, and hence the language of prose and reason had come to be regarded as the primary verbal expression of reality. This assumption is so firmly established that Sidney raises it only by implication. It is accepted that no poet can be regarded as having, in religion, the kind of authority that the theologian would have; and in history and morals too the language of poetry falls short of the language of what is considered literal truth. Many people in Sidney's day and later were obsessed with the values of a writing culture. Religion for most of them was derived from a book; it was spiritually dangerous to be illiterate, yet the religion had to be understood from the book in the plainest possible terms. Hence the attitude of such pamphleteers as Gosson, who demanded to know why Plato was not right, and why the poets with their outworn modes of thought and their hankering for the fabulous should still have a claim on our attention.

Gosson is something of a straw man in Sidney, if he is

there at all, and the sense of social threat is not very oppressive. The general critical position of Sidney is contained within the same Christian framework of assumptions as that of the detractors of poetry. For Sidney, the ultimate aim of education, in the broadest sense, is the reform of the will, which is born in sin and headed the wrong way. Truth, by itself, cannot turn the will, but poetry in alliance with truth, using the vividness and the emotional resonance peculiar to it, may move the feelings to align themselves with the intelligence, and so help to get the will moving. Thus the function of poetry is rhetorical or persuasive. When writing techniques develop in society, the central oral figure becomes the orator, and for Sidney the poet's training is very similar to the orator's rhetorical training, as laid down by Cicero and Quintillian. Rhetoric, said Aristotle, is an *antistrophos*, the answering chorus, of truth; and whatever genuine social function the poet has depends on the consonance between his rhetoric and the rational disciplines, with their more exact relation to reality. The same conception of poetry as an emotional support is applied to social action, more particularly military courage, where poetry is discovered to be not a corrupter of courage but "the companion of camps."

In countering the attack on poetry as "fabulous," Sidney follows the line of argument which had also descended from Aristotle, that the truthful statement is the specific and particular statement. Poetry withdraws from particular statements: the poet never affirms or denies, and thus is able to combine the example of the historian with the precept of the moral philosopher. As compared with the historian, the poet gives us not the existential but the recurring or essential event; as compared with the moralist, he tells us not the essential but the existential truth, the kind of truth that can only be presented through illustration or parable. One principle

119

emerging here, of which Sidney is as yet still imperfectly aware, is a distinction between what the poet says and what he illustrates or shows forth. What he says is of limited importance: whatever it is, other forms of verbal expression say it more accurately. He is, of course, greatly prized for his capacity to make sententious statements, of the kind that readers and schoolboys copied out in their commonplace books. But the more admirable the sentence, the more it is an echo of what we already know in a different way. What is distinctive about poetry is the poet's power of illustration, a power which is partly an ability to popularize and make more accessible the truths of revelation and reason. Hence the importance of the tag *ut pictura poesis:* poetry is a speaking picture. Gerard Manley Hopkins draws a distinction between a poet's "overthought," or explicit meaning, and his "underthought," or texture of images and metaphors. But in a writing culture a poet's underthought, his metaphorical or pictured meaning, tends to become the more important thought, and to some degree it even separates itself from the explicit statement.

The critical situation which Sidney is implicitly accepting may be stated something like this: in a writing culture the norms of meaning are established by the nonliterary writers. It is the discursive prose writers who really mean what they say, and align their words clearly with the facts or propositions they are conveying. Compared with them, the poet's meaning is indirect, or ironic, as we should say now. When we try to grasp a poem's meaning, we begin with the meaning which the poem has in common with nonliterary writing. We call this the literal meaning, though it is actually an allegorical meaning, something that relates the poem to something outside poetry. What the poem means apart from this is largely an emotional meaning, conveyed through various devices of rhetorical embellishment. For criticism based on this aspect of meaning, poems considered as content are essentially documents or records, whether of ideas or of the poet's experience: considered as forms they are products of rhetorical expertise. In either case the critic's function is primarily judicial or evaluative, concerned with the worth of what the poet is saying and with his success in saying it.

When we look at Shakespeare, we realize that Elizabethan culture is still very largely oral, and that the existence of a poetic theatre is evidence of the fact. In Shakespeare we see a good deal of the poet's original oral educating function still going on, most obviously in the histories. Shakespeare also shows the identification with the audience's attitude that the oral poet has. On the level of explicit statement, or what the play appears to be saying, he seems willing to accept the assumption, or implication, that Henry V was a glorious conqueror and Joan of Arc a wicked witch, that Shylock is typical of Jews and Judaism, that peasants are to be seen through the eyes of the gentry, that the recognized sovereign is the Lord's anointed and can cure diseases in virtue of being so, and many other things that the modern critic passes over in embarrassed silence. With Shakespeare we are still many centuries removed from T. S. Eliot's comparison of the explicit meaning of a poem to a piece of meat that a burglar throws to a watchdog to keep him quiet. But there is clearly something in the uncritical social postulates of Shakespeare that has to do with soothing popular anxieties and keeping a vigilant and by no means unintelligent censorship from getting stirred up. I am not of course speaking of a conscious policy on Shakespeare's part: I am merely applying to him a principle which extends to all poetry. Questionable or dated social attitudes, as expressed in what appears to be the surface meaning, do not affect the real meaning of poetry, which is conveyed through a structure of imagery and action.

The Elizabethan critics were less contradictory than they

may at first seem to be in saying, on the one hand, that the poet popularizes the rational disciplines, sugar-coats the pill, provides instruction for the simple, and on the other hand that great poetry is a treasure trove of esoteric wisdom which poets hid in parables "lest by profane wits it should be abused," as Sidney says. Both these views of poetry can be understood through the same axiom of *ut pictura poesis*. Spenser, for instance, attempted in *The Faerie Queene* "a continued allegory or dark conceit" which would return proportionate rewards for a good deal of work. At the same time it is clear that his friend Gabriel Harvey regarded the poem, with its use of magic, medieval romance, the fairy world, the folk play of St. George, and in general of what he called "Hobgoblin run away with the garland from Apollo," as a concession to the simpler tastes in Spenser's audience.

The more completely the techniques of writing and the mental disciplines they create pervade a community, the more difficult it is for the poet to retain his traditional oral functions. Prose becomes fully mature and in command of its characteristic powers, and thereby begins to break away from poetry, which has nothing like its capacity for conceptual expression, and has a limited tolerance for the abstract language which is now becoming even the ordinary language of educated people. Ambiguity, which simply means bad or incompetent writing in any logical or descriptive context, is a structural principle of poetry. In proportion as scientific and philosophical pictures of the world develop, the starkly primitive nature of poetic thought stands out more clearly. Poetry being founded, not in the sense of an objective order of nature, but in the sense of social concern, its approach to nature is intensely constructive and associational. Poetry attempts to unite the physical environment to man through the most primitive of categories, the categories of analogy and identity, simile and metaphor, which the poet shares with the lunatic and the lover, and which are essentially the categories of magic. The figure of the magician, who, like Orpheus, can charm the trees by his song is a figure of the poet as well. The function of magic, said Pico della Mirandola, is to "marry the world" (*maritare mundum*), and this naive anthropomorphic image remains close to the center of all poetic metaphor. But magic, as soon as writing develops, no longer seems contemporary with the rest of thought.

Such are some of the paradoxes that Peacock deals with in his brilliant satire *The Four Ages of Poetry*, perhaps the nearest to Vico of any piece of writing in English literature. According to Peacock, poetry began in primitive times as "the mental rattle that awakened the attention of intellect in the infancy of civil society." The chief form of primitive poetry was, Peacock says, panegyric, which points to the identification of the poet with his community that we find in oral cultures. Poetry has its greatest flowering, or golden age, in the times immediately following, where habits of thought are still close to the primitive. But as civilization develops, Plato's prophecy becomes fulfilled, and the poet becomes more and more of an atavistic survival. "A poet in our times is a semi-barbarian in a civilized community. He lives in the days that are past. His ideas, thoughts, feelings, associations, are all with barbarous manners, obsolete customs, and exploded superstitions. The march of his intellect is like that of a crab, backward."

Peacock's essay is in part a comment on the rise of the romantic movement, particularly on such features as its interest in the ballad and other forms of primitive verbal culture, its use of superstition and magic as poetic imagery, its withdrawal from urban culture and its tendency to seek its subjects in the simplest kinds of rural life. But everything that

Peacock says about the age of Wordsworth and Coleridge applies far more to the age of D. H. Lawrence and Ezra Pound. He illustrates a stage of poetry in which the poet has lost the traditional function inherited from preliterate days, and as a result has become separated from society. Yet the very isolation of the modern poet may indicate a turning point in literary history: at any rate, this is the principle on which Shelley's reply to Peacock is based. In Shelley the poetic or mythical habit of mind, however primitive, is seen as coming back into society, insisting on being recognized for itself and on being accorded some degree of autonomy and independence from the logical habit of mind.

We are first made aware, however, of the decline of the sense of the social relevance of poetry since Sidney's time, except insofar as it has become assimilated to the mental outlook of a writing culture. Sidney's case for the poet depends on a body of generally accepted social ideas and values. As society becomes more confident about these values, the help of the poet in publicizing them becomes less essential, and his role more curtailed. For Sidney the poet is, for example, potentially a religious influence. Sidney accepts the Christian conception of two levels of nature, an upper level of human nature as God originally planned it, man's unfallen state, and a lower level of physical nature which is theologically "fallen." When Sidney says that poetry develops a second nature, he is thinking of the power of the poet to present the ideal of the unfallen state in its most vivid possible form, as a speaking picture. But in a later age, under Boileau's influence, the mysteries of religion are thought to be too high for the poet's ornamentation: on the other hand, the puerilities of heathen mythology are too low, and the poet should outgrow his hankering for them. Of the traditional qualities of oral poetry, the one that chiefly survives, in the age of Pope, is the sententious, the capacity to formulate "What oft was thought, but ne'er so well expressed." The high value set on this aspect of poetry continues well into Victorian times. But otherwise the elements that make Homer the cornerstone of our poetic tradition are precisely the elements that come to be most despised. Catalogues and lists and mnemonic verses of the "Thirty days hath September" type, quoted by Coleridge, are now regarded as poetry's lowest achievement: the formulaic unit becomes the cliché; the reverence for convention, of doing things because this is the way they are done, gives place to a law of copyright and a cult of uniqueness.

The poet's role of telling his society what his society should know is even more drastically inverted. In this connection Peacock makes the comment:

As to that small portion of our contemporary poetry . . . which, for want of a better name, may be called ethical, the most distinguished portion of it, consisting merely of querulous, egotistical rhapsodies, to express the writer's high dissatisfaction with the world and every thing in it, serves only to confirm what has been said of the semi-barbarous character of poets, who from singing dithyrambics and "Io Triumphe," while society was savage, grow rabid, and out of their element, as it becomes polished and enlightened.

The most intellectually tolerant of critics, studying the ideas or opinions of Yeats, D. H. Lawrence, Ezra Pound, Robert Graves, or Wyndham Lewis, is bound to be puzzled, even distressed, by the high proportion of freakish and obscurantist views he finds and the lack of contact they show with whatever the ideas are that actually do hold society together. In the twentieth century an important and significant writer may be reactionary or superstitious: the one thing apparently that he cannot be is a spokesman of ordinary social values. The popular poems of our day are usually poems of explicit statement, continuing the sententious tradition, but such poems seem as a rule to be out of touch with the real poetic idioms of their times. Recently, in an interview program on the Canadian radio, a Toronto hippie remarked that the world would have no problems left if everyone would only read Kipling's "If" and live by it. One feels that in our day a remark of that kind could be attached only to a substandard poem. Those who express the ideas and symbols that hold society together are not the poets; they are not even the orators who succeeded them, so much as men of action with a power over the sententious utterance which operates mainly outside literature, and who usually arise in a revolutionary situation. Such men of action include Jefferson, and later Lincoln, in America, and the great Marxist leaders, Lenin and Mao. The "thoughts" of Mao in particular seem to have succeeded in putting Marxism into the aphoristic prose of concern, something that Marx himself, after the *Communist Manifesto*, hardly attempted except for the *Theses on Feuerbach*.

In spite of the close affinity between metaphor and magic, one might have thought that, as the authority of science established itself, poets would become the heralds of science, as they had earlier been the heralds of religion. Many great poets, such as Dante, had in fact absorbed and used most of the essential science of their day. But after about Newton's time it became increasingly clear that most really important poets were not going to make much more than a random and occasional use of imagery derived from science, or even from technology. Many poets from the eighteenth century onward have taken a keen and well-informed interest in science, but it is true even of Shelley and Goethe that their best poetry does not really absorb scientific conceptions and vocabularies and express them with full poetic resonance. Cosmological and speculative themes have been central to poetry throughout its history; versified science has always been eccentric to it. What had attracted earlier poets to the science contemporary with them was clearly a certain schematic and mythical quality in it, associations of seven planets with seven metals and the like, which science itself had outgrown. This schematic quality survived only in a kind of intellectual underground inhabited by occultists, theosophists, mystagogues, and scryers, yet curiously enough this was where many poets turned for intellectual support. Further, as we see in Yeats, such interests are so triumphantly vindicated in the poetry itself that it seems clear that they are connected with the actual language of poetry, and are not simply a removable obstacle to appreciating it. The relation of poetry to religion has been much closer, and many modern poets have been most eloquent in their support of the Christian religion. One wonders whether they may not be connected with the fact that Christianity is more primitive in its mythology than Judaism or Marxism or the highly intellectualized versions of Oriental religions that reach us.

Shelley begins his answer to Peacock by neatly inverting the hierarchy of values implied in Sidney. Sidney is concerned to show that poetry is a genuine instrument of education, along with religion, morality and law, but their claim to be educational is prior and unquestioned. Shelley puts all the discursive disciplines into an inferior group of "analytic" operations of reason. They are aggressive; they think of ideas as weapons; they seek the irrefutable argument, which keeps eluding them because all arguments are theses, and theses are half-truths implying their own opposites. Some of the discursive writers are defenders of the social status quo: not only do they fail to defend it, but they exasperate and embitter a society in which the rich get richer and the poor poorer.

There are also liberal and radical discursive writers: they are on Shelley's side and he approves of them, but being only the other half of the argumentative disciplines, the amount of good they can do is limited. The works of imagination, by contrast, cannot be refuted: poetry is the dialectic of love, which treats everything it encounters as another form of itself, and never attacks, only absorbs.

This view of poetry cannot be affected by the notion that Peacock pretends to accept, that mankind progresses through reason to greater enlightenment, and that poetry, like the less interesting types of religion, is committed to the values of an outworn past. The metaphor of creation, if it is a metaphor, is not new with the Romantics, and most of the better Elizabethan critics understood what is meant by "creative" very well. But in Sidney's day it was accepted that the models of creation were established by God: for Shelley, man had made his own civilization and is responsible for it, and at the center of his creation are the poets, whose work provides the models of human society. Thus poetry once again, as in primitive times, becomes mythopoeic, but this time its myths embody and express man's creation of his own culture, and not his reception of it from a divine source.

Shelley says that poetry is "that to which all science must be referred." There is a reality out there, a reality which is given and has in itself no moral significance, which science studies, and there is the reality which does not exist to begin with, but is brought into being through a certain kind of creative activity. This latter kind of created reality does have moral significance, and is in fact what we have been calling the myth of concern: the statement of questions and answers about man's destiny and situation, the meaning of his life and death, his relation to past and future, to God and to society. The articulating of concern cannot base itself on science or any discursive discipline, nor can it any longer echo or support what they say. The mythical confronts the logical, and assimilates it to the concerns of human existence.

Consequently it is no good attaching a pejorative meaning to the word "primitive." Poetry which is not primitive is of no use to anybody: every genuine work of the imagination comes out of the most primitive depths of human concern. I say "depths" because of all the subterranean and oracular imagery in Shelley. Poetry for him comes from an area which, though superior to consciousness, is metaphorically hidden and underneath, in what we now call the subconscious. Because this oracular power has assumed the authority formerly ascribed to God's revelation, it is surrounded with a good deal of resonant rhetoric about "that imperial faculty, whose throne is curtained within the invisible nature of man." Such a formulation may tend, in later romantics, to lead to a certain amount of displaced racism and an unhealthy emphasis on the immense difference between those few who are born geniuses and the rest of us mediocrities. The implications in Shelley, despite the rhetoric, are more interesting.

Shelley says that our perception of given reality, the world out there, tends to become habitual, hence a pernicious mental habit develops of regarding the unchanging as the unchangeable, and of assimilating human life to a conception of predictable order. But poetry, says Shelley, "creates anew the universe, after it has been annihilated in our minds by the recurrence of impressions blunted by reiteration." Hence the poetic and the revolutionary impulses are interdependent. No genuine change in society can take place except through realizing that the imagination, which conceives the form of society, is the source of the power of change.

Every great poem is a product of its time, and is consequently subject to the anxieties of its time. It is an implicit part of Shelley's argument that an authentic reading of poetry reads it by its imaginative "underthought" and not by its explicit conformity to contemporary prejudice, or what he calls, in connection with Calderon, "the rigidly-defined and ever-repeated idealisms of a distorted superstition." If, for instance, we read Dante's *Inferno* as a poem conforming to or coming to terms with anxieties about a life of unending torment after death awaiting most of those who do not make an acceptable deal with the Church, then, from Shelley's normal point of view, writing such a poem would be an act of treachery to the human race far lower than anything done by Dante's three traitors, Brutus, Cassius, and Judas Iscariot, all of whom must have acted from better motives. But, of course, we read the *Inferno* through its imagery and action, as a representation of the actual life of man. Reading all poems in terms of their presented or illustrated meaning, we come to realize that there are no dead ideas in literature. The imagination operates in a counterhistorical direction—it redeems time, to use a phrase which is Shelleyan as well as Biblical, if in a different context—and literature exists totally in the present tense as a total form of verbal imagination. Shelley speaks of this total form as "that great poem, which all poets, like the co-operating thoughts of one great mind, have built up since the beginning of the world."

We are brought back here to our original point about the insufficiency of allegorical or external meaning, which aligns poetry to something outside itself, when considered to be the whole work of criticism. Meaning is centripetal as well as centrifugal: words in a poem are to be understood by their function in that poem as well as by their conventional or dictionary meanings, hence the importance of explicatory criticism. But the words used in a poem are used in other poems as well as in nonliterary structures, and not only words but images and metaphors and rhythmical patterns and conventions and genres. This leads to a conception of poetic meaning which is not allegorical, taking us outside literature, but archetypal, placing the poem in its literary context, and completing our understanding of its structure by relating it to the rest of our literary experience. The lightning flash of Shelley's phrase illuminates the contemporary critic's *pons asinorum*, the bridge leading from the secure routines of explication and research over to the other shore of criticism.

Ever since Plato the question has been raised: In what sense does the poet know what he is talking about? The poet seems to have some educational function without being himself necessarily an educator. He knows what he is doing, but *qua* poet can say nothing beyond his poem. Hence the need for the educational aspect of his function to be taken over by someone else. In oral days he had only the rhapsode, who, as Socrates demonstrates in the *Ion*, really knows nothing at all. With the rise of writing and more sequential forms of thinking the critic appears as the social complement of the poet. In Sidney's view of poetry the critic retains his traditional role as judge, as a spokesman for society's response to poetry. But Shelley's conception of poetry makes the critic rather a student of mythology. The whole subject of which criticism forms part, then, on this view, is the study of how society produces, responds to, and uses its myths, or structures of concern, in which the poetic structures are central. This subject has not yet been defined, but it would embrace large segments of psychology, anthropology, philosophy, history, and comparative religion, as well as criticism.

We can see from Sidney's defense, then, how literature adapts itself to the canons of a writing culture by withdrawing from specific statements, and how it marks out its own field on the boundaries of history and philosophy. We can

131

also see how the documentary or "background" interests of literary criticism have originated. We can see too that poets do not forget their original function as teachers of the myth of concern, many traces of which still linger in the Bible, and that for them it is still true that their world is golden, and nature's only brazen, in Sidney's phrase. That is, their place is with the truth or reality that is created out of nature, not with the truth or reality that is presented by nature and studied. Here and there, as in Sidney's appreciation of the ballad of Chevy Chase, or the famous phrase about the poet coming to us "with a tale which holdeth children from play, and old men from the chimney corner," we are reminded that there is always something primitive and conservative about poetry, that the poet's world is built out of a flat earth with a rising and setting sun, with four elements and an animate nature, the concrete existential world of emotions and sensations and fancies and transforming memories and dreams. Truth of correspondence grows and progresses, and each age of science stands on the shoulders of its predecessors. But truth of concern knows nothing of progress, and poetry keeps revolving around its canon of classics, as religion does around its canon of sacred texts. Sidney is riding on the crest of the humanist revolution, but humanism, with its cult of classical authority and its contempt for the "jargon" of technical philosophy, had its reactionary as well as its liberal side.

The lurking primitiveness of poetry is suggested by only a few hints in Sidney's urbane apologetic, but after Peacock the "Luddite" tendencies of the literary attitude, as Sir Charles Snow calls them, come more into the open. For Shelley, religion as a creed and a social institution is a projected, and consequently a perverted, creation of the human imagination. The revolutionary element in the creation of literature, for Shelley, is connected essentially with the recovery by the imagination of what it has projected. But this act of imaginative recovery also separates the created reality of poetry from the presented reality of the objective world. Not only does poetry create for us "a being within our being," but it also "defeats the curse which binds us to be subjected to the accident of surrounding impressions." An imaginative revolution is envisaged here that goes far beyond political ones. Marxism returned to the view of Sidney, that poetry's social function is to echo and support the more specific approaches to truth made by the discursive verbal disciplines. The bourgeois culture of Shelley's day took the same view, in a more naive form. Hence Shelley's phrase "unacknowledged legislators." The poet's function is still his primitive oral function of defining and illustrating the concerns of the society that man is producing, but this fact is not generally realized. It is not realized partly because the language of poetry is still thought of as a rhetorical and sublogical language: the principles of mythical language are still largely unknown.

IV

The modern form of the conceptions of concern and freedom may be expressed somewhat as follows. Man lives in two worlds. There is the world he is actually in, the world of nature or his objective environment, and there is the world he wants to live in, the civilization he is trying to build or maintain out of his environment, a world rooted in the conception of art, as the environment is rooted in the conception of nature. For the objective world he develops a logical language of fact, reason and verification; for the potentially created world he develops a mythical language of hope, desire, belief, fantasy, and construction. Both languages are based on the arts, and the verbal arts are prominent in both, but the metaphorical language of poetry is essentially a mythical and not a logical language. It speaks the language of concern, of the beliefs and wishes that hold society together, not the language that describes the environment, however descriptive it may sometimes become as a technical tour de force.

Naturally, the study of man's environment cannot be confined to the nonhuman environment: human society, in the present as in the past, is an objective fact too. Sooner or later, therefore, the scientific spirit and the search for truth of correspondence are going to invade the structures of concern themselves, studying human mythology in the same spirit that they study nature. This collision between concern and freedom may well be the most important type of what is now called "culture shock" that we have. In weak or frightened minds such a collision produces immediate panic, followed by elaborate defensive reactions. Efforts to bring the spirit of enquiry into the Christian religion have been met with such responses as (to give a relatively mild example): "If you destroy our faith with your rational and analytical questions, what will you put in its place?" Marxist atheologians similarly insist that, as everybody exists in a specific social context, there is no such thing as complete detachment from a social attitude, and that consequently all enquiry is rooted in a social attitude which must be either revolutionary, and so in agreement with them, or counterrevolutionary. One still often hears the argument among student militants that because complete objectivity is impossible, differences in degree of objectivity are not important. In my own field, I have often observed how the critical study of literature meets with resistance and guilt feelings based on a fear that if a professional knowledge of literature involves a deeper understanding of it than casual readers possess, it will build up some kind of undemocratic elite. The resistance is especially strong when the critic holds, as I do, that criticism cannot be directed toward value-judgments, because every attempt to do this leads to ranking literary works in some irrelevant moral hierarchy. Such clichés as "It kills poetry to analyze it"; "Literature is life, not a critic's chess game," etc., etc., are typical of the anxieties thrown up by immature concern.

Others meet the collision from the opposite side, with a naive rationalism which expects that before long all myths of concern will be outgrown and only the appeal to reason and evidence and experiment will be taken seriously. It will, I hope, become clear in the course of this essay why I consider such a view entirely impossible. When we see a concern myth in process of formation, such as the current "black" myth, it is an oversimplified view that regards fidelity to historical or sociological fact the only important moral principle involved. It seems to be one of the unavoidable responsibilities of educated people to show by example that beliefs may be held and examined at the same time. The growth of nonmythical knowledge tends to eliminate the incredible from belief, and helps to shape the myth of concern according to the outlines of what experience finds possible and vision desirable. But the growth of knowledge cannot in itself provide us with the social vision which will suggest what we should do with our knowledge.

In its "pure" form, concern is expressed by an unquestioning belief that cares little for evidence or reason, or, at least, does not depend on them. But as the sense of the importance of truth of correspondence makes itself felt, concern attempts to absorb this sense by constructing a deductive attitude to experience. Thus as Christianity developed, it rationalized itself, asserting that it possessed the truth of correspondence as well, and was true by the tests of reason and historical evidence. In doing this its faith, or central body of verbally articulated concern, became a set of major premises for a deductive rational structure provided by theology, from which in turn principles of philosophy and science were, at least theoretically, to be deduced. Marxism is still struggling with a similar deductive scholasticism, maintaining that its principles are "scientific," that is, valid major premises of science. In proportion as this deductive synthesis breaks down, and individual sciences become autonomous, what we have called the myth of freedom begins to be effective, the feeling that tolerance and suspended judgment are good things in themselves and are not merely expedient. Christianity began to enter this phase with the humanist movement of the late fifteenth century, but the ferocity of the conflict between Catholic and Protestant versions of the Christian myth of concern delayed the development of a myth of freedom for centuries. Marxism appears to be entering the same phase in the smaller European countries, with similar obscurantist conflicts looming on the horizon.

In the democracies, too, a strong hankering for an encyclopedic synthesis of thought, which would have a solidly established body of scientific facts and laws as its foundation and the premises of belief and hope as its superstructure, keeps recurring in every generation. In the nineteenth century, such ambitions gave a strong cosmological slant to philosophy: in fact, constructing encyclopedic "systems," or verbal cathedrals of knowledge and faith, was often regarded as philosophy's primary task. In the twentieth century it has become more widely accepted that mythical and logical languages are distinct languages, connected mainly by analogy. (I use the term "language" in a metaphorical sense, not in a linguistically precise one.) Thus if a philosophical or social thinker bases his structure on the conception of evolution, what he is working with is not really the same principle as the biological hypothesis of evolution, but is rather a mythical analogy of that hypothesis. The vision of things as they could be certainly has to depend on the vision of things as they are. But what is between them is not so much a point of contact as an existential gap, a revolutionary and transforming act of choice. The beliefs we hold and the kind of society we try to construct are chosen from infinite possibilities, and the notion that our choices are inevitably connected with things as they are, whether through the mind of God or the constitution of nature, always turns out to be an illusion of habit.

I said above that as historical Christianity gained power in a writing culture, it took on the mental attitudes of that culture, and that no Christian poet, not even Dante or Milton, could be given the kind of authority that the theologian possessed. Classical mythology therefore provided some advantages for the poets because it belonged to imagination rather than directly to faith. Hence literature, especially the more explicitly mythopoeic literature, tended increasingly to go over to the classical and liberal opposition, as the kind of imaginative commitment that classical imagery demanded was very like the suspension of judgment that is so important for liberalism. By the time of the romantic movement this tendency was so marked that several romantic poets, including Shelley and many of the Germans, began to suggest that our real myth of concern was of classical rather than Christian origin. The culmination of this tendency was Nietzsche and his opposition of Christ and Dionysus; but more significant, for our present purposes, is its development by Matthew Arnold in *Culture and Anarchy*. I am writing in the centenary year of that book (1969), and nobody can be writing on such a subject as mine in this year without being aware that the confrontation of culture and anarchy has taken a very different form from the one that Arnold envisaged.

According to Arnold, the "Hebraic" revolutionary myth

of concern was losing its impetus, running into the desert sands of bourgeois morality. Other revolutionary movements were beginning to take shape. One was a cult of "doing as one likes," the other a working-class social movement that was making ominous noises after the passing of the Second Reform Bill. Both represented anarchy, and the remedy for them was culture, a myth of concern which held the essence of everything good in conservative, liberal, and radical values. It was conservative because it was aware of and accepted its tradition, and because it was a source of social authority. It was liberal because it was held, not through faith or dogma, but through reason and imagination, incorporating a sense of beauty and the virtues of the liberal attitude, including tolerance and suspended judgment. Consequently the real source of its tradition was Hellenic rather than Hebraic. It was radical because its authority was ultimately a spiritual authority, and so its long-run influence was an equalizing one, dissolving the hierarchy of classes by subordinating class conflict to a wider conception of social concern. Arnold also appeared to be saying, here and elsewhere, that literature would eventually assume the social function that religion then had.

Whatever one thinks of this last proposition, Arnold's doctrine in general was, for most humanists of my generation, the shadow of a rock in a weary land. Arnold gave a genuine social dimension to the study and teaching of the humanities, and did not, like John Henry Newman, insist that we sell out to some other interest, such as the anxieties of the Christian Church. But we notice that for Arnold literature, like Cressida, appears to have deserted the defending camp for the besieging one. The primitive social function of poetry was to teach the myth of concern; in Arnold's conception of culture, it seems to be associated with the values connected with individual freedom and the truth of correspondence.

Here Arnold was faithfully reflecting the cultural conditions of his time. One of the things that happens to literature, as it becomes assimilated to the mental habits of a writing culture, is that it comes to be thought of as an ornament of leisure, a secondary product of an advanced civilization. In the tenth book of Plato's *Republic*, Socrates asserts that the poet's version of reality is inferior, not merely to the philosopher's, but to the artisan's or craftsman's as well. The artisan makes what is, within the limits of his reality, a real bed; the painter has only the shadow of a bed. Most devaluations of poetry ever since, whether Platonic, Puritan, Marxist, or Philistine, have been attached to some version of a work ethic which makes it a secondary or leisure-time activity; and when poetry has been socially accepted, it is normally accepted on the same assumptions, more positively regarded. This seems a curious conception of poetry in view of its original social role. In a technologically simple society preoccupied with the means of survival, like that of the Eskimos, poetry appears to be a primary need rather than a superfluous refinement. But increasingly, as Western culture became more complex, works of art came to be thought of as a series of objects to be enjoyed and appreciated by a liberalized leisure class.

A necessary part of this view of art is a decline of the sense of convention and, in poetry, of a community of words. The poet no longer has a communal "word hoard," and only in the most subtle and indirect way is he thought of as possessing and retelling the essential myths of the society he lives in. The individual poem or novel comes rather to represent a unique or sealed-in experience, and a law of copyright assimilates literature to private property. Literature could not go as far in this direction as painting, where a picture acquires a purchaser or sole owner, but it went as far as it could. Kierkegaard, in contrasting Christian concern to the liberal and speculative attitude of his day, was so impressed by the similarity of the latter to the place of the arts in society that he called it the "aesthetic" attitude, and symbolized it by Mozart's *Don Giovanni*, more particularly by the catalogue of mistresses, the picture of the universal lover surrounded by a mass of attractive objects.

It would of course be nonsense, in any age, to think of the poet simply as producing luxury goods for an ascendant class. But after Edmund Burke's time, concern takes on the sense of continuity, the sense that we belong to something before we are anything, and that the community we join at birth completes our social context by attaching us to our traditions. The classical education that was so important as a status symbol at this time had much to do with the sense of continuity with the past as a basis of concern. Increasingly, from the romantic movement onward, the poet becomes a representative of cultural tradition, and his poem acquires the oracular, overdetermined emotional resonance of something that speaks to the depths of the mind of an age that has most of its conscious attention directed outside itself. Romantic poetry, in Keats and Coleridge, preserves the sense of a charm or spell woven around some guarded place, and a corresponding sense of separation from its audience. The later movement associated with Eliot, Pound, T. E. Hulme, and Wyndham Lewis thought of itself as revolting against this, yet Wyndham Lewis ridiculed what he called the "dithyrambic spectator," the member of the audience bumptious enough to imagine that his presence made any difference to the creative process. A similar attitude, in him and in many others, led to the exalting of primitive and archaic art, which the distance in time and culture had tended to make inscrutably authoritative. In Mallarmé, in Rilke, even in Flaubert, the artist becomes a secular and initiating priest. This last suggests a certain affinity between the arts and religion to the extent that both become a kind of palladium or cultural monument. The fact that in America today one is entirely free to be of what religion one pleases, or of no religion at all, means that religion is no longer a central area of social concern; and a similar tolerance, similarly based on indifference, appears to be enveloping the arts as well. The French impressionists, excluded from the Academy, set up their own *"salon des refusés,"* but it is difficult even to imagine what sort of works of art would go into a *salon des refusés* today.

And yet other movements were demonstrating a very different context for poetry, and for the arts generally. In English literature, the immense significance of William Morris, as a revolutionary artist trying to show how the arts could still recover something of their original social role, needs an essay to itself. Yet Morris never escaped from the paradox in his position. In theory, the "minor" or socially active arts could transform society by destroying mechanical and mass production and recreating a community of brains and hands; but in practice they merely diversified the middle-class scene with a new aesthetic perspective. The voice was that of a revolutionary Esau, but the hands were the smooth and accommodating hands of Jacob. Much earlier, William Blake, another revolutionary artist trying to get around the mercantile machinery of publishers by etching and designing his own books, also found that what he was actually producing were luxury goods for well-to-do connoisseurs.

A different type of revolutionary movement was starting up in the nineteenth century, mainly in France, having little in common with other revolutionary movements except its opposition to the bourgeois ascendancy. This was what the nineteenth century called Bohemianism, the way of life pursued by many creative artists, both poets and painters, in opposition to the mores of their society. The *vie de Bohème* was more hedonistic and freer in its sexual standards than its more respectable rival, and it carried on a guerrilla campaign against the kind of middle-class anxieties that are usually expressed by the word "decency." The symbols of its social opposition included drugs, specifically hashish, which is prominent in the imagery of Baudelaire, and a not-so-sweet disorder in the dress (*"Je m'encrapule les plus possible,"* said Rimbaud). When this movement revived in the twentieth century, it was less completely identified with artists and became rather the expression of a revolutionary life style, for which the spokesman was Freud rather than Marx. This was hardly a role that Freud would have envisaged for himself, but in the beat movement of the fifties, even in their hippie successors, one sees a curious effort to define a social proletariat in Freudian rather than Marxist terms. From its point of view, bourgeois society is a repressive anxiety-structure which is particularly disturbed by the sexual instinct, hence the renewal of society is bound up with the emancipating of that instinct, though this also involves associating it with the creative process.

Meanwhile the language of concern preserved in Christianity had begun to be examined more objectively, and this precipitated a crisis which we should take a moment to examine, as it is a model for our present subject, the difference between mythical and logical languages. The crisis is often called a crisis of belief, but it is really a crisis in understanding the language of belief, the growing realization that religion speaks the mythical and concerned language of poetry, and not the factual and evidential language of history.

When I am asked if I "believe in" ghosts, I usually reply that ghosts, from all accounts, appear to be matters of experience rather than of belief, and that so far I have had no experience of them. But the mere fact that the question takes such a form indicates that belief is usually connected in the mind with a vision of possibilities, of what might or could be true. We often use the term "believe" to mean a suspended sense experience. "I believe you will find a telephone on the next floor" means that if I were on the next floor I should see a telephone. In reference to past time this suspended sense experience becomes the acceptance of a historical fact: "I believe Julius Caesar existed" means that I think that if I had lived when and where he is said to have lived I should have seen him. "I believe in God" can hardly refer to a belief of this kind, but under the influence of the mental habits of a writing culture, concerned belief also has come to be associated with historical fact. This leads to such curious aberrations as "believing the Bible," i.e., of ascribing special virtue to asserting that in another culture, a few years ago and a few miles away, Jonah was swallowed by a great fish and Elijah carried up to heaven in a fiery chariot, and that if we had been present at those events we should have seen precisely what is described in the sacred text. Such belief is really a voluntarily induced schizophrenia, and is probably a fruitful source of the infantilism and the hysterical anxieties about belief which are so frequently found in the neighborhood of religion, at least in its more uncritical areas. One thinks of Don Quixote's remark to Sancho Panza, that the Golden Age would soon return if people would only see things as they are, and not allow themselves to be deluded by enchanters who make hundred-armed giants look like windmills. In the seventeenth century Sir Thomas Browne, reflecting on such matters as the fact that conditions in Noah's ark, after thirty-eight days or so, might become a trifle slummy, remarked "methinks there be not enough impossibilities in religion for an active faith." But of course when a faith beyond reason is looked at in this

143

sort of playful or ironic light, it tends to become unconcerned. The more genuinely concerned faith is, the more quickly a hierarchy is established in it, in which "essential" beliefs are retained and less essential ones regarded as more expendable. But this conception of "essential" belief is, in spite of the word, introducing an existential element into belief. What we really believe is not what we say or think we believe but what our actions show that we believe, and no belief which is not an axiom of behavior is a genuinely concerned belief. Marxism has a similar conception of unessential belief, the "ideology" which is to be talked about but not acted upon, and which has the function of decorating the facade of a conservative attitude. Many of my readers would call what I am calling a myth of concern an ideology, and though, as I have indicated, I have specific reasons for using the term myth, those who prefer ideology may substitute it in most contexts.

For Milton writing *Paradise Lost*, Adam and Eve were historical characters, his own literal ancestors, whose skeletons might conceivably be uncovered by an archeologist. Milton is fond of contrasting the plain and sober scriptural accounts with the extravagances of the heathen. Plainness, however, may result from a primitive as well as a credible element in the style, and we today are struck rather by the similarity of the Biblical stories of the Fall and the Flood to other myths in other cultures. As the Old Testament narrative proceeds, myth gives place to legend and what German critics call *Sage*, legend to historical reminiscence, historical reminiscence to didactic and manipulated history, and so on. But there are no clear boundary lines: all that seems clear is that whatever in the Old Testament may be historically accurate is not there because it is historically accurate, but for quite different reasons. Further, historical accuracy has no relation to spiritual significance. The Book of Job, which is avowedly an imaginative drama, is clearly more significant in the development of religion than the begats in Chronicles, which may well contain authentic records.

With the Gospels, however, surely things must be different, for Christianity has always insisted on the historical nature of its central event. We soon begin to wonder, however, whether the verbal presentation of that event is as historical as the event itself. We notice that the life of Christ in the Gospels is not presented biographically, as a piece of continuous prose writing founded on historical evidence, but as a discontinuous sequence of appearances (pericopes), which have a strongly mythical quality about them. If the approach were biographical we should want only one definitive Gospel, and of course the historical belief in them has always rested on some "harmony" of their narratives rather than on the four as they stand. Naturally many efforts have been made to extract a credible continuous narrative from what seems a mass of mythical accretions. Thus a century ago Ernest Renan, in his *Vie de Jésus*, began confidently with the statement that Jesus was born in Nazareth, the story that he was born in Bethlehem being inserted later to harmonize with Micah's prophecy that the Messiah was to be born in Bethlehem. But, arguing on those terms, if the only reason for associating Jesus with Bethlehem is the passage in Micah, the only reason for associating him with Galilee is a similar passage in Isaiah (ix), and the only reason for associating him with Nazareth is to enable Matthew to make a dubious pun on "Nazirite." Renan's historical and credible statement, on his own basis of argument, dissolves into two more myths.

As we go through the Gospels, with their miracles of healing and miraculous feeding and raising the dead and the like, we begin to wonder how much there is that must be historical, that is unambiguous evidence for a historical Jesus. The authors of the Gospels seem to care nothing for the kind of evidence that would interest a biographer; the only evidence they concern themselves with is coincidence with Old Testament prophecies of the Messiah. The result is that our historical evidence for the life of Jesus, besides being hermetically sealed within the New Testament, seems to melt away, as we try to grasp it, into echoes from the Old Testament or from contemporary Jewish ritual. As some factual basis for Jesus' life was obviously available to the authors, why did they make so oblique and limited a use of it? In any case, for any uncommitted reader of the Gospels, the question "Could it really have happened just like that?" is bound to occur with great frequency. But at a certain point the question begins to turn into the form: "If I had been there, is that what I should have seen and experienced?" At this point the doubts become overwhelming, because most of these doubts are of one's own capacity for spiritual experience. Sir Thomas Browne's "I thank God that I never saw Christ or his disciples" begins to sound like a very shrewd remark. If I had been out on the hills of Bethlehem on the night of the birth of Christ, with the angels singing to the shepherds, I think that I should not have heard any angels singing. The reason why I think so is that I do not hear them now, and there is no reason to suppose that they have stopped.

If, under the influence of the mental habits of a writing culture, we insist on regarding a myth as a disguised way of presenting a real situation, we should have to regard the accounts of Jesus in the Gospels as highly suspect, if not actually fraudulent. But the impression of authority they convey is so strong that nobody is likely to take this possibility very seriously. It is much more probable that it is our conception of myth that is wrong, and it seems better to think of the authors as too concerned about the importance of their message to entrust what they had to say to merely historical or biographical idioms of language. The historian tries to put his reader where the event is, in the past. If he is writing about the assassination of Julius Caesar, he tries to make us see what we should have seen if we had been there, while keeping the additional understanding afforded by the distance in time. The apostle feels that if we had been "there," we should have seen nothing, or seen something utterly commonplace, or missed the whole significance of what we did see. So he comes to us, with his ritual drama of a Messiah, presenting a speaking picture which has to be, as Paul says, spiritually discerned. Myth is the language of the present tense, even of what is expressed by that abominable word "confrontation." There is a moral aspect of literature, stressed by Sidney in particular, which literature possesses through its power of idealized example. When poetry is the "companion of camps," a heroic achievement in the past is linked to another in the future of which the reader is the potential hero. The best way to connect the two, for Sidney, is to present the former in its universal shape, combining the historical example with the abstract precept or model. If we wish to be inspired by Achilles we must read Homer, and may well thank God that we never saw Achilles or his myrmidons. What is true of literature is a fortiori true of religion, where "go thou and do likewise" is always a part of the presentation.

The Bible, it may be said, is not a storybook or an epic poem; but it is much closer to being a work of literature than it is to being a work of history or even doctrine, and the kind of mental response that we bring to poetry has to be in the forefront of our understanding of it. This is, I think, what Matthew Arnold meant when he suggested that poetry would increasingly take on a religious importance in modern culture. It is not that poetry will become a substitute or replacement for religion, a situation that could only produce phony literature as well as a phony religion. It is rather that religion will come to be understood increasingly as having a poetic rather than a rational language, and that it can be more effectively taught and learned through the imagination than through doctrine or history. Imagination is not in itself concern, but for a culture with a highly developed sense of fact and of the limits of experience, the road to concern runs through the language of imagination.

I remarked earlier that every myth of concern is religious, in the sense of establishing a *religio* or common body of ritual acts and beliefs for the community. Of course, such a religion may be theistic and deny the finality of death, like Christianity, or atheistic and assert it, like Marxism. Marxism, and Christianity as long as it had temporal power, have tended to assume that a definite position on such points was obligatory on society as a whole, and hence, even if they could tolerate a group with a different position, they could not recognize such a difference as inevitable, certainly not as desirable. Democracy, which was preoccupied a good deal with trying to pare the claws of Christian temporal power, envisaged, in the American Constitution and elsewhere, a social order which could contain within itself a plurality of myths of concern, and which would accept the responsibility for keeping the peace among them. This establishes the distinction that I have elsewhere made between "open" and "closed" mythologies, in which only the former are capable of a genuine and functional toleration. Jews, for instance, are a minority group with a myth of concern peculiar to themselves: consequently any society with a closed myth which contains Jews is bound sooner or later to turn anti-Semitic. Occasionally we find it suggested that breaking up closed myths of concern may be part of the historical function of Judaism: thus the King of

Persia complains, in (the Greek additions to) the Book of Esther: "In all nations throughout the world there is scattered a certain malicious people, that have laws contrary to all nations . . . so as the uniting of our kingdoms, honourably intended by us, can not go forward."

A society with an open mythology still has, of course, its own predominant myth of concern. Nobody would say that "the American way of life" was less concerned than any other community's way of life. The principle of openness, however, is, so far as I can see, the only possible basis for a world community. It is chimerical to expect any one myth of concern to establish itself all over the world: the more widely any such myth spreads, the deeper the rifts that develop within it. What is potentially world-wide is an assumption, too broad in itself to constitute a myth of concern, that life is better than death, freedom better than slavery, happiness better than misery, health better than sickness, for all men everywhere without exception. This forms a principle for a myth of concern analogous to what Milton called the "rule of charity" for reading the Bible. According to Milton, the Bible is the great manifesto of human freedom, hence any text in it which seems to support an authoritarian way of life is being read out of context. Similarly, the freedom and happiness of all mankind forms the context within which a contemporary myth of concern ought to operate. An open myth can accommodate itself to such a context; a closed one cannot. A closed myth can only pursue its own ends, deciding at each step how much misery and slavery may be necessary (of course only temporarily) to advance those ends.

There are two aspects of this distinction between a closed and an open mythology that are particularly relevant here. In the first place, an open mythology establishes the relativity of a myth of concern, and so emphasizes the element of con-

149

struct or imaginative vision in it. The view advanced above, that the language of Christianity is in its Biblical origin a mythical language, is an "open" view of it. It does not affect the reality of the Christian vision for anyone who holds it, but it puts it on the kind of basis on which communication, or what is now often called "dialogue," becomes possible with Jews or Moslems or Marxists, or even other Christians. When a myth of concern claims truth of correspondence as well as truth of vision, and assumes that its postulates are established facts, it can hardly produce any argument except the single exasperated formula: "But can't you *see* how wrong you are?" When it renounces this claim, it acquires the kind of humility which makes it possible to see intellectual honesty on the other side too. As for one's own side, one is not renouncing its truth: what one renounces is the finality of one's own understanding of that truth.

In the second place, the principle of openness in mythology is founded on the myth of freedom. Man is civilized by his social institutions, and those institutions provide a continuum which gives his individual life another dimension of meaning. Before he is born, he is predestined to be born of a certain race and social class and nationality at a certain point in time: thus before he has any personality he has a social context. The institutions to which he is attached are mainly products of concern, and they form the complex of temporal authority. He may spend his whole life in this context, but an educated man in a complex society also becomes aware, through his education, of another kind of authority, which has only an internal or inherent compulsion: the authority of the rational argument, the accurate measurement, the repeatable experiment, the compelling imagination. In times of crisis, when loyalty to temporal institutions is weakened, it begins to be clear that this purely spiritual authority is the permanent center of real authority in a civilized community, and that all temporal power is temporary as well. This does not mean that it can ever become expendable or replaced by spiritual authority. Temporal authority is the parental aspect of society: it is always there and always primary, every revolt against it being also an identification with it. But, as such historical titles as "The Decline and Fall of the Roman Empire" remind us, there is a rhythm of death and rebirth in it. Spiritual authority, on the other hand, which is closely associated with science and the acquiring of knowledge, keeps expanding as long as an organized social group is paying sufficient attention to it. This process of steady expansion has much to do, in our day, with the mortality of temporal power. We now appear to be going through one of those crucial periods of the death and rebirth of concern, and this situation forms the next stage of our critical path.

V

If our argument is on the right track so far, we get two kinds of education in life. The primary kind is an education in concern, an understanding of the axioms and assumptions on which the people around us act, or say they act. It is an education in loyalties, attachments, beliefs, responses, and ideals, along with a growing sense of dissonance between professed and genuine beliefs, between ideals and realities. We study relatively little of it, and get most of it out of the air from our parents, teachers, and contemporaries. But every society has ways of ensuring that we learn it, and learn it thoroughly and early, even though some aspects of it, such as the teaching of religion in a democracy, may be left to private enterprise. This is followed by a secondary education, mainly in the truth of correspondence, which is education properly speaking, and is the chief business of schools and universities. From the universities in particular, the concern of the educated minority, which is centered on the myth of freedom, leaks out to society as a whole. But whenever the sense of concern receives a shock, whenever the sense of a solid social order that we accept and go along with is weakened, we realize how primary social concern is. If concern is damaged, that damage must be patched up first, no matter what happens to the virtues fostered by reason and evidence.

This seems to be the kind of situation we are in now. In North America, at least, most of us take in, through the pores of our primary education, a concerned belief in democracy, as an inclusive social ideal that works toward giving equal rights to all its citizens. This ideal, many now feel, was kidnapped at the beginning by a social movement which was really oligarchical in tendency, based on various forms of exploitation, including slavery and later racism, and hence exclusive, which built up a hysterically competitive economy on a thunderous cannonade of advertising and other forms of systematic lying, and finally began to spill over into imperialistic crusades like the Vietnam war. The result is that many people, especially in the under-thirty age group, feel alienated from their own society, to the point of what is sometimes called an identity crisis. The lunatic obsessiveness of a foreign policy that keeps on making aggressive gestures at a time when any serious war would wipe out the human race forms the nucleus of this crisis. These are rationalizations of contemporary unrest: they cannot be causes (for causes we should probably look rather at such factors as noise, pollution, and overcrowding), but in the area of our argument rationalizations are extremely important.

As a result there has been a strongly revived sense of concern, which finds much of its focus in the universities. The universities are the social centers of the myth of freedom, and are, by necessity, devoted to the virtues of the truth of correspondence, including objectivity and detachment. These are felt to be insufficient virtues in the face of a direct threat to human survival, and hence there is a strong desire to transform the university into a society of concern, like a church or political party. The reason for this curious and confused situation is that education itself, during the last century, has taken on many of the features of a myth of concern: compulsory and universal schooling, combined with the attempt to instill concerned social attitudes as part of the educational process (saluting the flag and the like), have turned the schools into a kind of secular church. At the university level the distinction between the two types of education is more clearly understood; the attempts to make it a society of concern are resisted, and so a kind of "sartor resartus" situation develops. In the symbolism of Carlyle's book, clothes reveal the body, by enabling it to become publicly visible, and at the same time they conceal and disguise it. When society is properly functioning, according to Carlyle, its institutions are a clothing that fits it and reveals its form; when society has outgrown its institutions and is due for a radical change, those institutions have become merely a disguise. The present mood of concern regards the university as part of the facade or outworn clothing of an "establishment" whose naked reality is a death wish.

The impetus toward revealing nakedness, which often takes very literal forms, goes in both directions. In one direction is the attempt to tear off the disguises of tolerance and good will, of rationalization and liberal rhetoric, from the "establishment," and in the other there is the popularity of encounter groups and similar devices for uncovering one's "real" emotions. The ultimate result is assumed to be a confrontation of innocent with guilty nakedness. Prudery, it is felt, is an important element in ruling-class mythology for many reasons, one of which is a feeling that sex should be concealed and subordinated because it is something equally accessible to the working classes. Hence the shock tactics of "bad" words and an explicit emphasis on sexuality among contemporary radicals. These shock tactics have already largely accomplished, I should think, their original aim of changing the focus of the obscene expression. The celebrated four-letter words raise few eyebrows today, because the taboo on them never was based on much more than reflex. The real obscenities of our time, the words that no self-respecting person would seriously use, are the words that express hatred or contempt for people of different religion or nationality or skin color, and disapproval of such words is based on a more solid idea of what is socially dangerous.

The demand for "relevance" is another effort to develop a form of concerned thinking. This demand is of course most articulate in the departments of humanities and social sciences which are devoted to the study of social mythology. Here there is frequently a deadlock between students preoccupied with their own myths of concern and their teachers who are studying such matters in a more piecemeal way: the two groups do not always realize that they are talking about different things. The demand for relevance usually reflects something of the inner drive of all concerned thinking to become encyclopedic, covering every aspect of human life and destiny. The natural tendency for scholarship to become specialized, even any reference to a discipline or a structure of thought, is apt to meet with the protest that this is a fragmented and compartmentalized approach to knowledge, now dangerously outmoded. There are of course some anti-intellectual trends latent here: concern may often come close to the "think with your blood" exhortations of the Nazis, for whom also relevance (*Zweckwissenschaft*) was a watchword. The issue is partly one of attaching greater approval to liquid than to solid metaphors: it is better to "keep things stirred up" than to be imprisoned in a "structure." Still it continues to make sense to say that all knowledge founded on the truth of correspondence is "structured," and that whatever is "unstructured" is headed toward belief or concerned mythology, not knowledge. There is no contradiction between the fact that all knowledge is "structured," and the fact that there are no real boundaries or compartments in it, because of the total interconnection of knowledge, the fact that every field of knowledge is the center of all knowledge. But such matters are unlikely to become clarified in collisions between claustrophobic students and agoraphobic scholars.

It seems obvious that, for people on this continent at least, the real cure for the identity crisis I mentioned above is the recovery of their own revolutionary and democratic myth of concern. Of course it is not only the "establishment" that has a façade, and some radicals also profess a democratic mythology who actually hold a very different one. Bourgeois democracy with its open myth is on the whole as mature and flexible a form of society as we have; consequently closed myths and authoritarian systems hold a strong attraction for immature and inflexible minds. But the great majority of those who are disaffected and restive are trying to articulate a democratic myth of concern, which is, after all, the only one they really know. Certainly there is a tremendous radical force in American culture, in Whitman's *Democratic Vistas*, in Thoreau's *Walden* and *Civil Disobedience*, in Jefferson's view of local self-determination, in Lincoln's conception of the Civil War as a revolution against the inner spirit of slavery, which could give a very different social slant to the American myth of concern. Ezra Pound, for all his crankiness, was trying to portray something of this innate radicalism in his John Adams Cantos. And while some American radicals may look for the illustration of their social ideals in whatever Marxist leadership appears to be still in the age of innocence, like that of Che Guevara, this search for a heroic ideal just beyond the frontier is itself a central part of American mythology, and, as with the pool of Narcissus, the real source of its attractiveness is not difficult to find. There is of course a right wing that would like to make the American way of life a closed myth, but its prospects at the moment do not seem bright.

Thirty years ago, during the depression, the last thing that anyone would have predicted was the rise of anarchism as a revolutionary force. It seemed to have been destroyed by Stalinist Communism once and for all. But there are many reasons why the present radical mood is so strongly anarchist. In the first place, the radical American tradition just referred to, especially in Jefferson and Thoreau, shows many affinities with the decentralizing and separatist tendencies of anarchism, in striking contrast to orthodox Marxism, which had very little in the American tradition to attach itself to. There are some curious parallels between the present and the nineteenth-century American scene, between contemporary turn-on sessions and nineteenth-century ecstatic revivalism, between beatnik and hippie communes and some of the nineteenth-century Utopian projects; and the populist movements at the turn of the century showed the same revolutionary ambivalence, tending equally to the left or to the right, that one sees today. Secondly, today's radical has inherited the heroic gloom of existentialism, with its doctrine that all genuine commitment begins in the revolt of the individual personality against an impersonal or otherwise absurd environment. The conception of the personal as inherently a revolutionary force began in a Christian context in Kierkegaard and was developed in a secular one by French writers associated with the resistance against the Nazis, the direct ancestor of the more localized revolutionary movements of our day.

The myths of concern and of freedom are ultimately inseparable, and the genuine individual can exist only where they join. When a myth of concern has everything its own way, it becomes the most squalid of tyrannies, with no moral principles except those of its own tactics, and a hatred of all human life that escapes from its particular obsessions. When a myth of freedom has everything its own way, it becomes a lazy and selfish parasite on a power-structure. Satire shows us in *1984* the society that has destroyed its myth of freedom, and in *Brave New World* the society that has forgotten its myth of concern. The emphasis on individuality makes it possible for the anarchism of our time to absorb more cultural elements than the Stalinism of the last generation seemed able to absorb. One of these is a middle-class disillusionment with the values of what is called an affluent society. This kind of disaffection is not, like orthodox Marxism, directed at the centers of economic power: it is rather a psychologically based revolution, a movement of protest directed at the anxieties of privilege. It does not fight for the workers against the exploiters: it attacks and ridicules the work ethic itself. It does not see Negro segregation or the Vietnam war merely as by-products of a class struggle: it sees the fears and prejudices involved in these issues as primary, and the insecurity that inspires them as the real enemy. Thus the revolutionary feeling of our time is, as previously indicated, at least as psychological as economic, as Freudian as it is Marxist, and many aspects of it carry on the "Bohemian" life-style revolution of the previous century already mentioned.

A revolutionary movement of this partly psychological kind is one in which the arts can play a central and functional role.

A Marxist novelist or poet who finds his enemy in capitalism has to construct a literary analogue or illustration to a philosophy, like Sidney's poet. But in the situation around us the artist has an enemy that he can recognize and deal with in his own terms: the enemy of anti-art, the psychological defenses of advertising and propaganda which occupy the place of the arts if they are not dislodged. A militant art of this kind can hardly find itself in the position of the simple old-line Marxism, with its formula of protest before revolution, panegyric afterward. The revolution it fights for can never "take place": it is permanent revolution in the strictest sense, society engaged in a perpetual critique of itself, reforming and reclarifying its own mythology, its own troubled and inconsistent but still crusading vision of what it might be.

The growth of a new sense of concern brings with it the urgent necessity of understanding, not merely its psychology, but its mythical and poetic language. The greater relevance of the arts to social protest today is connected with another cultural fact of the greatest importance in our present argument: the quite sudden revival of oral culture, at least in the North American and European democracies. Oral culture had been fostered a good deal in Communist countries, where in any case the traditions of oral poetry had been much more active. But for us it is a new experience to think of contemporary poetry as consisting not so much of a small group of great poets as of a kind of diffused creative energy, much of which takes quite ephemeral forms. It used to be assumed that every creative effort worthy the name was aiming at permanence, and so was really addressed to posterity, but this notion does not have the prestige it once had. A fair amount of this creative energy takes the form of a poetry read or recited to listening groups which is close to improvisation, usually has some kind of musical accompaniment or background, and includes commentary on current social issues. Wyndham Lewis's contempt for the "dithyrambic spectator" seems very remote today: we are now in a culture of formulaic units and semi-improvised "happenings," where the role of the audience is of primary importance, and which demands a consolidation of social opinion. We shall not, I hope, go so far as to retribalize our culture completely around formulaic units, as China is now doing with the thoughts of Chairman Mao. But a similar oral context, and a similar appeal to immediate emotional response, is obviously reappearing in our literature.

When I began teaching, a generation ago, literature had become so assimilated to a writing culture that it was being looked at in reverse, and taught the wrong way round. Poetry is at the center of literature; literary prose, in novels and plays and the like, forms the periphery; outside that again is utilitarian prose, the use of words for nonliterary purposes. Educational theory assumed that literature was first of all an art of communication, interpreting the word communication in anti-imaginative terms. So its center of gravity was utilitarian prose, which moved on to literary prose by way of relaxation, and finally, with the greatest reluctance, approached poetry, though as cautiously as if it were boiling oil. Students were told that the conventionalizing of speech known as prose, which is actually a very difficult and sophisticated convention, was in fact the natural way to talk and to think; hence they were compelled to compose sentences in what for them was a dead language, with nothing of the actual rhythms of speech in it. However, by the time they reached the university they had become convinced that prose was the language of ordinary speech, though they often still could not write it and seldom or never spoke it, and that poetry was a perverse way of distorting ordinary prose statements. Educators today appear to be as ignorant and confused as ever, but their victims are less helpless. They have educated themselves, partly through movies and television, art forms with an unparalleled power of presenting things in terms of symbol and archetype, and partly through the oral tradition, as it reaches them through folk singers and similar forms of poetic expression. As a result many students have come to think of poetry as a relatively normal form of thought and speech, and even such difficult poets as Wallace Stevens or the later Yeats are regarded with less panic than they were.

Along with this, and partly as a result of the influence of science fiction, there has grown up a new tolerance for schematic patterns in thinking, of a kind congenial to poetry, even for what a few years ago would have been considered superstitious nonsense and nothing more. Astrology, Tarot cards, the I Ching, maverick writers like Velikowski or Gurdjieff, all have their student following. It seems clear that the revival of oral culture and the growth of a revolutionary sense of concern are part of the same social process. This does not mean that a great age of poetry is about to dawn upon us: it means rather the opposite, an absorption of the poetic habit of mind into ordinary experience. We still read poetry by its symbolic "underthought," and have developed very subtle techniques of doing so. The general assumption is that, as Auden says of Yeats, if a poet seems to be "silly like us," time pardons all poets who can write well. But such poets as folk singers with a listening audience have to make a surface of explicit statement a part of their communication as well. Perhaps even silliness is not always a wholly unpoetic quality, nor is time always the most important critic.

This situation is so new that not all its social implications are clear yet. It is still not quite realized that the closer an art is to improvisation, the more it depends on a rigorous convention, as we see in the *commedia dell' arte*. The oral poet is concerned with the ritualized acts, or what Yeats called the ceremony of innocence, around which social activity revolves in an oral culture. Both oral poetry and the life it reflects rely on a spontaneity which has a thoroughly predictable general convention underlying it. It is consistent with this kind of culture that young people should be concerned, in McLuhan's formulaic phrase, more with roles than with goals, with a dramatic rather than a teleological conception of social function. One sees them throwing themselves into roles with great passion and conviction; but while the role solves the problem of sincerity, as the actor's sincerity consists in putting on his show and not in believing what he says, it does not solve the far greater problem of identity. The role is usually a part in someone else's play, and a great deal of youthful spontaneous idealism is obviously being exploited by leaders who do not share it, but who understand its predictable basis.

Then again, because the myths of concern and freedom stand and fall together, one's social function is inseparably a part of one's personality. Hence when the sense of concern is weakened, the sense of the continuity of the individual is weakened too. The individual life breaks down into a disconnected sequence of experiences, in which the sexual experiences bulk very prominently. One reason why they are so prominent is that one's sexual life, as such, is not so much individual as generic: people may love in individual ways, but copulation in itself, like birth and death, is of the species. I spoke of Kierkegaard's use of Leporello's catalogue of mistresses in *Don Giovanni* as a symbol of the "aesthetic," or falsely individualized, attitude to experience, and of course there is a sense in which all Don Giovanni's mistresses are the same woman, or more accurately the same female object. In the mechanical sexuality of so much contemporary drama and fiction there comes back into our culture something of the fetishism that we have in that quaint little paleolithic object called the Venus of Willendorf, all belly and teats and gaping vulva, but no face. The confusion between the physically intimate and the genuinely personal is parallel to, and doubtless related to, the confusion between the introverted and the creative experience in the drug cults.

I have spoken of the importance of the sententious utterance in literature, the existential commentary on life in general, which is so frequently embedded in a literary work. From medieval times until as late as the nineteenth century, such utterances were often regarded as the pearls of literature, worth opening the oyster to get. They descend historically from the oracles and proverbs which are typically the concerned prose of an oral culture. In both Greek and Hebrew literature the line of descent from actual oracles to the dark sayings of the wise is easy to see, though as usual the Hebrew development holds much more tenaciously to its origin. Proverbs, on the other hand, are popular rather than esoteric in reference, and collections of proverbs (there being something about the proverb, in all ages, that seems to stir the collector's instinct) appear in the "wisdom literature" of the Bible and elsewhere. In later literature we find oracular aphorisms more frequently in tragedies and proverbial ones in comedy and satire. The convention of beginning a story with a sententious comment, already well established in Boccaccio, is still going strong in the opening sentences of *Anna Karenina* and (in the key of delicate parody) *Pride and Prejudice*. The language of concern or belief is instinctively sententious and aphoristic, as anyone challenged to produce a statement of "What I Believe" would soon begin to demonstrate. Such aphorisms have a discontinuity about them that indicates a context rather than that of logical or sequential connection.

So the question arises, to what context do such statements of concern belong?

Statements of belief or concern are existential, and therefore the most obvious context for them is the life of the person who makes or inspires them, and who is usually a leader or culture-hero of some kind. In religious leaders particularly we notice the link with the oral tradition: Jesus, Buddha, even Mohammed, do not write, but make their utterances usually in connection with specific occasions, some of their disciples acting as secretaries, like the author of the collection of sayings of Jesus (Q) which is preserved in Matthew and Luke. In all theistic religions God speaks and man listens. Neither conception is simple, for all the efforts to make them so. God speaks, by hypothesis, in *accommodated* language, putting his thoughts and commandments into a humanly comprehensible form. And once the primary revelation is received, in prophecy or gospel or sura or oracle, man's listening takes the form of interpretation, which means critical reconstruction. There is no "literal" way of receiving a message from an infinite mind in finite language. Once a myth of concern is socially established, the personal focus falls on the leader or interpreter who is centrally responsible for sustaining the myth in history. This line of succession may derive from such a canonical organizer as Paul, whose letters, like the pamphlets of Lenin later, deal with specific tactical decisions in a way that leads to far-reaching theoretical principles. The succession of leaders may be regarded as definitive interpreters of the myth of concern, like the Pope with his ex-cathedra infallibility in Catholic Christianity or the Marxist leaders. Such figures are really incarnations of a dialectic, like Plato's philosopher-king. In other contexts the incarnation may be a purely symbolic figure like Elizabeth II, in her role of "defender of the faith." The most primitive form of such a conception is the kind represented by the *Führerprinzip* of Nazism: a much more open and sophisticated one is that of the Constitution of the United States, which was theoretically dictated by an inspired people to a prophetic group of founding fathers. When two myths of concern collide, this personal focus is usually prominent in the collision. It was the repudiation of the largely symbolic cult of the deified Caesar that marked Christians and Jews off from the Roman world; and when Julian the Apostate tried to set up a more philosophical and "open" alternative to Christianity he could not avoid putting his own cult at the center of it.

The earlier stages of a myth of concern usually include a development of a mainly oral oracular philosophy, associated with wise men, prophets, or gurus whose sayings are also usually recorded, often very haphazardly, by disciples or scribes. A strong esoteric tendency to distinguish between an inner and an outer court of hearers, or between deep and shallow comprehension of the same doctrines, is notable here. The practice of reserving special teachings for a smaller group of initiates has run through philosophy from Pythagoras to Wittgenstein. Similar esoteric movements make their way, sometimes in the form of philosophical heresies, into the great religions, producing various Gnostic developments in Christianity, Sufism in Islam, and what eventually became the Mahayana vehicle in Buddhism. Any personality at the center of a myth of concern whose life is the context of a body of teaching must be regarded as having reached a definitive level of truth. But as truth of concern is not truth of correspondence, and cannot strictly be verified and expanded like the established principles of a science, it follows that such a central personality is bound to create a hierarchy of response. This hierarchy of response may be represented, as above, by an inner group of specially enlightened followers, but in a socially ascendant myth it tends to become formalized in an institution, which becomes the acknowledged interpreter of the myth of concern, again on a hierarchical basis.

The more open the myth, the more the task of interpreting it begins to show analogies to literary criticism. The myth of concern usually exists as a body of words drawn up in the past, sometimes a remote past, and this body of words is, like the critic's text, unalterable. The variable factor is the new social situation provided by the interpreter's age; and as there is an indefinite series of such new situations, it follows that the original structure, again like the critic's text, is not only unalterable but inexhaustible in application. Thus the Supreme Court in America may not alter the Constitution, but must say what an eighteenth-century principle means in a twentieth-century world. The assumption is that the principles are comprehensive enough to be applicable to any current situation. At one extreme of this assumption would be the effort to keep twentieth-century America within an eighteenth- or nineteenth-century framework, giving it the ossified stability of some primitive societies. No one advocates this, but conservative and nostalgic pastoral myths, idealizing "old-fashioned" morality or ways of life, cluster near this extreme. At the other extreme would be the assertion that the Constitution means nothing in the contemporary scene at all and must be scrapped for a new myth of concern. What such an interpretive activity does is to establish a pattern of continuity in time, linking the present both to the past and to the future so far as the future can be surmised.

The analogy with literary criticism is becoming clearer: the critic dealing with Shakespeare, let us say, has to try to grasp the implications of the fact that Shakespeare still holds the stage and still communicates with the present age, for reasons that would have been unintelligible to Shakespeare's contemporaries and probably to Shakespeare himself. At the same time Shakespeare lived in a specific age and addressed a specific audience which was remote from ours in cultural assumptions. The critic has, as one impossible extreme of his interpretation, the attempt to understand Shakespeare as Shakespeare's contemporaries may be supposed to have understood him. At the other extreme is the view that the historical Shakespeare does not really exist any longer, and that only the contemporary critical revaluation of him exists. This view is sometimes advanced by critics as a paradox, but it is not very fruitful even as a paradox. Shakespeare's relation to his own time is the "liberal" or academic element in the study of Shakespeare; it brings us into contact with an alien culture, and expands our own notions of cultural possibilities. His relation to us is that of one more voice of concern, speaking with the authority of what Wallace Stevens calls the essential poem at the center of things. It is not a contemporary voice, and it has the oracular quality of something definitively revealed in the past. The critic, like the Christian or Marxist theologian or atheologian, or like the legal interpreter of the Constitution, has to establish a pattern of continuity linking present culture with its heritage, and, to some degree, with its inheritors.

But the analogy of literary criticism to the interpreting of a myth of concern reminds us that statements of belief or concern can have another context than the existential one of a leader's life or body of thought and exhortation. In literature they have the context of a story, from which they emerge as comments or applications. From a literary point of view every statement of belief or concern can be seen as the moral of a fable. Thus statements of Christian belief are inseparable from the story of the Bible, which is, in its literary form, a comic romance. Similarly the Greek belief in fate, or whatever was meant by such words as *ananke*, *moira*, and *heimarmene*, is essentially chorus comment on the narrative form of tragedy which the Greeks invented. In our day we tend to go from the three R's in our education as directly as we can to a belief in, or at least an assent to, the three A's: anxiety, alienation, and absurdity. But these concepts again are noble sentiments derived from a prevailingly ironic age of fable.

When Raphael in Milton's *Paradise Lost* was sent down to talk to Adam, the reason for sending him was to impress Adam with the importance of not touching the forbidden tree. Raphael, however, refers only obliquely to the tree: what he mainly does is to tell Adam the story of the fall of Satan. The implication is that teaching through parable, the typical method of Jesus, is the appropriate way of educating a free man, which of course is what Adam is before his fall. After his fall, he gets from Michael a similar emblematic and illustrative instruction, though within his new and fallen category of time, where the events are prophecies of an inevitable future to him, records of an inescapable past to the reader. Yet education is still by story or "speaking picture," with morals attached, and the total containing structure of the teaching is the Christian romantic comedy of salvation. Angels, evidently, teach by fable; teaching by morals is merely human, and only the officially and institutionally human at that.

Every statement of belief or concern, then, has a context in a vision of society or of man's relation to his gods or his destiny, and such visions make up what is expressed imaginatively by the total body of literature. It then becomes clear that literature, conceived as a total structure, is not in itself a myth of concern: what it presents is the *language* of concern, the total range of its imaginative possibilities, the encyclopedia of visions of human life and destiny which forms the context of all belief. "The Old and New Testaments are

167

the Great Code of Art," said Blake, indicating the context of his own work, and similarly literature is the "great code" of concern. The Christian myth of concern derives ultimately from the Bible, and the Bible presents Christian beliefs in the context of visions or fables. Many of these, such as the stories of the Fall or the Flood, remain imaginatively sterile if one tries to rationalize or historicize them, but approached in the universalized terms of the imagination, they become conceivable as visionary sources of belief. Other myths of concern, democratic, Marxist, or whatnot, are also founded on visions of human life with a generic literary shape, usually comic. Literature as a whole also is to be related to a life, but it is the life of all humanity, the total verbal imagination of man.

Educating through the fable rather than through the moral involves all the responsibilities of a greater freedom, including the responsibility of rejecting censorship. Of all the things that Milton says about censorship in the *Areopagitica*, the most far-reaching in its implications seems to me to be his remark that a wise man will make a better use of an idle pamphlet than a fool would of Holy Scripture. That is, the reader is responsible for the moral quality of what he reads, and it is the desire to dodge this responsibility, either on one's own behalf or that of others, that produces censorship. Statements of concern are either right or wrong, which means, as the truth involved is not directly verifiable, that they are accepted as right or wrong. For the deeply concerned, all arguments are personal, in the bad sense, because all arguments are either for them or against them, and hence their proponent needs simply to be identified as one of us or one of the enemy. A censorship or index expurgatorius which separates all the works of the latter seems logical to certain types of concerned mentality. One sees the hierarchical institution beginning to take shape here, with the censors forming an elite. The most unattractive quality of the censor is his contempt for other people. The censor says: "I want this play banned, because, while it can't possibly do me any harm, there are all those people over there who will be irreparably damaged in their morals if they see it." Similarly, the person who attaches a smear label to whatever he disagrees with is really saying: "It may be all very well to appeal to me with logical arguments, because I can see through them; but there are all those people over there who are not so astute, and who in any case will not act unless they are stampeded by slogans." The same habit of mind is common among all those whose main effort of thought is to save themselves trouble. I note in several Freudian books a tendency to dismiss Freudian revisionists or heretics like Jung or Adler as "reactionary." I mention Freud because he was in so many respects a conservative, pessimistic, even "reactionary" thinker who has been made into the founder of a myth of revolutionary optimism. In other words, no writer is inherently revolutionary or reactionary, whatever his views in his own lifetime may have been: it is the use made of him which ultimately determines what he is, and any writer may be potentially useful to anybody, in any way.

A more difficult assumption of responsibility relates to the poet's beliefs, and the particular concerns that he participates in. We have already met the principle that in reading poetry the "overthought," or explicit statement, is expendable to some degree, and that the "underthought" or progression of image and metaphor is the decisive meaning. When a myth of concern is derived from the teachings of a single man, or series of accredited teachers, those teachers must be regarded as in a very special sense wise or inspired men. No such respect need be accorded the poet so far as he represents a belief or attitude, however important and essential the belief may be to the poet himself. Hopkins and Claudel would probably never have bothered to keep on writing poetry without the drive of a powerful Catholic belief; but what makes them poets is their skill in using the language of concern, and hence they can be studied with the greatest devotion by readers who share none of their commitments. Still, most reasonable readers would respect a Catholic belief, whatever their own: a much more crucial example would be, say, Céline, who is a significant and important writer to many readers who could not possibly regard his views with anything but contempt.

The principles involved here which seem to me to be important to the present discussion are, first, that while the teacher of a myth of concern must be a wise or great or inspired man to his followers, the poet, or speaker of the language of concern, may be an important poet and yet, in certain crucial respects, almost any kind of a damned fool. Second, the subordination of reader to poet is tactical only: he studies his author with full attention, but the end at which he aims is a transfer of the poet's vision to himself. Poetry is not, then, to be merely enjoyed and appreciated, but to be possessed as well. Third, there are no negative visions: all poets are potentially positive contributors to man's body of vision, and no index expurgatorius or literary hell (to borrow a figure of Milton's) exists on any basis acceptable to a student of literature. Therefore, fourth, criticism does not aim at evaluation, which always means that the critic wants to get into the concern game himself, choosing a canon out of literature and so making it a single gigantic allegory of his own concern.

I have suggested that the restiveness we find all around us today, particularly in universities, derives from a weakening of the sense of concern, in a society where the need for social coherence is primary and the values of freedom and tolerance and rationality are derivative from it. In modern times the classical statement of this position is Kierkegaard's *Either/Or*, from which the existentialist traditions of our day mainly descend. For Kierkegaard the detached, liberal, and impersonal attitude fostered by the study of an objective environment, and which flowers into comprehensive intellectual systems like that of Hegel, is an "aesthetic" attitude, and the crisis of life comes when we pass over into the commitment represented by "or," and enter the sphere of genuine personality and ethical freedom. Once one takes this step, one realizes that the "aesthetic" attitude was projected, because with this attitude man tries to fit himself into a larger container, the general outlines of which he can see with his reason, and forgetting that his reason built the container. The postulates of Kierkegaard's ethical freedom are Christian postulates, and his commitment is an acceptance of faith. The acceptance is essentially uncritical, because, so the argument runs, man is not a spectator of his own life. But, we have seen, the context of Christian faith in the Bible is a context of vision and fable and myth, and Kierkegaard does not really come to terms with the implications of this fact. Milton's portrayal of Adam looking at the sequence of Adamic life presented in the Bible, where the Christian faith becomes a total informing vision which Adam contemplates as a spectator, shows a far profounder grasp, not only of Christianity, but of the whole problem of concern. We cannot stop with the voluntary self-blinkering of commitment: on the other side of "or" is another step to be taken, a step from the committed to the creative, from primitive concern to a full awareness which derives from it and retains its values but carries them into a higher state. Man *is* a spectator of his own life, or at least of the larger vision in which his life is contained, but this vision is nothing external to himself and is not born out of nature or any objective environment. Yet it is not subjective either, because it is produced by the power of communication, the power

171

that enables men, in Aristotle's phrase, not merely to come together to form a social life, but to remain together to form the good life.

VI

A certain critical element in one's education, which consists in becoming increasingly aware of one's own mythological conditioning, obviously has an important function in any open mythology. For example, a good many of the subjects studied in the university are the myths of concern themselves, in their various aspects: these constitute, as previously remarked, the mythological subjects: literature, religion, and large areas of other subjects in the humanities and social sciences. The mythological subjects are not identified as a group in any university curriculum, but the distinction between studying a myth of concern and promoting it is quite familiar in practice. In a democracy, a publicly supported university is supposed to teach a religion within the orbit of the truth of correspondence, presenting it as a faith that as a matter of historical fact has been or is held. Similarly, the university's role with other myths of concern is to study, for example, Marxism, but not to support the kind of seminar on Marxism which consists only of charging the batteries of the Marxist faithful. The same principle applies to the myth of democracy itself: it is not the function of a university to indoctrinate even that myth, because the public indoctrination of any myth tends to close it.

The principle of openness in a myth of concern does not, I said, prevent a society from having a myth of concern. What it does is to break up what is so often called its "monolithic" aspect. Expressions of faith in such a myth of concern as medieval Christianity may range from the philosophy of St. Thomas Aquinas to the crudest forms of relic fetishism. But

all intense orthodoxy, however subtle or sophisticated, rests
on a compromise with less enlightened versions of the same
views. The latter can be deprecated, but not repudiated.
Erasmus may ridicule or Luther denounce the popularity of
indulgences and relics, but the Council of Trent must reaffirm
the genuineness of these phenomena. Our own society is less
orthodox in that sense. As in all societies, we are first introduced in childhood to popular social mythology, the steady
rain of clichés and prejudices and assumptions that come to
us from elementary schooling, from mass media, from entertainment, from conversation and gossip. In a society with an
open mythology this process has little if any conscious aim,
but unconsciously it aims, very precisely, at the same goal
as that consciously sought in societies with closed myths, that
is, the docile and obedient (or "adjusted") citizen. A few
years ago (things have improved lately) the bulk of American
education up to about grade eight was essentially an education in the clichés of American social mythology, the teaching
of what purported to be literature being almost entirely so.
But in an open mythology we encounter, as we go up the
educational ladder, other forms of social mythology, some
confirming the more elementary ones, others rejecting or
repudiating them.

Although I remarked earlier that the collision between
democratic faith and oligarchic fact in American society has
produced an acute sense of social alienation, I have so far said
nothing about "capitalism," which according to Communists
is the central myth of concern in non-Communist countries.
The belief in capitalism, so far as capitalism commands a
belief, appears to rest mainly on an analogy between laissez-
faire and liberalism, between the entrepreneur and the creative,
adventurous, or emancipated individual, of the kind that the
phrase "free enterprise" suggests. This analogy is deeply em-

bedded in the elementary social mythology I just referred to, and of course many Americans hold it for life. Others find it dishonest, or, at best, vague and unconvincing, and feel that social education involves outgrowing it. In general, it is perhaps true to say that in the countries technically called capitalist, capitalism is not a belief that is very seriously defended as a myth of concern. It rests for its dissemination on advertising, in the broadest sense; and advertising seems to be related to an open mythology much as propaganda is to a closed one. Advertising contains a residual irony: most of its statements are not expected to be literally believed by normal adults, and the gullible and impressionable audience it assumes is a largely fictitious one. In propaganda, of course, this residual irony disappears, and with it most of the means for escaping from the pressure of what it says.

This situation has the great advantage, not merely of keeping American social mythology open, but of making a critical attitude toward that mythology, along with the education which fosters the attitude, functional in society. It has the disadvantage of making disillusionment so much a part of social education that it tends to leave one's permanent loyalties unformulated and undefined. There are those who accept the capitalist and oligarchical aspect of American society as a part of their loyalty, there are those who reject it in theory but come to terms with it in practice, and there are those who repudiate it in practice but are unable to say where their real loyalties belong. Much of the social energy that a myth of concern generates leaks away through the openings of critical and analytical attitudes. This is not a bad thing in itself, as a free society must have these attitudes, but it creates other problems.

Social mythology is polarized by two mythical conceptions, the conception of the social contract and the conception

174

of the Utopia or ideal state. These two conceptions operate as informing principles in the mind: however much one may theoretically equate the Utopian with the illusory or the chimerical, it would be a very cynical person who could participate in society without some implied social ideal at some level of his consciousness. Similarly with the contract, which stresses the fact already mentioned, that our major social roles, along with our position in time and space, are prescribed for us before birth. These two principles of contract and Utopia descend historically, as myth, from their Christian predecessors, the alienation myth of the fall of man and the fulfillment myth of the City of God.

Of the new secular myths of concern that came into Western thought as the monopoly of Christianity declined, one, already referred to, was the conservatism expounded by Edmund Burke, which was based on the positive aspects of the social contract. For Burke, the development of the individual in society is largely a matter of growing organically out of the roots of one's social context. We are given our loyalties before we are capable of choosing them, and to try to reject what one is already committed to can only lead to chaos, both in one's life and in society. Further, it is the permanence and continuity of social institutions, including church and state, that not only civilizes man, but adds the real dimension of historical significance to his life.

This conservative view was liberalized by a gradualist and sequential myth of progress, which after Darwin's time became a mythical analogy of evolution. I often turn to a favorite book of my childhood, H. G. Wells's *Outline of History*, which is a fascinating source book for progressive mythology. There, the "outline of history" is appended to a brief introductory account of the evolution of life, on the assumption that history follows the same direction of development that evolution does. We read near the beginning of a Neanderthal man who was "quite a passable human being," in spite of not being able to walk erect "as all living men do." I understand that the evidence for this statement depended on a single specimen who was later proved to have had arthritis. The important thing for the present context is not the adequacy of the evidence, but the symmetry of a gradualist myth, in which somebody had to shamble before homo sapiens could walk upright. A gradualist myth, in other words, needs inferior races, in order to lead up dramatically to the final epiphany of what Wells calls the "true men." Wells not being a fool, he does not identify these inferior races with Mongol hordes or the accursed progeny of Ham, so he puts them at the beginning of history, where they are both out of harm's way and are more convincingly related to their natural superiors, who have proved their superiority in two gradualist ways: by coming later and by still surviving.

The overtones of the social contract are ironic, even tragic; but nearly all popular historical myths are, like the myth of Christianity itself, derived from comic romance, the story of the successfully achieved quest. As G. K. Chesterton remarks, the Victorians assimilated history to a three-volume novel, with themselves as the happily-ending third volume; and a theory of gradual progress is the obvious way of providing a narrative shape for history without giving too much importance to revolution. Wells's post-Victorian version of this romance myth emphasizes the sequential structure inherent in all romance. The successful quest in romance is usually the third attempt, and in the passage referred to we have the evolution of man summarized in three stages: pithecanthropoid, Neanderthaler, and finally the true men.

The weak spot in the conservative emphasis on the contract, on playing the hand dealt to one at birth, so to speak, is the uncritical element in it. The primary justification for all social phenomena, in the conservative view, is simply the fact that they are there, and this makes it extremely difficult to distinguish reality from appearance in them, what they really are from what they seem or pretend to be. Being involuntarily born into a certain nation seems hardly enough to compel one to adopt the maxim "my country right or wrong." The radical view of the social contract focuses on this uncritical element, and feels that maturity and development are a matter of becoming aware of our social conditioning, and so of making a choice between presented and discovered loyalties. The only real loyalty, from this point of view, is the voluntary or self-chosen loyalty, which is often loyalty to a social ideal not yet in existence. This transfer of loyalty from one's native society to another society still to be constructed creates an intensely Utopian state of mind.

The Marxist revolutionary movement is the Utopian counterpart to conservative gradualism in the modern world. When Engels contrasted Utopian and "scientific" socialism he was really completing the Utopian myth. In a world like ours a limited Utopia in a restricted or enclosed space is an empty fantasy: Utopia must be a world-wide transformation of the whole social order or it is nothing. But for it to be this it must be conceived, not as an a priori rational construct, as in most Utopian romances, but as the *telos* of history, the end to which history points. The "scientific" element in Engels's socialism, then, is a religious belief in the teleology of history. We see this particularly in the intensely teleological nature of Marxist revolutionary tactics, in which every strike or demonstration is one more step in the advance to the final takeover. Thus the Marxist myth of concern also has the shape of a comic romance, but one that puts its main attention on the final dragon-killing achievement and the separation of the

177

hero's world from the threats and menaces surrounding him.

The belief in the continuity and in the manifesting of an inner purpose in history, and in the movement of time generally, had been built into Western religious and political thought from the earliest times. It was still there in the culture of the nineteenth century, not only in its thought but in the long novels that rolled through complication and crisis to an inevitable conclusion, in the symphonies that took off from and returned to the same tonality, in the pictures that were moments of arrested movement, like the self-portraits of Van Gogh or the dancers of Dégas. Nothing is more striking in our own day than the disappearance of this sense of continuity. The bourgeois progressive myth, which assumed a benevolent future on the whole, began to break down under the shocks of twentieth-century disasters, and the inherent paradox in the myth, that progress is a good thing and yet leads to increasing stability, became more obvious. Marxism could interpret the disasters more plausibly as the death-agonies of bourgeois culture, but the prevailing revolutionary mood of our time being anarchist, contemporary radicals have largely lost interest in the "historical process." The two teleological myths continue to dominate much of our thinking, but they do so increasingly out of habit rather than genuine conviction. The progress of science and technology produces an uneasy sense of a confused and rapid process of change that is just about to become clear: this sense has of course nothing to do with either science or technology, but is a social mirage, like flying saucers.

There is a very cruel donkey's carrot concealed in both progressive myths. Both project an ideal into the future; both can rationalize the most atrocious present acts as leading to a future good; both promise the gratitude of some hazy posterity for very real sacrifices of life and happiness to be made now; both present us with leaders who have the abstracted gaze of the car driver, looking forward to the imminent; both constantly tell us that we can really enjoy the blessings of our civilization only after some particular social hurdle is got over first. The appeal seems plausible until we start noticing that there is a series of hurdles, that the series never comes to an end, and that the earlier religious view was probably more realistic in assuming that the temporary hurdle could only be life itself, and could only be cleared by death. In the society of our day the unhappiest people are those who, in Sir Charles Snow's phrase, have the future in their bones: who convince themselves, every night, that Godot will infallibly come tomorrow.

The conservative acceptance of the social contract throws a strong emphasis on what is now called "commitment" or "engagement." These are not only largely uncritical attitudes, but also somewhat humorless: their instinct is to rationalize whatever they find existing in society, instead of recognizing injustices, anomalies, or absurdities in it. Commitment and engagement are attitudes that imply the superiority of the continuum of society to the person who is involuntarily caught up by it. The authority of the social contract is a *de facto* authority: it lacks a genuinely ideal dimension, and thereby keeps social ideals in an empty world of wish or hope or promise. The radical Utopian attitude begins in detachment from conservative commitment and in moral judgment on what the conservative accepts. It transfers its loyalty to an ideal, and works toward gathering enough force around this ideal to smash the existing contract in its turn, thereby becoming a new *de facto* authority. But of course its potential society also demands commitment, of a much more intense kind. It recognizes anomalies and absurdities in existing society, but its own loyalty is still less critical, even more eager to rationalize, more impatient with dissent. In a time of a conflict of concerns, instead of getting more liberalism and tolerance we eventually get less, as each side tries to identify these qualities with the disguise of its enemy. The trouble is that myths of concern nearly always are in conflict, because concern, unless very open, must have an enemy. Marxist countries must have imperialistic aggressors; bourgeois societies must have Communist subversives, just as medieval Christendom had to have a pretext for starting the Crusades.

It has been fairly obvious all along that the myths of contract and of Utopia are interconnected. Every future ideal is the fruition of one supposed to have existed, actually or potentially, in the past. The heaven of the Christian myth, which we reach after death, returns us to a state of bliss set up before the beginning of history. The revolutionary future goal achieves the society of nature and reason that is the true social contract, buried under exploitation and tyranny. The conservative acceptance of the contract ensures a serene, or relatively serene, future by preserving the inner balance of society. All such mythologies connect the past and the future by building a bridge over the present. And yet this double dislocation of time seems to lead us into a curiously unreal world. We notice how frequently a myth of concern rests on a false version of history, or, at best, on a very strained interpretation of it. The future is similarly distorted, as ideals which are projected into the future get us involved in a pernicious means-to-an-end process which ignores the fact that means cannot lead to ends, because they condition and eventually replace those ends. One suspects that there must be some reality in the middle, and in the present moment, from which these past and future fictions have been projected.

If we look at the greatest writing about contracts and Utopias, the works of Plato, More, Locke, or Rousseau, we

notice, for example, that Socrates in the *Republic* is not concerned about setting up his ideal state anywhere: what he is
concerned about is the analogy between his ideal state and the
structure of the wise man's mind. The latter is an absolute
dictatorship of reason controlling desire through the will, and
these three elements correspond to the philosopher-king,
soldiers, and artisans of the political myth. The ideal state
exists, so far as we know, only in such wise minds, who will
obey its laws whatever society they are actually living in. In
More's *Utopia*, the narrator Hythlodaye, who has been to
Utopia, has returned a revolutionary communist, convinced
that nothing can be done with Europe until its social system
has been destroyed and a replica of the Utopia set up in its
place. But More himself, to whom the story is being told,
suggests using the knowledge of Utopia rather as a means of
bringing about an improvement in European society from
within. Thus the real Utopia becomes the social vision of the
wise counselor's mind. Plato and More realize that while the
wise man's mind is rigidly disciplined, and while the mature
state is ordered, we cannot take the analogy between the disciplined mind and the disciplined state too literally: if we did
we should get the most frightful tyranny in the latter. The
real Utopia is an individual goal, of which the disciplined
society is an allegory. The end of commitment and engagement is the community: the logical end of detachment is the
individual. But this is not an antithesis: the mature or fully
rounded individual is so only after he has come to terms with
his community. This is the reason why the individual goal is
symbolized by a political analogy. The Utopian ideal points
beyond the individual to a condition in which, as in Kant's
kingdom of ends, society and individual are no longer in
conflict, but have become different aspects of the same human
body.

We do not now think of the wise man's mind as a dictatorship of reason, of which an authoritarian society could be an allegory: in fact we do not think about the wise man's mind at all. We think rather, in more Freudian terms, of a mind in which a principle of sanity is fighting for its life against a thundering herd of chaotic impulses, which cannot be simply suppressed but must be frequently indulged and humored, allowed to have their say even when it is silly or infantile. In short, we think of the mind as a participating democracy, and our social ideals become, as before, an idealized political allegory of such a mind. In this analogy there is no place for the inner-directed person who resists society, like Socrates, or More himself, and for that very reason the analogy seems more compelling. It is felt that because it is therapeutic for the individual to talk out his aggressions and get rid of his inhibitions and "hangups," a society in which everyone was doing this would be the ideal society of innocent nakedness referred to earlier. But here, as with earlier thinkers, the analogy is a tricky one. Several decades of sublimated violence have not made society any less violent, and the social response to sexual stimulation in entertainment is as itchy and prurient as it ever was. The moral I should draw from such facts is that the release of inhibitions is just as compulsive and hysterical an operation as the suppression of them could ever be.

When we take a second look at our great Utopian and contract writers, we begin to suspect that they are not really writing about contracts or Utopias at all, but about the theory of education. It is education that Plato and More and Locke and Rousseau really care about, and all their fictions about what happened in a remote past or might conceivably happen in a remote future are expendable. Wisdom, or whatever education is looking for, joins the individual to a community, but a different community from that of concern. It is the community of those who appeal to evidence, reason, experiment, and imagination, the largely nonmythical features of civilization which suggest an environment outside the immediate society and its enemies. This community constitutes the only genuine *de jure* or spiritual authority in society. The social contract and the ideal state, then, are projections, into the past and the future respectively, of a source of social authority that sits in the middle of our society, and which I shall call the educational contract. By the educational contract I mean the process by which the arts and sciences, with their methods of logic, experiment, amassing of evidence, and imaginative presentation, actually operate as a source of authority in society. What they create is a free authority, something coherent enough to form a community, but not an authority in the sense of being able to apply external compulsion. The sense of the permanence and continuity of social institutions, so powerful in Burke's day, is now greatly weakened, along with the belief that they are any better for being permanent. There still remains the continuity of the arts and sciences. This is not a gradual continuity: every subject of knowledge has gone through a long series of revolutionary transformations. But the continuity is there, nevertheless, and is something that everyone experiences in his own education, as he recapitulates the earlier stages of the subjects he studies. From the point of view of educational experience, the continuity of knowledge is really the source of the continuity of social institutions, and the source to which we have to return in times of crisis.

This conception of an educational contract was the main contribution made by the development of educational theory in nineteenth-century England, usually regarded as one of the world's greatest eras of liberal thought. The educational contract is the area of free thought and discussion which is at the center of John Stuart Mill's view of liberty, and which is thought of as a kind of intellectual counterpart of Parliament. It differs from Parliament, for Mill, in that the liberals can never have a majority, which is why democracy has to function as an illogical but deeply humane combination of majority rule and minority right. In Matthew Arnold the educational contract is called culture, and Arnold is explicit about culture's being the source of genuine authority in society and at the same time operating in a Utopian direction by breaking down the barriers of class conflict. Newman draws a distinction between liberal and useful knowledge, in which only the former belongs to the educational contract, but this is really a difference between two aspects of knowledge rather than two kinds of knowledge.

The educational contract is what the university in society primarily stands for. The conceptions of Mill, Arnold, and Newman are wider than the university, but the university is their engine room, and their authority can last only so long as the university keeps operating. The university, then, is the source of free authority in society, not as an institution, but as the place where the appeal to reason, experiment, evidence and imagination is constantly going on. It is not and never can be a concerned organization, like a church or a political party, and the tactics of trying to revolutionize society by harassing and bedeviling the university are not serious tactics. The university is, of course, relatively easy to harass, and hence doing so may give a false sense of accomplishment.

In all societies the pressure in the direction of a closed myth is also the tendency within society to become a mob, that is, a social body without individuals or critical attitudes, united by slogans or clichés against some focus of hatred. A myth of concern, by itself, cannot prevent this kind of social degeneration. I have said that faith, or participation in a myth of concern, is not in itself verifiable. But to some extent it can be verified in experience. Some myths of concern obviously make a fuller life possible than others do. I spoke earlier of a "rule of charity" in a myth of concern which compares its activities to the total welfare of mankind. This is doubtless the primary criterion, but there is an important secondary one: the ability of a myth of concern to come to terms with the nonmythical criteria of truth and reality. Thus a religious faith which permits intellectual honesty is clearly better in practice than one which tries to deny elementary facts of history or science. I have tried to show that no myth of concern is really scientific, or is itself based on nonmythical criteria, but the necessity for a working arrangement between the two aspects of culture is clear enough. And perhaps the two standards, of charity and of intellectual honesty, are ultimately the same standard. Certainly such a myth of concern as Nazism, which ranks very low on the scale of charity because of its racism and exclusiveness, could not avoid the falsifying of history and science, and I suspect that the two vices always go together.

In its relation to literature the university is primarily a place of criticism. The university is a first-rate place for studying literature, but at best a second-rate place for producing it. And literary criticism in our day has to be aware of many things that many literary scholars do not yet see to be relevant to that subject. One is the fact that all myths of concern are founded on visions of society, and that all visions of society have literary shapes, generally romantic and comic shapes. Another is the result of the revival of oral culture, the decline of belief in the teleological myths, and the rise of a new anarchism for which "confrontation" is to some extent its own end. This result has been a concerted effort to break down the distinction between art and life, between stage and audience, drama and event or "happening," display and par-

185

ticipation, social role and individual life style. We thus have, among other things, new forms of social activity which are really improvised symbolic dramas. One example that I witnessed recently was the extraordinary sleepwalking ritual of the "people's park" crisis in Berkeley. Here a vacant lot with a fence around it became assimilated to the archetype of the expulsion from Eden, dramatizing the conflict of the democratic community and the oligarchical conspiracy in a pastoral mode related to some common conventions of the Western story. A student editorial informed us that the lot was "covered with blood" because, like all the rest of the land in North America, it had been stolen from the Indians (murder of Abel archetype). The expelling angels in this symbolism were (as in Blake's version of it) demonic, and the police, with their helmets and bayonets and gas masks, were endeavoring, with considerable success, to represent the demonic in its popular science fiction form, of robots or bug-eyed monsters from outer space.

It is not such casual recognitions of traditional symbolic patterns, however, that give the critical study of literature so much importance for our time. Criticism is the attempt to attain knowledge of the language of concern and belief, and hence it has a central role in the study of human society. In developing this role it is bound to become more closely associated with neighboring disciplines, especially those in which the conceptions of myth, symbol, and image are functional.

The distinction I have been drawing between the mythical and the logical, which is partly the ancient and traditional distinction between faith and knowledge, is, I think, valid for the kind of considerations that I have been dealing with here. There clearly is a difference in attitude, and in the direction that a given writer is facing. But theoretically the distinction is very vulnerable, as no doubt some of my readers are already impatient to tell me. Words are one of the languages, along with mathematics and the pictorial arts, for informing our knowledge of the world. But how far do words inform, as compared with equations or diagrams, and what are the distinctively verbal methods and characteristics of providing a form for knowledge? Then again, we cannot express any knowledge of the world in words without providing a verbal structure for it. How does this structure differ from a myth? A descriptive writer may produce an informing structure which "follows" the facts, or arranges them in the way that, as many such writers hopefully say, the facts themselves suggest. At what point do such arranging structures become wish-fulfillment or manipulating structures? Where does reason become rationalization? A closed myth of concern can readily answer these questions: for it, a writer is using reason when following that myth, and only rationalizing when he departs from it. More disinterested philosophers, however, find such questions very difficult, and I doubt if we can get much further with them without taking literary elements into account. Every arrangement of words is a narrative, and so has a narrative shape, and a study of narrative shapes involves the study of literature. Such are some of the "hermeneutic" problems awaiting the critics of the future. They indicate that the critical path, like all well-conducted paths, ends where it began, with the possibility of a new beginning.

The first principle of this discussion is that the social context of literature can only be understood after the conception of "literature" itself has been grasped. Literature has its own forms of statement, its own conventions, its own history. Society does not simply produce plays and poems and novels, but develops a literature, and writers draw their themes and genres and technical skills from that literature, not from their experience of life in general. Literature is therefore autonomous in the sense in which any coherent human activity is autonomous. It is literature and not life which "inspires" or gives form to a writer's output, just as it is science which inspires or gives form to a scientist's investigations. One runs into various simplistic antitheses at this point, many people telling us that a work of literature has to be directly resolved into its social and historical background, and that if we refuse to do this we are separating literature entirely from its social context. The assumption behind this view is that the literary form of a work of literature is a negligible and arbitrary feature, and that only the content of literature need be taken seriously. I tried to trace the origin of this attitude to the mental habits of a writing culture, for which "literal" or genuine meaning is established by nonliterary forms. Such antitheses, however, are quite pointless obstacles to critical theory, as are the cliché phrases they use, such as "art for art's sake." I can understand that a writer may often feel that what he has done is its own justification and its own end, and that his art is for the sake of art in that sense, but what the phrase could mean to a critic I do not know.

Literature begins, I have tried to suggest, in that undifferentiated period of society where culture is mainly oral, where history, philosophy, religion, and politics are all united in a common mythical complex, which the poet is largely responsible for remembering, arranging, and transmitting. As writing develops, language becomes more conceptual and descriptive, and the sense of an objective order of nature begins to take shape. In this situation myths of concern attempt to preserve themselves by shifting their language to the rational and historical, but this in its turn creates a tension with nonmythical standards of judgment which bring in new criteria of truth and reality. In our society this tension has finally produced an "open" or pluralistic mythology with several myths of concern competing within it. Elsewhere in the world, notably in the two great Marxist empires, a closed myth of concern has taken over, and has harnessed literature to it, on the ground that literature must always be a means to a political end, and can only speak either for or against whatever myth of concern is in power. This attitude is based on the simplistic social/antisocial antitheses just mentioned. Those outside Marxist countries can see more clearly that such an attitude to literature is morally wrong and that the argument used to rationalize it is hysterical nonsense. The prescriptions of "social realism" have been notoriously incapable of coming to terms with anything in twentieth-century art which is genuinely revolutionary in form, and not merely in content.

It seems clear that a crucial test of a society's maturity is its ability, not merely to permit freedom of thought, but to release the language of concern itself, allowing the poets to follow whatever paths the conventions of literature in their time suggest. Left to itself, literature follows the encyclopedic pattern of concern, and covers the entire imaginative range from romance to irony, although of course every age stresses certain conventions more than others. The critic's function is not to tell the poet what he should do, but to study what he does do: such a phrase as "of course I don't like this *kind* of poetry" can never be uttered by a serious critic. Hence the critic, like the poet, can function properly only in a society with an open mythology.

Poets are the children of concern: they show a liking for being converted to dogmatic creeds of all kinds, sometimes showing the greatest contempt for the toleration they receive; they are a competitive and traditionally an irritable group; their genius is one of intensity rather than wisdom or serenity. Nevertheless, as they lose their primitive social role and seem to become more and more isolated from the thought and material culture of their societies, another social function grows up in the original place. They give pleasure. And how on earth—an earth which after several civilized millennia seems to be as ferocious and psychotic an earth as ever—can pleasure grow out of concern? Concern is constantly on the borderline of anxiety, and anxiety is only a hairsbreadth away from bigotry and fanaticism, violence and terror. Yet the poet's role clearly has to do with providing pleasure, even though all the demons of obsession are inside his magic circle.

I touched on the pleasure of poetry earlier, in connection with what Kierkegaard calls the aesthetic attitude to experience. What is insufficient about that conception of pleasure is its association with passivity, the vision behind it being one of a pleasantly stimulated subject contemplating an inscrutably beautiful object. This leads to an idolatry of art, a second-rate pseudo concern in which art itself becomes an object of concern, something to be believed in. This attitude is out of fashion now, in theory, but some of its assumptions can still be found in the criticism, and still more the teaching, of literature. Even at its best it impoverishes the teaching process, because it ignores, or tries to get rid of, the vast pyramid of verbal experience which builds up to "worthwhile" literature. It commits itself to trying to impose a minority culture on the whole of society, an object which we must recognize as futile even if we sympathize with its aim. It seems better to realize that the highest forms of play are not spectator sports, and that the student is actively engaged with literature, not so far as he studies its classics, but so far as he uses words at all. The end of literary education, we said, is not a contemplative end, however much the admiration of masterpieces may form part of it. Its end is rather the expanding of the verbal creative power of the student, a power which does not necessarily operate in literature, though it cannot be expanded except through the study of literature.

190

Throughout this discussion of myth one mythical shape has constantly recurred: the theme of an original descent from a higher world, preserved in the Judaeo-Christian story of the fall from the garden of Eden into history, in the Classical legend of the decline from the Golden Age, in the Hindu and Buddhist conception of an unborn world beyond the wheel of life and death, in Rousseau's primitive society of nature and reason, in Heidegger's "being" as a state antecedent to the "thrownness" of "being there," and so on. There is no myth of concern that I know of which does not employ this framework of two levels of the world, the upper or ideal one associated either with the past or with the future, or, more commonly, with both. Yet as we looked at some of these myths, we began to suspect that all the social contracts established at the beginning of history and all the Utopias glittering at the end of it were really projected from something in the present, something connected with education and the good life.

For the critic, these worlds are the two verbal worlds, the upper world of imagination and the lower world of belief, concern, argument, and every form of verbal defense or aggression. The two worlds are, we saw, distinguished in Sidney as the golden world of poetry and the brazen world of nature, a distinction which aligns them with their Christian counterparts, and the same distinction forms the organizing structure of Shelley's treatise. In Shelley its counterpart is not the Christian fallen and unfallen worlds, but the Romantic distinction of *Verstand* and *Vernunft*, analytical and imaginative knowledge. The myths of belief enable members of a society to hold together, to accept authority, to be loyal to each other and courageous against attack. Such myths are verbal constructions designed for specific social purposes. In literature myths are disinterested: they are simply forms of human creativity, and as such they communicate the joy—a more concrete word than pleasure—that belongs to pure creation. They are formed out of every conceivable horror and iniquity of human life, and yet an inner exuberance lifts them clear of that life. Belief becomes imagination and concern pleasure, as the concerned myth, rooted in a specific culture and told for instruction, is emancipated into the nomadic folk tale, traveling freely around the world and told for fun. The function of criticism is to go on doing what literature itself does, by making its language intelligible to those remote from it in space or time or cultural attitude.

The world of imagination is the holiday or Sabbath world where we rest from belief. On earth and in history, Christianity destroyed the belief in the classical gods, but the classical gods promptly went to the imaginative heaven of poetry, and Venus was perhaps more genuinely revered in Renaissance Europe, as one of what Emily Dickinson calls "our confiscated gods," than she ever was in her temple at Cyprus. As a Sabbath world, literature is a temporary refuge from life, not because it is an unreal world of empty fantasies of escape or wishfulfillment, but for the opposite reason. In life what we are united by must always include what we are united against: the enemy of concern is its inseparable shadow. It is difficult not to feel the force of the axiom, which comes down from Lucretius, that the social effects of religions, or structures of belief and concern generally, including the secular and atheistic ones, are evil, in direct proportion to their temporal power as closed myths. In the previous century Samuel Butler tried to show that it was a cultural disaster to exchange an old and sophisticated myth, which had been deprived of its inquisitorial powers and been forced to come to terms with tolerance and suspended judgment, for a young and naively dogmatic one, obsessed with the superiority of expediency to truth. It is better to know that one is lying than to feel that truth is expendable in a crisis, for there is always a crisis. But we have limited powers of choice in such matters, and whenever a new and powerful myth of concern develops we can see a dark age, or what Gibbon called the triumph of barbarism and religion, in its penumbra. An open myth of concern is infinitely better for human life than a closed one, yet an open mythology is by no means a panacea. Not only is there always a pressure within society to close its mythology, but the efforts to keep it open have to be strenuous, constant, delicate, unpopular, and above all largely negative.

One would arrive at a very pessimistic conclusion about the role of concern in society if it were not for the imagination, which, positively in comedy and romance and negatively in tragedy and irony, takes us from the brazen world of conflict into the golden world of peace. The world it discloses is, as is often said for very different reasons of New York, a place to visit and not to live in. Bob Dylan rightly says that there are no truths outside the garden of Eden, but the innocence needed to live continuously in such a world would require a nakedness far beyond anything that removing one's clothes could reach. If we could live in it, if we could lift our entire verbal experience from belief and concern to imagination, criticism would cease and the distinction between literature and life would disappear, because life would then be the incarnation of the creative word.

GEOFFREY HARTMAN

Toward Literary History

> "Go to Art, and tell him Pop sent you."
> *Chafed Elbows*

I AM concerned with the idea of history by which men live, and especially with the idea of history by which poets have lived. No one has yet written a history from the point of view of the poets—from within their consciousness of the historical vocation of art. To write decent literary history is, of course, important in itself: We are all disenchanted with those picaresque adventures in pseudo causality that go under the name of literary history, those handbooks with footnotes that claim to sing of the whole, but load every rift with glue. Twenty years ago René Wellek and Austin Warren were forced to ask, "Is it *possible* to write literary history, that is, to write that which will be both literary [in subject] and a history?" Most histories of literature, the authors continued, "are either social histories, or histories of thought as illustrated in literature, or impressions and judgments on specific works arranged in more or less chronological order."[1]

The dissatisfaction with literary history is not limited to this country. In 1950, Werner Krauss, the distinguished East

[1] *Theory of Literature* (New York, 1948), chap. 19.

German scholar, published an essay on literary history as a historical duty; and Hans Robert Jauss recently delivered an inaugural lecture at Konstanz, "Literary History as Provocation."[2] American scholars, in fact, have been slower than their European colleagues to shake off that distrust of speculative ideas that came in reaction to the giddy era of *Geistesgeschichte* and the equally dubious if more sober pomps of the history of ideas. This cautiousness has long degenerated into the positivist's medley of fact and fashionable ideas or into a formalistic kind of literary criticism only vaguely in touch with history writing.[3] Yet if I raise the question of literary history, it is not merely to urge its importance as an intellectual discipline or to deplore the absence of methodological thinking in that area. There are just too many areas in which one could be thinking more clearly and generously. My argument will be that literary history is necessary less for the sake of intellect than for the sake of literature; it is our "historical

---

[2] Krauss, "Literaturgeschichte als geschichtlicher Auftrag," in *Studien und Aufsätze* (Berlin, 1959), pp. 19–72; Jauss, *Literaturgeschichte als Provokation der Literaturwissenschaft* (Konstanz, 1966); also Max Wehrli, "Sinn und Unsinn der Literaturgeschichte," *Neue Zürcher Zeitung* (February 26, 1967), Number 813, Blatt 5.

[3] There are honorable exceptions. American Studies, strongly in touch with the idea of national character, has Howard Mumford Jones' *Theory of American Literature* (1948), the product of a cosmopolitan mind working in a national context. See also Charles Feidelson, *Symbolism and American Literature* (New Haven, 1953), antithetical yet complementary, the product of a cosmopolitan mind working in a specifically literary context. The call for an "inside history" was revived by Roy Harvey Pearce, *The Continuity of American Poetry* (Princeton, 1961). Renato Poggioli engages the subject through Pareto's theory of history in *The Spirit of the Letter* (Cambridge, Mass., 1965), and Claudio Guillén has recently remarked that "to explore the idea of literary history may very well be the main theoretical task that confronts the student of literature today" (*Literature as System* [Princeton, 1971]).

duty" because it alone can provide today a sorely needed defense of art.

Since Aristotle, the best defense of art has been to call it "more philosophical" than history. Despite recent advances in sociology, literature continues to escape historical research at some point. To demonstrate, as Lucien Goldmann has done, that the dramas of Racine participate in the public thought of his time, that there is nothing in his plays not illuminated by the conflict within church or state, is a significant authentification of the reality principle guiding even the most abstract or stylized art, and a cogent reminder that literature is never as self-centered as it seems to be.[4] But the influence of Racine, the continuing resonance of his language and form, even for those who do not know of the topical historical issues, remains unclarified. There exists, in other words, a principle of authority in art that is purely authorial: It seems to derive from art alone or from the author's genius rather than from the genius of his age. Werner Krauss, troubled by this characteristic autonomy of literature, by this "capacity of art-forms to outlast the destined hour," admits that Marxist theory has not been able to understand the phenomenon. Whether or not poetry is more philosophical than history, it is more formal: That is the brute yet elegant fact that we must appreciate without falling into idealistic or unhistorical explanations.

Thus the formality of art becomes a central issue in any literary history. How do we ground art in history without denying its autonomy, its aristocratic resistance to the tooth of time? Is it not a monument rather than a document; a monument, moreover, of the soul's magnificence, and so a richly solipsistic or playful edifice?

To understand the "art" in art is always essential. But it is even more essential today, for we have clearly entered an

[4] Lucien Goldmann, *Le Dieu caché* (Paris, 1955).

"era of suspicion" in which art seems arty to the artist himself. The artist, indeed, is often the severest critic of his own medium which turns against itself in his relentless drive for self-criticism. Artistic form and aesthetic illusion are today treated as "ideologies" to be exposed and demystified; this has long been true on the Continent, where Marxism is part of the intellectual milieu, but it is also becoming true of America. If literary history is to provide a new defense of art, it must now defend the artist against himself as well as against his other detractors. It must help to restore his faith in two things: in form and in his historical vocation.

Toward a Theory of Form

It may seem strange, this suggestion that we suffer at present from a shame of form. But the modern insistence on process, on openness, on mixed media, and especially on the mingling of personal and technological elements indicates more than the usual difficulty with inherited patterns or the desire to "make it new." The older way of achieving a form impersonal enough to allow the new to emerge was to subordinate the individual talent to the tradition. Eliot still thought it possible. Then what is wrong with the old forms? Why do they appear less exciting, less viable—even less "pure"—than mixed or technological forms? Take the example of a man from whom Eliot learned his craft: No one was more interested in purity of form, or form as such, than Ezra Pound. Yet Pound's Cantos, which ransack the high culture of both West and East, remain a nostalgic montage without unity, a picaresque of styles.

We look back at Pound and Eliot,[5] at Bridges and Yeats,

[5] Eliot's dictum in *Notes towards the Definition of Culture* (London, 1948), "civilization cannot simultaneously produce great folk poetry at one cultural level and *Paradise Lost* at another," is examined

and we realize that their elitist view of culture is dead. Though their art aimed for the genuine vernacular, it could not resist the appeal of forms associated with high culture, forms that remained an "ideological" reflex of upper-class mentality. To purge this ideological stain, and to rescue art from the imputation of artiness, the writer had to become his own enemy. Today all art stands in a questionable relation to elite modes of thought and feeling. But while the artist moves closer to self-criticism, the critic moves closer to art by expanding the notion of form until it cannot be narrowly linked to the concerns of a priestly culture or its mid-cult imitations.

I want to examine modern criticism in the light of this tendency. Is there a larger conception of literary form in the making? There are four significant theories to be considered: first, Marxist criticism which raises explicitly the issue of elitism; then Northrop Frye's theory of archetypes; and finally two kinds of structuralist theory, that of Claude Lévi-Strauss, and that of I. A. Richards and the Anglo-American critics. I hope to persuade you that an important new theory of form is gradually emerging.

Let me illustrate the Marxist preoccupation with form by a work of art that provides its own critical perspective. Jean-Luc Godard's *Weekend* is cinematic self-criticism of an extreme kind. The title of the film points to the theme of leisure or, rather, of "ignoble leisure"; and Godard engages in the film on a ruthless violation of taboos, especially the "taboo" of form. Not only are the unities of time, place, and action killed once again, or rather parodied to death, but just about every art-movie cliché, from the films of Antonioni, Fellini, Bunuel, Resnais, Truffaut—and Godard himself—is exposed to

---

by Raymond Williams in *Culture and Society* (London, 1958), pp. 231–232. He points to the contemporaneity with *Paradise Lost* of *Pilgrim's Progress*.

massive lyrical ridicule. The result is strangely operatic, since opera tends to be pure superstructure, its form having but an absurd or magical connection with the passions staged. The Antonioni promenade, the Fellini harlequinade, the Bonnie-and-Clyde relationship, the Truffaut tenderness, the Bunuelian symbols—everything is mocked in this bloody, endlessly interrupted pastoral.

What remains? It is the problem of the elitist status of art, expressed in powerful visual graffiti. One scene shows a truck driver playing Mozart on a huge concert piano that has somehow found its way into a farmyard. Various laborers and old peasant women seem as entranced by that music as the beasts were by Orpheus. It is Godard's gentlest scene, but also the most mocking vis-à-vis the Marxist theory of a proletariat pastoral. What reconciliation is possible between Mozart, the proletariat *régisseur*, and the barnyard setting? "What are the conditions," asks Werner Krauss, "which compel a breakthrough from the base (*Unterbau*) of society and which might rectify its relation to the superstructure (*Überbau*)? In what way can literature belong to the superstructure of society?"[6] There is nothing that belongs authentically to either the social base or superstructure in Godard's *mise en scène*. We are left with a few lyrical images of old women who seem to listen to the incongruous music and a farmhand walking to its rhythm and yet not to its rhythm. All the rest is— ideology.

If we insert this film into a history of the concept of form, we would have to say that, for Godard, form was less important than its violation. He writes about the problem of

[6] "Was sind die Bedingungen die einen Durchschlag aus den Unterbau der Gesellschaft erzwingen und damit das Verhältnis zum Überbau richtigstellen? In welcher Weise gehört überhaupt die Literatur zum Überbau der Gesellschaft?" (Werner Krauss, *Perspektiven und Probleme* [West Berlin, 1965], p. 19).

form in blood—in the lifeblood of his medium. He hopes that by violating all taboos something deeper than the gratuitous values of a leisure class might emerge: real pastoral values, perhaps; something from the *Unterbau* or Marxist "deep structure." Yet this movie, which begins as sophisticated pornography, ends with a totally undelicious scene of anthropophagy: a progress which suggests that to destroy through revolution or some other mode of cleansing the forms of our high culture will simply result in primitivism, in the naked substructure. We are therefore forced to consider a second reason for Godard's violation of taboos. The movie medium, instead of discovering new values, is shown to participate necessarily in the old values, in the capitalistic desire for conspicuous consumption. All the totems of movie culture are therefore offered up to the reluctant viewer in this movable feast which is like the massacre of matériel in American spectaculars. To go beyond this movie means to go beyond a movie-centered culture and no longer to confuse participation with consumption.

We come away from Godard with two observations about the authenticity of art forms in contemporary society. The first is that the only forms that all classes of society enjoy are primitivistic; the second, that the most we can expect from art is not authenticity but purity—the fissure of the work of art into ideology on the one hand and pure form on the other. Godard's "alienation effects" are more Mallarméan than Brechtian and substantiate the view that poetry is detachable from a more continuous prose base. Thus form remains a lyrical and dying effect, a falling star in the twilight of taboos.

The theory of form advanced by Northrop Frye is more familiar. He removes the elitism of the art object by pointing to similarities between the structure of primitive myths and the formal principles of all art. The structure of a sophisticated novel by Henry James or Virginia Woolf is like that of any story; and the historical difference between stories is due to what Frye calls the displacement of myth, that is, its accommodation to rules of verisimilitude that differ for different cultures. In a culture, for example, that is "realistic," a writer cannot depict supernatural figures directly, yet he invents characters with daemonic attributes or with the capacity for violating social norms. Thus Frye can talk of the pharmakos or sacred scapegoat in Virginia Woolf and Henry James; and Ihab Hassan expands that insight to cover a broad range of modern works in *Radical Innocence*.

The virtue of Frye's system is that it methodically removes the one barrier that prevents art from exerting wide influence: the distinction of kind between sacred and secular, or between popular and highbrow. His sense for the commonality of art is radically Protestant: Every man is imagination's priest. All art that is good expands imagination; all art that is bad restricts it. Mystery and its brood—secret religion, secret sex, secret government—are simply imagination gone bad. For Frye as for Blake, bad art argues a sick society, one that has the power to block our imagination. And the blocking agent is always a priesthood: some political or religious or artistic elite.

It is clear that Frye's theory has affinities with Marxist thought. But the latter is more dialectical and realistic in its view of history. Where Marxist critics confront the individual work and evaluate it according to its struggle with the proletariat-elite, base-superstructure split, Frye's structural observations are developed for descriptive and not for evaluative purposes. His idea of literary history is certainly abstract: not only less sweaty than Marxist literary history, but also less concrete than most scholarly versions. Though he expands our concept of form and redeems individual works from the isolation imposed on them by cult and culture, he may do so at the cost of a false idea of universality and an elite idea of literary history. The illusion that a world-wide culture is already within reach is fostered by evading the question of national difference and large-scale social (East-West) conflict. I suspect that for the Marxist his vision of cultural dissemination is a technocrat's ideal and betrays an American perspective. Werner Krauss would surely commend Frye, as he does other American scholars, for his "radical break with all monopolistic attitudes in the writing of literary history," but he would also criticize a method that bypasses national or ideological differences till literature becomes an "All-Souls, in which Cervantes and Rabelais, Dante and Voltaire, amicably drink tea together."[7] It is, in short, bad comparative literature.

We return later to this problem of how the nationality of literatures is to be respected; but it is important to add that Frye writes about criticism rather than about literature, and he seems more interested in improving the consumer than in evaluating the product. His whole effort is an attempt to improve the public relations of art. His vision of an expanding cultural universe includes literary works, but they are not the reified apples of his eye. On the contrary, he is less interested in the marmoreal object than in a change of perception from which the object would profit. To Eliot's thesis that the advent of the authentically new work of art revises our view of all preceding works, Frye adds an important footnote: This change is a change in our consciousness of art and can only occur, therefore, if mediated by criticism. Whatever totemic or elitist elements remain in the literary work, this interplay between art and critic, between product and

[7] *Ibid.*, p. 372, translated freely. "Weltliteratur ist dann zu einem Pandämonium geworden, in dem sich Cervantes und Rabelais, Dante und Voltaire zunicken." The specific context is Krauss's attack on a concept of world literature as superliterature or metahistorical assemblage of masterpieces.

consumer, expands both and anticipates the Marxist hope (itself a version of Christian communism elaborated around the time of Blake, Pierre Ballanche, and Claude Henri Saint-Simon)[8] that the forms of social life dissolve into the form of man—into the expanding humanistic consciousness of a classless society.

It is, hence, a question whether Frye is dealing with "form" at all. He seems to approach the concept of "structure" with which structuralism (the third of our theories) is concerned. This structure is a mental fact and supposedly intersubjective: common to every man as man, to priest and peasant, sophisticate and primitive. The shift in linguistics from individual languages (or sign-systems) to language in general (or semeiotics) and from there to structures of the mind parallels Frye's shift from the individual work of art to literature as a totality and from there to a "verbal universe" which exhibits archetypes basic to science as well. Yet the "structures" isolated by Claude Lévi-Strauss differ from Frye's in an essential respect. They are solutions to real social problems—which is why structuralism can call itself a science, a *science humaine*. The principles of structure described by Frye solve a problem only in the sense that they free art from the stigma of archaism or elitism, and so publish it once again. Tradition is extradition; art must become transitive vis-à-vis its original site in history. Frye teaches us a lot about tradition, handing-on, but less about what is handed on. He fails to bring together the form of art and the form of its historical consciousness—which is the ideal of the science we seek.

Claude Lévi-Strauss also fails in this, but he does bring together the form of myth and a kind of *social* consciousness. Myth, according to him, resolves a societal hang-up or articu-

[8] See, for example, P. S. Ballanche, *Essais de palingénésie sociale* (1827).

lates its solution. Since every society has conflicts of interest that cannot be resolved without great mental anxiety, every society will have its myths. If all myths use the same basic method to resolve these social conflicts, then a science of myth would be possible. And this possibility is the claim of anthropological structuralism.

Let us look more closely at the structuralist's description of myth. The form of myth is always twofold: Its surface structure reflects local traditions and may be esoteric, but its deep structure is logical and can be formulated in mathematical terms. Myths dealing with the incest taboo, for example, should project in their totality a theory of kinship that makes it clear that the generative problem is how to distribute women fairly—how to pry them loose from father or clan and make them "go around." The incest taboo, therefore, is neither absolute nor eternal, but a humane and logical institution, part of a system of exchange as complex as the monetary system today.

Here, as in Frye, myth is both story and a principle of structure: a primitive narrative and a functional type of logic. Myth and mathematics join in a mysterious way more reminiscent of Plato than Aristotle. What is lacking in this description is precisely the middle ground between myth and mathematics that art occupies. Where in this description are the qualities of storytelling that actually involve us—tone, rhythm, humor, surprises, and displacements? A sense of hidden structure or a delight in exotic surface is only a part of this involvement. Surely, even if literature proves to be a problem-solving form, it must be of a more liberal and chancy kind than Claude Lévi-Strauss suggests. And since, for Lévi-Strauss, form is totally explained by its social function, we cannot ask which myths are viable universals and which empty or chauvinistic versions of what Blake called "the Human Abstract." The structuralist science of myth does not allow us to cross over from its theory of form to a descriptive or critical account of the artist's historical consciousness.

Our last theory, and in many ways the one most clearly focused on the literary work, is that of I. A. Richards and the New Criticism. Richards' concept of form is as functional as that of Lévi-Strauss, and it may have a common source with the latter in Bronislaw Malinowski.[9] What ritual, according to Malinowski, does for primitive societies, literary form, in Richards, does for the civilized (and perhaps over-civilized) individual; it reconciles tensions and helps to unify. Richards, however, does not specify what the basic tensions or "hang-ups" are. He is content with the common-sense observation that tensions always exist and that the deeper they are and the more complexly respectful of them the reconciling form, the better the work of art or the harmony of the person. We seem to have a very open theory of form that defines neither the contents reconciled nor the exact, perhaps organic, structure by which they are unified.

This theory is open, except for the very insistence on unity or reconciliation, which has become a great shibboleth developed by the New Critics on the basis of Eliot and Richards. Only William Empson tried to escape it by postulating "types" of ambiguity which showed how precarious this unity was, or how rebellious language. It is important not to be deceived by the sophisticated vagueness of such terms as "unity," "complexity," "maturity," and "coherence," which enter criticism at this point. They are code words shored against the ruins. They express a highly neo-

[9] Cf. Malinowski, "The Problem of Meaning in Primitive Languages" in C. K. Ogden and I. A. Richards, *The Meaning of Meaning* (London, 1923).

classical and acculturated attitude, a quiet nostalgia for the ordered life, and a secret recoil from aggressive ideologies, substitute religions, and dogmatic concepts of order. Out of the passionate intensity of the post-war period, out of the pressures of politics, press, and propaganda comes a thoughtful backlash that attempts to distinguish the suasion of literary statements from more imperative kinds. A poem, we learn, does not "mean," but "is"; art, we are told, is pseudo statement or pseudo action. Thus the literary work, though nominally democratic—inclusive of anything—is thought of as exclusive by its structure. Art turns out to be a mental purification of the impulses to action: an idea that has eastern resonances in I. A. Richards, but is associated in Cleanth Brooks with testing the simplifications by which we live.

Richards' concept of the functional unity of the work of art is far from narrow, of course. By modeling it on the psychology of communication, which includes reader or auditor in the aesthetic transaction, he opened a path to a theory of participatory form and helped to revive the academic interest in rhetoric still important today when new and sophisticated notions concerning the "entrapment" of reader by writer are emerging. He may also have influenced Kenneth Burke's refusal to equate rhetorical forms with aristocratic or privileged ideas of order and to examine anew both their psychological function and social participatory (Burke continues to call it "ritual") aspect. Sigurd Burkhardt's emphasis on the "troth-value" of words is a further echo of these explorations.[10]

There is, nevertheless, the distinct afterglow of an elitist idea of culture in Richards' work. The function of art moves closer to that of ordinary language and normal psychological transactions, but it remains reminiscent of Plato's "dia-

[10] *Shakespearean Meanings* (Princeton, 1968).

lectic." Art's therapeutic virtue is to Richards what the intellectual virtue of dialectic was to Socrates: purging fixed ideas, it still leads upward to the one form of truth. The Socratic assumption, moreover, of a basic identity of questioner and questioned evades the issue of class or nationality —it assumes a society of equals whose upward mobility is intellectual in essence. Join Plato's dialectic to communications theory, and you get the idea of art as an elite communications medium. What you do not get is a concrete understanding of how this medium mediates: of how in history it actually reconciles or unifies different persuasions. For this we need quite another kind of dialectic, which Hegel and Marx tried to develop. We still have not found a theory linking the form of the medium to the form of the artist's historical consciousness.

Toward a Theory of Literary Vocation

It is time I showed my hand and proposed such a theory. Let us construct it on the basis that literary form is functional and that its function is to keep us functioning, to help us resolve certain "hang-ups" and bring life into harmony with itself. But let us also agree that art can divide as well as heal and that its healing power may be complicated by its power to hurt. Wordsworth, in the "Preface to Lyrical Ballads," defines the poet as one who "considers man and the objects that surround him as acting and reacting upon each other, so as to produce an infinite complexity of pain and pleasure." Art cannot be expected to "bring us together again" by metaphysic, by an occult virtue of unification.

Since we are looking for a theory of *literary* as well as *functional* form, the essential ingredient is whatever makes the theory specifically relevant to literature. Otherwise we might quote Housman's "For Malt does more than Milton can/To justify the ways of God to Man," and leave it at that. But are there perhaps specifically *literary* hang-ups? And are we not forced by this question into the psychology of art on the one hand, but also into an analysis of literary history on the other?

Take the contemporary situation. Many artists today doubt art to the point of becoming incapable of it. The reason for their extreme self-questioning has already been suggested. The artist has a bad conscience because of the idea that forms, structures, and so on always reconcile or integrate, that they are conservative despite themselves. To create a truly icono-clastic art, a structure-breaking art, to change the function of form from reconciliation and conservation to rebellion, and so to participate in the enormity of present experience—this is the one Promethean aim still fiery enough to inspire. It is the psychic state of art today. But let us think, in addition, about other periods. Is the problem of the present era unique or a special case of a more inherent, perhaps universal dilemma besetting the writer's consciousness of himself? Were not Keats and Milton, those great formalists, also great iconoclasts, and did they not think about the historical vocation of art?

Pursuing this question we come on the probability that no great writer is without an identity crisis. The shape of that cri-sis can be generalized. Though we may not always discern what developmental impasse occurs within the poet's private life, we can describe the vocational crisis that occurs in the poet as poet, in his literary self-consciousness. No great artist is without the ambition to seize (and hand on) the flame of inspiration, to identify the genius of art with his own genius or that of a particular age (*genius loci*). But this is the crisis of self-consciousness in its purity: of emergence and commitment to being manifestly what one is. In the modern era with its problem of "legitimacy," the artist is especially aware of the

211

need for self-justification.[11] The basic problem, however, is as old as history: how is spiritual authority to be transmitted if not through an elite of persons or communities? There seems to be no *recorded* greatness without the driving force of an idea of election or the search for evidences of election.

All societies have rituals for the passage out of latency and into the public light. They seek to guide it and to assure the individual a formal maturity. Arnold Van Gennep, who studied these ceremonies, called them *"rites de passage."* His findings have a complex but real bearing on the function of literature, whether in society or in the individual consciousness of artists. Take Shakespeare's Hamlet, a figure that has fascinated generations. It is widely agreed that an important function of art is to create character types of universal or general appeal, and that Hamlet is the type of a man deprived of typical existence: of vocation or role or the possibility of commitment. The paradox, a simple one, is clarified by reference to Van Gennep: Hamlet is *"le seigneur latent qui ne peut devenir"* (Mallarmé) because he cannot assume his real (regal) self by innocent means—by the formal rite. Ceremony itself, in its legal and ludic aspects, in its justifying and mediating functions, is wounded. Deprived of kingship and shunning the outlaw role of avenger, Hamlet is doomed to remain a liminal person in an action (the play) that is an abortive rite of passage. He becomes the "juvenile shadow of us all" in his psychic struggle with *"le mal d'apparaître."*[12]

[11] Cf. Hans Blumenberg, *Die Legimität der Neuzeit* (Frankfurt am Main, 1966); William Collins, "Ode on the Poetical Character" (1747); Otto Rank, *Art and Artist* (New York, 1932), especially the chapter "Creative Urge and Personality Development"; and Erik Erikson, *Young Man Luther* (New York, 1958).

[12] A. Van Gennep, *Les Rites de passage* (Paris, 1907; English trans., Chicago, 1961); Victor W. Turner, *The Ritual Process* (Chicago, 1969); and Mallarmé, "Hamlet," *Crayonné au théâtre* (1886).

Yet every artist is like Hamlet. The artist must always find his own way to "appear"; he has no ritual to guide him. The presumption of his act, the daring of his art is all. The conventions at his disposal do not lessen the agony of self-election: If he admires the ancients, he trembles to rival them; if he does not admire, he trembles before a void he must fill. No wonder art continually questions the hopes for art; no wonder also that it endures irony and negativity to the point of substantiating Yeats's comment, so appropriate to Mallarmé: "The last kiss is given to the void."

The plea for literary history merges here with that for phenomenology or consciousness studied in its effort to "appear." Consciousness can try to objectify itself, to disappear into its appearances, or to make itself *as* consciousness the vocation. Social anthropology is involved because rites of acculturation and the structure of public life provide many of the collective forms that could allow self-objectification. Indeed, the very multiplicity of terms used to characterize the dynamics of phenomenology (appearance, manifestation, individuation, emergence, being-in-the-world, and so forth) imply a concern that incorporates the human sciences, or all sciences to the extent that they are humane. This concern centers on the problem of "civilization" and encompasses both nature and nurture, "those frontiers of biology and sociology from which mankind derives its hidden strength."[13] We have only to look at the crisis point in Keats's *Hyperion* to see this struggle for "appearance" accompanied by all the suggestiveness that hidden frontiers bestow.

In the third book of *Hyperion*, Apollo, the young sun-god, attempts to rise—to emerge into himself helped by the mem-

[13] Philip Aries, *Centuries of Childhood* (London, 1962), p. 11. Cf. the tendency of Elizabeth Sewell's *The Orphic Voice* (New Haven, 1960).

ory-goddess, Mnemosyne. The sun never rises, however; *Hyperion* begins and ends in twilight. While attempting to dawn, Apollo suffers pangs like those accompanying childbirth or sexual climax or the biomorphic passage from one state of being to another. His "fierce convulse" is comparable to that of the snake Lamia in her transformation to womanhood (*Lamia*, Part I, ll. 146ff.). We expect Apollo to become the sun: "from all his limbs/Celestial" a new dawn will break. But the poem breaks off, as if Apollo's metamorphosis had tied itself into a knot and entered a developmental impasse. Though the impasse cannot be reduced to ego psychology—it is clearly related to the Enlightenment assumption of a "progress" of religion and literature—Apollo, in bringing his identity to light, is also bringing his father to light. In the psychotheology of art, as Keats depicts it here, the ephebe god, under the influence of "knowledge enormous," is about to replace the sun-god Hyperion. To bring his identity to light means to bear a father-god *out of himself*. The poem stops on that uncanny yet familiar truth.

To stress the "phenomenological" dimension is not to transcend the "literary" aspect. Apollo is the god of art by traditional equation. The knowledge that floods him,

> Names, deeds, gray legends, dire events, rebellions,
> Majesties, sovran voices, agonies.
> Creations and destroyings . . .

is "epic" knowledge, mediated by literature or by Mnemosyne as mother of the Muses. It signals the change from a lower to a higher mode of consciousness, from pastoral romance to that kind of heroic verse which *Hyperion* seeks to be. Yet Keats does not succeed in passing from pastoral to epic any more than Apollo does from ephebe state to Phoebus. What he writes is *hot pastoral* rather than epic. The very rituals that wing him into a new sphere prove too literary, too magical-archaic, and do not prevent fresh anxieties about the authenticity of his "passage." The marble steps the dreamer barely ascends in *The Fall of Hyperion* or Moneta's face "deathward progressing/To no death" are images raised up by his anxiety. Literature is breaking with an archaic mode that has been its glory and remains influential; yet the very idea of ritual transition is part of this archaism and makes the poet aware of his lateness or inauthenticity. His art, a new star, finds itself in the arms of the old by a fatal if fine repetition.

The impasse, then, is that Keats believes in poetry, in its "progressive" character, yet cannot see an authentic catena between old and new. In a sense *he* is the catena and his art the "passage." The past masters haunt him: Their glory is his guilt. The burden of *traditio*[14] leads to a preoccupation with *transitio,* and transition has two very different aspects in Keats. It may infer a real passing-over, a transcendence of past stages enabled by the "grand march of intellect"—Keats's phrase for the Enlightenment. Wordsworth, he speculates, thinks more deeply into the human heart than Milton, whether or not he is a greater poet. Transition can also, however, infer the obverse of transcendence: transience, or abiding the *consciousness* of change by "negative capability." That is the real test of the fallen gods in *Hyperion,* by which they become human. All rites lead only to further "dark passages" and not beyond. "We are in a Mist—*We* are now in that state." If the first aspect of the idea of transition requires a philosophy of history, the second elicits the watchword, "The creative must

[14] Cf. W. J. Bate, "The English Poet and the Burden of the Past, 1660–1820," in *Aspects of the Eighteenth Century,* ed. E. R. Wasserman (Baltimore, 1965); Harold Bloom, "Keats and the Embarrassments of Poetic Tradition" in *From Sensibility to Romanticism,* ed. H. Bloom and F. Hilles (New York, 1965); and G. H. Hartman, "Romanticism and Anti-Self-Consciousness," in *Beyond Formalism* (New Haven, 1970).

create itself." "The Genius of poetry," Keats also says, "must work its own salvation in a man."

We are close to the era that makes transition a historiographical concept, as in "The Age of Transition." But this concept is a compromise and belies the rich gloom of Keats's verse. While he fails to place us where we can see the historical vocation of poetry, he does somehow transmit deeply, feelingly, an existential or temporal consciousness. This is not only by the sensuous or empathic highpoints of his art. His famed sensuousness exists as one pole in this temporal rhythm, the other being the mind's irritable, positivistic "reaching after fact and reason." A sharp revolution of tempi or moods, the alternation of an overwrought questing with "silence and slow time," is what catches us. In the odes, which traditionally permit bold transitions, this is less remarkable than in the *Hyperion*. Moments before Mnemosyne brings Apollo to the flood stage of recollection, he is steeped in forgetful, even indolent sensation. ("Beside the osiers of a rivulet/Full ankle-deep in lilies of the vale. . . .") This direct, precipitous transition from puberty to epiphany, from pastoral to apocalypse —which aborts historical vision proper—puts all progress by "stages" in doubt.

What remains is almost purely existential: a birth which is a forgetting, and a dying into recollection. But the poetry also remains and the question of its relation to this "existential metaphysics." There is a metaphysical element, because Apollo "dies" into an antelife by a kind of platonic anamnesis. On examination, however, this antelife proves to be Wordsworth, Milton, Spenser, the Bible, Plato . . . the *paradise of poets*.[15] Keats is not less a humanist for being visionary; what pre-exists is not metaphysical or transcendent of life, but souls that are logoi, "sovran voices" mediated by each great poet.

[15] Cf. H. Bloom, p. 517.

So Milton "descends" into Keats: Apollo's birth is predicated on an overcoming of the father-gods just as in *Paradise Lost* (itself "descended" from Biblical tradition) Adam's birth presupposes the fall of the angels. The fledgling god's dying into the life of recollection is, similarly, comparable to Adam's falling into knowledge or the ambiguous career of the soul in Wordsworth's "Immortality Ode," its humanizing passage from a birth that is "a sleep and a forgetting" to the compensating radiance of the philosophic mind. Keats's invention trails clouds of glory. It is itself a recollection, or anamnesis, which either justifies or devours the literary identity of its poet.

Genius and *genius loci*

On the surface there is some naivete in claiming that literary history should be written from the point of view of the poets or of poetry. It is like saying naval history should be written from the point of view of sailors or ships. Hence it becomes important to stress the relatedness of the literary and the phenomenological points of view, as is implied by the previous section. The artist's struggle with his vocation—with past masters and the "pastness" of art in modern society—seems to be a version of a universal human struggle: of genius with Genius, and of genius with the *genius loci* (spirit of place).

It is always hard to defend the analytic categories one chooses. I have found the above terms useful and flexible. They have some kinship, obviously, with race, milieu, and moment, but they are free of special sociological meaning and may be as old as Western religion. A study of their history and prevalence must still be made,[16] but I would guess that

[16] See Edgar Zilsel, *Die Entstehung des Geniebegriffes* (Tübingen, 1926); W. Lange-Eichbaum and Wolfram Kurth, *Genie, Irrsinn und Ruhm* (6th ed., Munich, 1967), chap. 1; and sources cited in note 1 to my "Romantic Poetry and the Genius Loci," in P. Demetz *et al.*, eds., *The Disciplines of Criticism* (New Haven, 1968).

the *genius loci* concept, at least, becomes visible with the nationalization of culture in Roman times and the revival of literary nationalism in the modern period. It also appears, from very preliminary observations, that whatever credence was given to the *genius loci* as a myth, it was an important principle of structure or an informing idea in literature and art from the sixteenth through the nineteenth centuries. One reason for its importance (to which I will return) is that it helped to mediate the conflict between the universal and nationalistic aspirations of art.[17]

In general, the artist's struggle with past masters corresponds to the struggle of genius with Genius, and his anxiety about the outmodedness of art to his anxiety about the genius of his country or time. To begin with the genius/Genius contest: This opposes, or conjoins, the personal "ingenium" in its unmediated, forgetful vigor, and the starry guide whose influence accompanies us from birth,[18] but is revealed mainly at crucial—"historical" or "self-conscious"—junctures. The

[17] "Romantic Poetry and the Genius Loci"; also my "Blake and the 'Progress of Poesy,'" in A. Rosenfeld, ed., *William Blake* (Providence, 1969).

[18] "Natale comes qui temperat astrum" (Horace). The Genius-genial-genital link, common from Roman times in which Genius personified the male procreative power, apparently helped to establish, in the Renaissance, the connection between Genius and ingenium. (See, for example, Otto Rank, chap. 2.) Zilsel concludes that genius, in the modern sense of the term ("Sondergift der Natur," "Personifikation der Eigenart"), became prevalent toward the middle of the sixteenth century as the *learned* revival of astrological and demonological symbolism joined with a surviving *popular* belief in genii and guardian spirits. (But J. Burckhardt, *The Civilization of the Renaissance in Italy*, describes astrology influencing the higher classes as early as the thirteenth century.) On the relation between "ingenium" and "vocatio," see Richard M. Douglas, "Talent and Vocation in Humanist and Protestant Thought," in T. K. Rabb and J. K. Seigel, eds., *Action and Conviction in Early Modern Europe* (Princeton, 1969).

contest is like that of Jacob with the Angel, which results in a name (or a new name), one that is generic as well as personal. In the Romantic period, Genius appears to genius as Memory: as an internalized guardian self or fateful shadow. This is as true of Hegel as it is of Wordsworth and Keats.[19] But in every period something pre-exists: original sin, or the world of the fathers, or Plato's Ideas or Husserl's *Ideen,* or the mythic forms of *illud tempus.* And in every period there is an *ingénu* to be tested by vision, to be led out of the state of natural light by a muse who opens an "everlasting scryne" where the "antique rolles" (rôles and scrolls) lie hidden.

To restrict literary or cultural history to the genius/Genius relation skirts two errors. One is that art is seen as a puberty rite or adolescent crisis, localized in personal time even if recurring periodically. The other is that art becomes the story of Humanity, in which Genius appears as a hero with a thousand faces (and therefore no face, like the ecumenical God) pursuing a gnostic odyssey. Much literary biography or existential criticism falls prey to the first, most myth-criticism to the second, error. These errors, however, are fruitful and complementary. We must manage to embrace both; only singly do they lead to an impoverishment in our understanding of art. Apollo's crisis, for example, is clearly that of adolescence. He has left the "chamber of Maiden-Thought" and hovers darkling between ephebic state and godhead. He is at once too young and too old: The middle state is what is obscure, and to emerge from it as a decisive, individuated being, there may have to be something equivalent to infanticide or parricide. His metamorphosis can only be toward pure youth

---

[19] Cf. H. Marcuse, *Eros and Civilization* (new ed., Boston, 1966), p. 232. The modernist conflict between historical memory and "the temptation of immediacy" is scrupulously analyzed by Paul de Man in this volume.

(and the mythic figure of the divine child) or pure eld (the divine *senex*) or theriomorphic (and the figure, for example, of the snake). But these are the very transformations studied by gnostic or myth-critical thought. The philosophers of individuation, from Plotinus through the modern school of Jung and Newmann, reveal how improbable it is for anyone to become truly individual, having wrestled with Genius and received the blessing and curse of identity.

Yet a poet is even more—because more *inobviously*—besieged than they describe. The dramatic encounter of genius with Genius is accompanied by the commonplace quarrel of genius with *genius loci:* of art with the natural religion or dominant myth of its age. To the burden of vision which rouses the poet's sense of his powers is added a combat with insidious habits of thought or perception. "Reasonings like vast Serpents/Infold around my limbs, bruising my minute articulations" (Blake). "A weight/Heavy as frost, and deep almost as life" (Wordsworth). The *genius loci* can rival Genius as an influence, for it suggests the possibility of a more "natural" (unself-conscious) participation in a pre-existent or larger self. England as Gloriana or America as Virgin Land is a visionary commonplace indistinguishable from an "idol of the tribe" or "collective representation."[20] Though bounded by period and place, the *genius loci* is as all-pervasive in its domain as a climate of opinion—which makes it harder to confront than

[20] Myth is expressive of Genius in Northrop Frye, but of the *genius loci* in Henry Nash Smith's *Virgin Land* (1949). The difference, though significant, is not absolute and shows the need for a unified theory. Is the Old Man of Wordsworth's "Resolution and Independence" a Genius or a *genius loci?* We have only the sparsest beginnings of a literary iconography on the subject of Genius. See, for example, C. S. Lewis, "Genius and Genius," in *Studies in Renaissance Literature* (New York, 1966), pp. 169–174. Also the analysis of the relation between sense of place and sense of self in my *Wordsworth's Poetry* (New Haven, 1964), especially pp. 211–219.

a Mnemosyne. What arms does one take up against a *spirit?* Who will challenge a temperament, tilt with a weather? It is as absurd as the Beatles fighting the Blue Meanies: They try the solvent of music, but their true arms, one suspects, are counter-visionary, obliging the enemy to recrudesce by pop or parody art. One best engages the lurking, many-headed *topoi* or fixed ideas of a culture by sending against them their own image, enlarged and purified. "Bring me my chariot of fire." This is still a *topos,* but more than commonplace. We see the spirited form, not the nebulous. The imagery of the tribe is given bounding outline, the imaginative vigor of national prejudices acknowledged and faced.

Should there be conflict in an artist between *genius loci* and Genius, it takes the form of humanity versus nation or local integrities versus abstract conceptions or art itself versus party allegiance. In the case of Keats, there is evidence that *Hyperion* was meant to depict a geopolitical "progress of poetry" from antiquity to modern England. The "beautiful mythology of Greece" was to have been revived or rivaled by "home-bred glory"—by the "Sister of the Island," as Keats calls the muse of his native land in *Endymion,* Part IV. This is the context of the poet's famous, formalistic-sounding statement that "English ought to be kept up." A contradiction remained (as also in Blake) between the Genius of Poetry and the national genius. Keats thought Milton had shown the way to their reconciliation, and he began *Hyperion* in that belief, but he eventually put Chatterton's "English Idiom in English words" against Milton's "artful or rather artist's humour." There are always, it seems, two genii fighting for the soul of the artist: two stars or visions of destiny, or Genius and the *genius loci.*

Starry persons, of course, are an inveterate poetical superstition, and the astrology of genius revives explicitly in Yeats's

221

Vision, but all literary judgment, insofar as it is historical, adjudicates the claims of Genius and *genius loci.* Here is Jules Michelet on the greatness of Rabelais:

Rabelais collected wisdom from the old, popular idioms, from sayings, proverbs, school farces in the mouths of fools and clowns. But mediated by follies of this kind the genius of the age and its prophetic power are revealed in their majesty. Where he does not reveal, he glimpses, he promises, he guides. In this forest of dreams, one can see under each leaf fruits which the future will harvest. The entire book is a golden bough.[21]

Compare this with Bronson Alcott. Thoreau's friend, praising *A Week on the Concord and Merrimack Rivers* as "purely American, fragrant with the lives of New England woods and streams, and which could have been written nowhere else," then because "the sod and sap and flavor of New England have found at last a clear relation to the literature of other and classic lands . . . Egypt, India, Greece, England." Alcott seems more interested than Michelet in harmonizing native and classical *genii loci,* but when he adds that "especially am I touched by this soundness, this aboriginal vigour, as if a man had once more come into Nature,"[22] he appeals beyond the *genius loci* to the genius of the artist in its unmediated relation to Nature.

The *genius loci* is especially significant for modern, that is, vernacular art, for it is then that the assertion of a national genius becomes vital, and a Dante, Ariosto, or Milton turns to the "adorning of their native Tongue." Native and national are not always identical, of course; and this, in the Renaissance, is part of the general problem of constructing a "national universal" from the genius of different localities. In Rabelais,

[21] *Histoire de France,* X, 58.
[22] Odell Shepard, ed., *The Journals of Bronson Alcott* (Boston, 1938), pp. 213–214.

Panurge at one point answers Pantagruel in seven languages, two of which are nonexistent; and M. M. Bakhtin has shown how this problematic abundance of linguistic "masks" fosters a peculiarly modern awareness of concrete historic space.[23] The literary self-consciousness of the modern era is intimately linked to a reflection on the fall of culture into nationality and its redemption into a new universality.

Finding a more "concrete" universal, one with truly national or native roots, proves to be, in the Renaissance, a highly liberative and creative endeavor. In Rabelais, Cervantes, and Shakespeare, those vernacular giants, popular culture joins the learned muses. The neoclassical or purist reaction merely showed how these giants traumatized later writers. Even before Shakespeare, Gabriel Harvey had doubts about Spenser —hardly a pop artist, yet to the genteel he seemed "hobgoblin run away with the garland from Apollo." With the signal exception of France, which identified culture once more with the purification of language and the achieving of a new latinity —an ideal that dominated Europe from about 1660 to 1760— Apollo retrieved his garland by hobnobbing with hobgoblin. If literary creativity becomes problematic toward the end of the eighteenth century, it is not because of a sudden mysterious uncertainty about the vocation of the artist, but on the contrary, because that vocation, in the light of the failure of French universalism, is only too clear. An intensely programmatic consciousness arises that defines the vocation of literature as "Art seeking Pop"—art seeking its father figure in folk

[23] *Rabelais and His World* (Cambridge, Mass., 1968), especially pp. 465ff. on the birth of modern literature "on the boundaries of two languages" (that is, Latin and the vernacular). Borges, from this perspective, is a modern Rabelais with a significantly different space-language relation. For remarks on the birth of a more contemporary literature, cf. Octavio Paz, "A Literature of Foundations," *Triquarterly*, 12–14 (1968–69), 7–12.

culture. Genius merges confusingly with *genius loci* as *Volks-boden* or autochthonous art. We see this most clearly among the German and English romantics. In the 1770's Herder wrote an influential essay attributing his nation's literary poverty to the fact that, unlike England, it had produced no poets to revitalize the learned muse by bringing folklore into the mainstream of art. Where are *our* Chaucer, Spenser, and Shakespeare? he asks. Or, as Keats will say: "Let us have the old poets, and Robin Hood."[24]

There is, then, a model that haunts the consciousness of vernacular artists. The "vegetable gold" of great art is to bring Sancho Panza into relation with Don Quixote. Patrician and plebeian are to be fellow travelers, part of the same human family. Genius, in expelling a false or discovering a true *genius loci*, discovers itself and enlarges us.

In our own day, this model is often dangerously simplified. Art, we are told, seeks to revitalize, and, if need be, rebarbarize man. There must be contact with devil or drug or forbidden areas. Thomas Mann's *Dr. Faustus* is the definitive expression —and critique—of that simplification. Yet, simplified or not, this model for creativity becomes an animating force, a

---

[24] Herder, "Von Ähnlichkeit der Mittlern Englischen und Deutschen Dichtkunst" (*Deutsches Museum*, 1777). Keats, letter to J. H. Reynolds, February 3, 1818. The idea survives into the present: "the English language—that was Shakespeare at the beginning of the seventeenth century—the English language grew up through the brains and the mouths of English people as such; I mean the nobility and the common people as well. But here, here in our country, the educated people and nobility spoke German, and just the people spoke Czech" (Jan Werich in A. Alvarez, *Under Pressure: The Writer in Society* [London, 1965]). These remarks differ vitally from an absolutist perspective of popular culture. ("Let us have pop art and *not* the old poets.") For a critique of the educational importance of popular culture, see G. H. Bantock, *Culture, Industrialization and Education* (New York, 1968).

psychic silhouette with which the artist strives to coincide. There is also a countermodel, inspired by the French tradition, in which art seeks to purify *"les mots de la tribu."* Both models, however, are functions of the rise of the national literatures. The nationalization of art is a cultural analogue of the Fall (perhaps a fortunate Fall);[25] and true literary history, like true theology, can help to limit the curse and assure the promise. At least it makes us honor the paradoxes of an era in which the tenth Muse is Pop.

Milton as Example:
Form and the Historical Vocation of Art

Milton's *Arcades* is a version of pastoral Empson left un-examined and which Godard might enjoy. It is hard to imagine a piece more elite in conception than this courtly interlude. A pastoral in little, it depicts the unmasking of shepherds as noble primitives. An opera in little, it is all opsis, like the *tableaux vivants*, the staged devices common from Elizabeth's time. A drama in little, its action is a single recognition, complete in the first stanza of the first song, and confirmed by the Genius of the Wood. As this sophisticated mixture of genres—pastoral, drama, and masque—it tends in its contracted yet leisurely form toward a fourth and undermining genre. Composed of but three songs and the "recitative" of the *genius loci*, the lyrical form of an ode clearly appears. If genres here, in their very multiplicity, their very formality, are the super-structure, the deep structure is nothing less than the spirit of song itself, questing like the "secret sluice" of Arethusa for a new country or local form, which turns out to be England— that is, the possibility of a truly native lyricism.

[25] Cf. "The presupposition of *Weltliteratur* is a *felix culpa:* mankind's division into many cultures" (Erich Auerbach, "Philologie und Weltliteratur" [1952], trans. M. and E. Said, *Centennial Review*, 13 [1969], 2).

Arcades begins with the fulfillment of a quest:

> Look Nymph and Shepherds look
> What sudden blaze of majesty
> Is that which we from hence descry
> Too divine to be mistook
> This, this is she. . . .

The cry practically ends the action: "here our solemn search hath end." It is the formal sign of an epiphany or theophany, of a "present deity" being revealed. It is a show-cry, the equivalent of the Lo, Behold, O see. But who is this new god? A lady of seventy, the Countess Dowager of Derby. The whole thing seems to be an extravagant courtly compliment; and after the Genius of the Wood has confirmed the perception of these displaced magi as well as acknowledged their own "bright honour," the piece concludes by inviting us to attest that a new deity has been found, one who makes England a greater Arcady.

Is there in this spectacle more than meets the eye? Is the compliment all that extravagant, the form all that gratuitous? The setting is not only the estate of a noble lady but the English countryside, and the masque was probably performed in the open air. Although Milton's literary code is classical and the allusions Italianate, the plot, what there is of it, depicts a journey from a southern to a northern Arcadia and the discovery that England, despite its dank climate, has deities worth celebrating:

> Who had thought this clime had held
> A deity so unparallel'd?

In the last song of the masque, the Dowager Countess is directly identified with a transcendent nature-spirit, the *genius huius loci:*

> Here ye shall have greater grace
> To serve the Lady of this place.

These words invite the nature-spirits haunting more classical shores to emigrate and grace the English countryside. "A better soil shall give ye thanks." Thus Milton's *Arcades* is really a farewell to Arcades, a "we'll to [Italian] woods no more," or "we'll to Fresh woods, and Pastures new." It is a nativity hymn for English nature poetry, in which nymphs, shepherds, and the *genius loci* make their formal submission.

Milton's simple sooth is never simple. The real discovery here is that of a pastoral within a pastoral. The old gods, the old forms—the elite superstructure—must serve a "rural Queen" identified with the *genius loci* of England. But is it not ridiculous to make of this septuagenarian Dowager a new Gloriana? Is what we find here the authentic expression of a national idea of poetry or its misuse as a courtly compliment? Is not *Arcades* at most *dirigisme, Kulturlenkung*, rather than poetry grappling authentically with the spirit of English history and countryside?

It is a question I want to explore rather than answer. If the Countess of Derby is a personal patron, she is also, not without authority, a patroness of English poetry as a whole, being a distant relative of Edmund Spenser and appearing as Amaryllis in "Colin Clout Comes Home Again." Spenser's homecoming, of course, was bitter: Promises of "chere of court" were not fulfilled. He used the pastoral disguise of Colin Clout as a *topos* of modesty, but also took secret pride in his resumption of vernacular poetry. Milton's version of pastoral foresees Spenser's redemption and a true homecoming of the spirit of poetry to England. He associates the aristocracy with the poet's game: The unmasking of artificial shepherds as guardians of the realm (nobles) also unmasks the simple sooth of his poetry as not so simple, as having a tutelary function and lineage as old as theirs. Poetry's tutelary function appears even more clearly in *Comus*, Milton's second pastoral masque,

227

which introduces young aristocrats both to society and the truth of fable.

Thus, by glorifying the lineage of the Countess, Milton at the same time glorifies the lineage of vernacular poetry. He honors Spenser, all the more so because Spenser had first taught English poets how to transfer the Virgilian genres to England and so to increase the honor of the line, revivified rather than interrupted by national ideals. There was schism in the Church, but there would be no schism in poetry. Spenser had more than imitated Virgil: He had *Englished* him by understanding how the idea of form merged with that of the historical vocation of art.

Artists may always have had a bad conscience, have always felt themselves Colin Clouts; but Virgil gave his feelings direct expression at the end of the *Georgics* where he accused himself of practicing an art of "ignoble leisure" (*ignobile otium*) compared to the victorious military exploits of Caesar Octavianus. Make war, not poetry. Later commentators saw Virgil's poetry as a conscious progression from pastoral to georgic to epic, a movement which is thought to express a mounting sense of vocation. We go from sheep and the man, to tools and the man, to arms and the man: from the silly arts and the competitive songs of rural life to the more cultic, warlike tasks of agriculture, and finally to those martial and political qualities that extend the empire of civilization. The Virgilian progress was a commonplace in the Renaissance: One may refer to the stanzas introductory to the *Faerie Queene* in which Spenser promises to exchange his "oaten reedes" for "trumpets sterne," or to Marvell's ode on Cromwell which begins,

> The forward Youth that would appeare
> Must now forsake his Muses dear
> Nor in the Shadowes sing
> His numbers languishing.

Here Cromwell is a male debutant: To "appear" or to "come out"—the humanistic equivalent of epiphany—he must leave the pastoral sphere and exchange plow or harp for sword.

The debut of the Countess Dowager of Derby is somewhat belated (she is seventy years old, the span of human life according to the Bible), but then Milton himself is a belated poet, uncertain, despite the greatness of the poetical era just passing, whether there is true public recognition of the poet as a seeing mouth. Though *Arcades* still looks toward the epiphany of poetry, the courtly culture that could have recognized it is clearly at the term of its life. Seven years later, in *Lycidas*, Milton almost stages his own debut as a poet-prophet who sings independent of any class but his own, the class of all great poets. But he vacillates, returns to swainishness at the end, and does not "appear" in the Marvellian sense till after Cromwell and the Civil War, when he finally passes from pastoral to epic and to a more than national idea of poetry.

An Objection

Is not the theory presented here a throwback to nationalistic speculation? That is its danger, yet a lesser danger for us than to remain trapped in the rhetoric of an Esperanto history. Substantive thought about the racial or ideological components in a culture became especially suspect after the Nazis; the American ideal of assimilation then appeared the only pragmatic answer to ethnic stresses in a nation-state. Now that assimilation has proved to be not false, but certainly an imperfect reality, we are facing the agony of pluralism all over again: conflicts of allegiance, cultural transvestism, and a splintered national identity. Most criticism before the present era was a matter of defining the national genius rather than a particular work of art; and literary history established the native or foreign influences carried forward by an artist. Such determinations could be crassly nationalistic, but they acknowledged that the community was struggling for self-definition and that art played its role in that struggle. No one, of course, wishes to return to the nineteenth-century racial calculus, even when practiced by so sensible a critic as Matthew Arnold:

Science has now made visible to everybody the great and pregnant elements of difference which lie in race, and in how signal a manner they make the genius and history of an Indo-European people vary from those of a Semitic people. Hellenism is of Indo-European growth, Hebraism is of Semitic growth; and we English, a nation of Indo-European stock, seem to belong naturally to the movement of Hellenism. But nothing more strongly marks the essential unity of man than the affinities we can perceive, in this point or that, between members of one family of peoples and members of another; and no affinity of this kind is more strongly marked than that likeness in the strength and prominence of the moral fibre, which, notwithstanding immense elements of difference, knits in some special sort the genius and history of us English, and of our American descendants across the Atlantic, to the genius and history of the Hebrew people. . . .[26]

It may be needful, however, to take back into consciousness what was too quickly subsumed. "An era comes," said a French contemporary of Arnold's, the philosopher and mathematician Antoine Cournot, "which will see the value of ethnic characteristics increase relatively, though decrease in an absolute sense; and Europe seems now [circa 1860] to be entering that era." The *relative* increase in the importance of ethnic distinctions he laid to the very advance of civilization which levels or blunts purely social or historical distinctions and so raises the more ancient or indelible ones. Cournot's anxiety

[26] *Culture and Anarchy* (London, 1869). Cf. E. Renan, *De la Part des peuples sémitiques dans l'histoire de la civilisation* (Paris, 1862).

for the organic nurture of cultural forms—an anxiety first arising in the romantic age—springs from the same insight concerning the advance of civilization. He fears that the expansion and availability of historical forms will burden emerging talents to the point of endangering their growth:

If it is true that everything living, everything which bears the cachet of native beauty must emerge from a seed . . . how can we conceive of the birth and nurture of a truly original art, a truly innovative style, in an era where all genres, all styles are understood historically, explained, liked, and imitated. . . . When one preserves so well all the dead no place is left for the living. . . . The new type will not be able to sustain the competition with existing types already at a high degree of maturity and evolution. Art will therefore arrive by the very progress of historical criticism at a syncretistic and erudite stage . . . incompatible with conditions favoring its organic development.[27]

A return to Herder and the romantic historians—or simply to E. R. Curtius[28]—may be painful. We have tended to forget such "unhappy, far-off things" as the birth-struggle of cosmopolitanism, and the foundation of the idea of world literature in the cultural effects of persecution, which made the Muse an emigré many times over. Without "racist" events like the revocation of the Edict of Nantes, which "drove the

[27] *Traité de l'enchaînement des idées fondamentales dans les sciences et dans l'histoire* (Paris, 1861), sec. 543, and *Considérations sur la marche des idées* (Paris, 1872), book 5, chap. 4.

[28] "Es wäre eine wichtige Aufgabe der vergleichenden Literaturgeschichte, den Entwicklungsgang der einzelnen Literaturen und ihre Selbstinterpretationen herauszuarbeiten. Was ich das französische Literatursystem nannte, ist eine solche Selbstinterpretation und d.h. eine Ideologie, die bewusst gemacht werden kann. Die Literaturvergleichung würde, wenn sie die bezeichnete Aufgabe ergreift, einen wichtigen Beitrag zur Analyse der modernen Nationalideologien leisten. Diese sind nicht weniger bedeutsam und wirksam als die Klassenideologien" (E. R. Curtius, *Gesammelte Aufsätze zur Romanischen Philologie* [Bern and Munich, 1960], pp. 20–21).

national genius abroad,"[29] we might never have had that cross-fertilization of talents that modernism takes for granted. In re-evaluating the prevalence of so many national, religious, or geopolitical ideals—superstitions we still live with despite the universalisms around us—the *genius loci* concept may help to prevent our collapsing national into nationalistic. It reminds us how flexible, if necessary, the idea of community is.

If art is the offspring of a precarious marriage between genius and *genius loci*, the place of which it is the genius is not necessarily a nation-state. Art can express a people (an emerging class or suppressed majority) or region (a Galilee whose genius becomes triumphant) or speech-community (as large as an empire, as small as a professional body). Hence literary study often combats the premature universalism that urges the institution of a common tongue or perfect language. This ideal of a *caractéristique universelle* has haunted intellects from Leibnitz to Noam Chomsky. Turning skeptical and sensuous, it ends in the aggressive, ecumenical utopianism that makes the law go forth from the Zion of T-groups. But a pentacostal ideal of the plurality or mingling of tongues seems preferable to a one-dimensional, deracinated language. "Would to God that all the Lord's people were prophets," was Moses's reply to those who urged him to put down rival sayers. At the end of the eighteenth century, Rivarol claimed with elegant contempt that "Leibnitz was seeking a universal language, and we French were creating it all around him,"[30] but by the

---

[29] Joseph Texte, *Jean-Jacques Rousseau and the Cosmopolitan Spirit in Literature*, trans. J. W. Matthews (London, 1899), p. xiii. Texte, one of our first scholarly comparatists, sees the cosmopolitan spirit founded not by an abstraction from nationality, but a convergence of the "Germanic" (northern) and "Latin" (southern) genius in Rousseau, who consolidated the eighteenth-century influence of England on France.

[30] Rivarol, *De l'Universalité de la langue française* (Berlin and Paris, 1784).

middle of the nineteenth—the great period of philological discovery—even a rationalist could defend the secularity of language against ideals of *une langue bien faite:*

It is language, in its abstractness or general form, which must be considered as essentially defective, while spoken idioms, formed slowly by the lasting influence of infinitely varied needs, have, each in its own way and according to its own flexibility, compensated for this radical defect. They have accommodated themselves to the special expression of a certain kind of imagery, emotion, or order of ideas according to the genius and destiny of each race, and the exceedingly divers influence of geographical region or climate. Our intellectual faculties would be greatly augmented and refined, when multiplying and varying our means of expression and transmitting ideas, if it were possible to have available to us—at our will and according to need—all spoken languages, rather than depending on one constructed language-system which, for most occasions, would prove a most imperfect medium.[31]

Conclusion

"I believe in Eternity. I can find Greece, Asia, Italy, Spain and the Islands—the genius and the creative principle of each

[31] C'est . . . le langage, dans sa nature abstraite ou dans sa forme générale, que l'on doit considérer comme essentiellement défectueux, tandis que les langues parlées, formées lentement sous l'influence durables de besoins infiniment variés, ont, chacune à sa manière et d'après son degré de souplesse, paré à cet inconvénient radical. Selon le génie et les destinées des races, sous l'influence si diverse des zones et des climats, elles se sont appropriées plus spécialement à l'expression de tel ordre d'images, de passions et d'idées. . . . Ce qui aggrandirait et perfectionnerait nos facultés intellectuelles, en multipliant et en variant les moyens d'expression et de transmission de la pensée, ce serait, s'il était possible, de disposer à notre gré, et selon le besoin du moment, de toutes les langues parlées, et non de trouver construite cette langue systématique qui, dans la plupart des cas, serait le plus imparfait des instruments" (A. Cournot, *Essai sur les fondements de la connaissance et sur les caractères de la critique philosophique* [Paris, 1851]).

and of all eras, in my own mind." This confession of a comparatist is Emerson's. Only a century old, it already seems dated in its optimism and deceptively easy in its transcendence of nationality. Yet some such faith has always governed the study of literature when humanistic in its aim. Some such faith makes each national book a Book of the Nations. Studied this way, literature might do what Seneca attributed only to philosophy. It could open "not some local shrine, but the vast temple of all the gods, the universe itself."[32]

The one literary historian, however, who came closest to Emerson's sense of Eternity or Seneca's of Universality was strangely pessimistic about it. Erich Auerbach's *Mimesis*, written in exile and published after World War II, foresaw the end of western history as we know it—of history as a rich, parti-colored succession of events, with personalities and writers dramatically divided by the pressure of class or conscience. Auerbach looked at this canvas of history, on which he saw consciousness strive with consciousness in the Hegelian manner, with something of Virgilian regret. Like Cournot, he surmised that we were moving toward a *nivellement* that would reduce the autochthonous element and gradually eliminate both local and national traditions; and for him this beginning to conformity augured the end of history. When one sees an airline ad with the motto "Introducing the Atlantic River" or hears André Malraux speak of technology creating an "Atlantic civilization," the forerunner of a world-wide humanistic culture, one is almost inclined to agree with Auerbach that historical time and space may be fading into the uniformity of landscapes seen from the air. But then one remembers the source of Auerbach's own strength as a historian of literature, how he traced the interaction of genius and *genius loci*,

[32] Ralph Waldo Emerson, *Complete Works* (Boston, 1903-04), II, 9. Seneca, *Ep.* 90.28.

of Latin and the *lingua franca,* of the vernacular and the high style. Surely in that dubious cultural millennium, in that predicted mass-cult era, a Gloriana will appear once more to a Colin Clout, like another angel to another Caedmon, and say "Sing to me."

PAUL DE MAN

Literary History and
Literary Modernity

To write reflectively about modernity leads to problems that put the usefulness of the term into question, especially as it applies, or fails to apply, to literature. There may well be an inherent contradiction between modernity, which is a way of acting and behaving, and such terms as "reflection" or "ideas" that play an important part in literature and history. The spontaneity of being modern conflicts with the claim to think and write about modernity; it is not at all certain that literature and modernity are in any way compatible concepts. Yet we all speak readily about modern literature and even use this term as a device for historical periodization, with the same apparent unawareness that history and modernity may well be even more incompatible than literature and modernity. The innocuous-sounding title of this essay may therefore contain no less than two logical absurdities —a most inauspicious beginning.

The term "modernity" reappears with increasing frequency and seems again to have become an issue not only as an ideological weapon, but as a theoretical problem as well. It may even be one of the ways by means of which the link between literary theory and literary praxis is being partly restored. At other moments in history, the topic "modernity" might be used just as an attempt at self-definition, as a way of diagnosing one's own present. This can happen during periods of considerable inventiveness, periods that seem, looking back, to have been unusually productive. At such actual or imaginary times, modernity would not be a value in itself, but would designate a set of values that exist independently of their modernity: Renaissance art is not admired because it may have been, at a certain moment, a distinctively "modern" form of art. We do not feel this way about the present, perhaps because such self-assurance can exist only retrospectively. It would be a hopeless task to try to define descriptively the elusive pattern of our own literary modernity; we draw nearer to the problem, however, by asking how modernity can, in itself, become an issue and why this issue seems to be raised with particular urgency with regard to literature or, even more specifically, with regard to theoretical speculations about literature.

That this is indeed the case can be easily verified in Europe as well as in the United States. It is particularly conspicuous, for example, in Germany where, after being banned for political reasons, the term modernity now receives a strong positive value-emphasis and has of late been much in evidence as a battle cry as well as a serious topic of investigation. The same is true in France and in the United States, perhaps most clearly in the renewed interest shown in the transfer of methods derived from the social sciences to literary studies.

Not so long ago, a concern with modernity would in all likelihood have coincided with a commitment to avant-garde movements such as dada, surrealism, or expressionism. The term would have appeared in manifestoes and proclamations, not in learned articles or international colloquia. But this does not mean that we can divide the twentieth century into two parts: a "creative" part that was actually modern, and a "reflective" or "critical" part that feeds on this modernity in the manner of a parasite, with active modernity replaced by theorizing about the modern. Certain forces that could legitimately be called modern and that were at work in lyric poetry, the novel, and the theater have also now become operative in the field of literary theory and criticism. The gap between the manifestoes and the learned articles has narrowed to the point where some manifestoes are quite learned and some articles—though by no means all—are quite provocative. This development has by itself complicated and changed the texture of our literary modernity a great deal and brought to the fore difficulties inherent in the term itself as soon as it is used historically or reflectively. It is perhaps somewhat disconcerting to learn that our usage of the word goes back to the late fifth century of our era and that there is nothing modern about the concept of modernity. It is even more disturbing to discover the host of complications that beset one as soon as a conceptual definition of the term is attempted, especially with regard to literature. One is soon forced to resort to paradoxical formulations, such as defining the modernity of a literary period as the manner in which it discovers the impossibility of being modern.

It is this complication I would like to explore with the help of some examples that are not necessarily taken from our immediate present. They should illuminate the problematic structure of a concept that, like all concepts that are in essence temporal, acquires a particularly rich complexity when it is made to refer to events that are in essence linguistic. I will be less concerned with a description of our own modernity than with the challenge to the methods or the possibility of literary history that the concept implies.

Among the various antonyms that come to mind as possible

opposites for "modernity"—a variety which is itself symptomatic of the complexity of the term—none is more fruitful than "history." "Modern" can be used in opposition to "traditional" or even to "classical." For some French and American contemporaries, "modern" could even mean the opposite of "romantic," a usage that would be harder to conceive for some specialists of German literature. Antimodernists such as Emil Staiger do not hesitate to see the sources of a modernism they deplore in the *Frühromantik* of Friedrich Schlegel and Novalis, and the lively quarrel now taking place in Germany is still focused on the early nineteenth-century tensions between Weimar and Iena. But each of these antonyms—ancient, traditional, classical, and romantic—would embroil us in qualifications and discriminations that are, in fact, superficial matters of geographical and historical contingency. We will reach further if we try to think through the latent opposition between "modern" and "historical," and this will also bring us closest to the contemporary version of the problem.

The vested interest that academics have in the value of history makes it difficult to put the term seriously into question. Only an exceptionally talented and perhaps eccentric member of the profession could undertake this task with sufficient energy to make it effective, and even then it is likely to be accompanied by the violence that surrounds passion and rebellion. One of the most striking instances of such a rebellion occurred when Friedrich Nietzsche, then a young philologist who had been treated quite generously by the academic establishment, turned violently against the traditional foundations of his own discipline in a polemical essay entitled *"Vom Nutzen und Nachteil der Historie für das Leben"* (Of the Use and Misuse of History for Life). The text is a good example of the complications that ensue when a genuine impulse toward modernity collides with the demands of a historical consciousness or of a culture based on the disciplines of history. It can serve as an introduction to the more delicate problems that arise when modernity is applied more specifically to literature.

It is not at once clear that Nietzsche is concerned with a conflict between modernity and history in his second *Unzeitgemässe Betrachtung*. That history is being challenged in a fundamental way is obvious from the start, but it is not obvious that this happens in the name of modernity. The term "modern" most frequently appears in the text with negative connotations as descriptive of the way in which Nietzsche considers his contemporaries to be corrupted and enfeebled by an excessive interest in the past. As opposed to the Greeks, Nietzsche's "moderns" escape from the issues of the present, which they are too weak and sterile to confront, into the sheltering inwardness that history can provide, but that bears no relation to actual existence.[1] History and modernity seem to go hand in hand and jointly fall prey to Nietzsche's cultural criticism. Used in this sense, modernity is merely a descriptive term that designates a certain state of mind Nietzsche considers prevalent among the Germans of his time. A much more dynamic concept of modernity, far-reaching enough to serve as a first definition, appears in what is here directly being opposed to history, namely what Nietzsche calls "life."

"Life" is conceived not just in biological but in temporal terms as the ability to *forget* whatever precedes a present situation. Like most opponents of Rousseau in the nineteenth century, Nietzsche's thought follows purely Rousseauistic

---

[1] "Vom Nutzen und Nachteil der Histoire für das Leben," *Unzeitgemässe Betrachtung II*, in Karl Schlechta, ed., *Werke 1* (Munich, 1954), pp. 232–33, 243.

patterns; the text starts with a contrasting parallel between nature and culture that stems directly from the *Second Discourse on the Origins of Inequality*. The restlessness of human society, in contrast to the placid state of nature of the animal herd, is diagnosed as man's inability to forget the past.

[Man] wonders about himself, about his inability [to learn] to forget, and about his tendency to remain tied to the past: No matter how far and how swiftly he runs, the chain runs with him. . . . Man says "I remember," and envies the animal that forgets at once, and watches each moment die, disappear in night and mist, and disappear forever. Thus the animal lives unhistorically: It hides nothing and coincides at all moments exactly with that what it is; it is bound to be truthful at all times, unable to be anything else.[2]

This ability to forget and to live without historical awareness exists not only on an animal level. Since "life" has an ontological as well as a biological meaning, the condition of animality persists as a constitutive part of man. Not only are there moments when it governs his actions, but these are also the moments when he reestablishes contact with his spontaneity and allows his truly human nature to assert itself.

We saw that the animal, which is truly unhistorical and lives confined within a horizon almost without extension, exists in a relative state of happiness: We will therefore have to consider the ability to experience life in a nonhistorical way as the most important and most original of experiences, as the foundation on which right, health, greatness, and anything truly human can be erected.[3]

Moments of genuine humanity thus are moments at which all anteriority vanishes, annihilated by the power of an absolute forgetting. Although such a radical rejection of history may be illusory or unfair to the achievements of the past, it never-

---

[2] *Ibid.*, p. 211.
[3] *Ibid.*, p. 215.

theless remains justified as necessary to the fulfillment of our human destiny and as the condition for action.

> As the man who acts must, according to Goethe, be without a conscience, he must also be without knowledge; he forgets everything in order to be able to *do* something; he is unfair toward what lies behind and knows only one right, the right of what is now coming into being as the result of his own action.[4]

We are touching here upon the radical impulse that stands behind all genuine modernity when it is not merely a descriptive synonym for the contemporaneous or for a passing fashion. Fashion (mode) can sometimes be only what remains of modernity after the impulse has subsided, as soon—and this can be almost at once—as it has changed from being an incandescent point in time into a reproducible cliché, all that remains of an invention that has lost the desire that produced it. Fashion is like the ashes left behind by the uniquely shaped flames of the fire, the trace alone revealing that a fire actually took place. But Nietzsche's ruthless forgetting, the blindness with which he throws himself into an action lightened of all previous experience, captures the authentic spirit of modernity. It is the tone of Rimbaud when he declares that he has no antecedents whatever in the history of France, that all one has to expect from poets is *"du nouveau"* and that one must be "absolutely modern"; it is the tone of Antonin Artaud when he asserts that "written poetry has value for one single moment and should then be destroyed. Let the dead poets make room for the living . . . the time for masterpieces is past." (la poésie écrite vaut une fois et ensuite qu'on la détruise. Que les poètes morts laissent la place aux autres . . . on doit en finir avec les chefs-d'oeuvres.)[5] Modernity exists in the form

---

[4] *Ibid.*, p. 216.

[5] *Le Théâtre et son double, Oeuvres complètes*, vol. IV (Paris, 1956).

of a desire to wipe out whatever came earlier in the hope of reaching at last a point that could be called a true present, a point of origin that marks a new departure. This combined interplay of a deliberate forgetting with an action that is also a new origin reaches the full power of the idea of modernity. Thus defined, modernity and history are diametrically opposed to each other in Nietzsche's text. Nor is there any doubt as to his commitment to modernity, the only way to reach the metahistorical realm in which the rhythm of one's existence coincides with that of the eternal return. Yet the shrill grandiloquence of the tone may make one suspect that the issue is not so simple as it may at first appear.

Of course, within the polemical circumstances in which it was written, the essay has to overstate the case against history and to aim beyond its target in the hope of reaching it. This tactic is less interesting, however, than the question of whether Nietzsche can free his own thought from historical prerogatives, whether his own text can approach the condition of modernity it advocates. From the start, the intoxication with the history-transcending life-process is counterbalanced by a deeply pessimistic wisdom that remains rooted in a sense of historical causality, although it reverses the movement of history from one of development to one of regression. Human "existence," we are told near the beginning of the essay, "is an uninterrupted pastness that lives from its own denial and destruction, from its own contradictions." ("Das Dasein ist nur ein ununterbrochenes Gewesensein, ein Ding, das davon lebt, sich selbst zu verneinen und zu verzehren, sich selbst zu widersprechen."[6]) This description of life as a constant regression has nothing to do with cultural errors, such as the excess of historical disciplines in contemporary education against which the essay polemicizes, but lies much deeper in the nature of things, beyond the reach of culture. It is a temporal experi-

[6] Nietzsche, p. 212.

ence of human mutability, historical in the deepest sense of the term in that it implies the necessary experience of any present as a *passing* experience that makes the past irrevocable and unforgettable because it is inseparable from any present or future. Keats gained access to the same awareness when, in *The Fall of Hyperion*, he contemplated in the fallen Saturn the past as a foreknowledge of his own mortal future:

> Without stay or prop
> But my own weak mortality, I bore
> The load of this eternal quietude,
> The unchanging gloom . . .

Modernity invests its trust in the power of the present moment as an origin, but discovers that, in severing itself from the past, it has at the same time severed itself from the present. Nietzsche's text leads him irrevocably to this discovery, perhaps most strikingly (because most implicitly), when he comes close to describing his own function as a *critical* historian and discovers that the rejection of the past is not so much an act of forgetting as an act of critical judgment directed against himself.

[The critical student of the past] must possess the strength, and must at times apply this strength, to the destruction and dissolution of the past in order to be able to live. He achieves this by calling this past into court, putting it under indictment, and finally condemning it; any past, however, deserves to be condemned, for such is the condition of human affairs that they are ruled by violence and weakness. . . . "It takes a great deal of strength to be able to live and forget to what extent life and injustice go together." . . . But this very life that has to forget must also at times be able to stop forgetting; then it will become clear how illegitimate the existence of something, of a privilege, a caste, or a dynasty actually is, and how much it deserves to be destroyed. Then the past is judged critically, attacked at its very roots with a sharp knife, and brutally cut down, regardless of established pieties. This is always a dangerous process, dangerous for life itself. Men and eras that serve life in this manner, by judging and destroying the past, are always dangerous and endangered. For we are inevitably the result of earlier generations and thus the result of their mistakes, their passions and aberrations, even of their crimes; it is not possible to loosen oneself entirely from this chain. . . . Afterwards, we try to give ourselves a new past from which we should have liked to descend instead of the past from which we actually descended. But this is also dangerous, because it is so difficult to trace the limit of one's denial of the past, and because the newly invented nature is likely to be weaker than the previous one.[7]

The parricidal imagery of the passage, the weaker son condemning and killing the stronger father, reaches the inherent paradox of the denial of history implied in modernity.

As soon as modernism becomes conscious of its own strategies—and it cannot fail to do so if it is justified, as in this text, in the name of a concern for the future—it discovers itself to be a generative power that not only engenders history, but is part of a generative scheme that extends far back into the past. The image of the chain, to which Nietzsche instinctively resorts when he speaks of history, reveals this very clearly. Considered as a principle of life, modernity becomes a principle of origination and turns at once into a generative power that is itself historical. It becomes impossible to overcome history in the name of life or to forget the past in the name of modernity, because both are linked by a temporal chain that gives them a common destiny. Nietzsche finds it impossible to escape from history, and he finally has to bring the two incompatibles, history and modernity (now using the term in the full sense of a radical renewal), together in a paradox that cannot be resolved, an aporia that comes very close to describing the predicament of our own present modernity:

[7] *Ibid.*, p. 230.

For the impulse that stands behind our history-oriented education—in radical inner contradiction to the spirit of a "new time"
or a "modern spirit"—must in turn be understood historically;
history itself must resolve the problem of history, historical
knowledge must turn its weapon against itself—this threefold
"must" is the imperative of the "new times," if they are to achieve
something truly new, powerful, life-giving, and original.[8]

Only through history is history conquered; modernity now
appears as the horizon of a historical process that has to remain
a gamble. Nietzsche sees no assurance that his own reflective
and historical attempt achieves any genuine change; he realizes
that his text itself can be nothing but another historical document,[9] and finally he has to delegate the power of renewal and
modernity to a mythical entity called "youth" to which he
can only recommend the effort of self-knowledge that has
brought him to his own abdication.

The bad faith implied in advocating self-knowledge to a
younger generation, while demanding from this generation
that it act blindly, out of a self-forgetting that one is unwill-
ing or unable to achieve oneself, forms a pattern all too familiar
in our own experience to need comment. In this way Nietzsche, at this early point in his career, copes with a paradox
that his thought has revealed with impressive clarity: Modernity and history relate to each other in a curiously contradictory way that goes beyond antithesis or opposition. If
history is not to become sheer regression or paralysis, it depends on modernity for its duration and renewal; but modernity cannot assert itself without being at once swallowed up
and reintegrated into a regressive historical process. Nietzsche
offers no real escape out of a predicament in which we readily
recognize the mood of our own modernity. Modernity and

[8] *Ibid.*, p. 261.
[9] *Ibid.*, p. 277.

history seem condemned to being linked together in a self-destroying union that threatens the survival of both.

If we see in this paradoxical condition a diagnosis of our own modernity, then literature has always been essentially modern. Nietzsche was speaking of life and of culture in general, of modernity and history as they appear in all human enterprises in the most general sense possible. The problem becomes more intricate when it is restricted to literature. Here we are dealing with an activity that necessarily contains, within its own specificity, the very contradiction that Nietzsche discovered at the end point of his rebellion against a historically minded culture. Regardless of historical or cultural conditions, beyond the reach of educational or moral imperatives, the modernity of literature confronts us at all times with an unsolvable paradox. On the one hand, literature has a constitutive affinity with action, with the unmediated, free act that knows no past; some of the impatience of Rimbaud or Artaud echoes in all literary texts, no matter how serene and detached they may seem. The historian, in his function as historian, can remain quite remote from the collective acts he records; his language and the events that the language denotes are clearly distinct entities. But the writer's language is to some degree the product of his own action; he is both the historian and the agent of his own language. The ambivalence of writing is such that it can be considered both an act and an interpretative process that follows after an act with which it cannot coincide. As such, it both affirms and denies its own nature or specificity. Unlike the historian, the writer remains so closely involved with action that he can never free himself of the temptation to destroy whatever stands between him and his deed, especially the temporal distance that makes him dependent on an earlier past. The appeal of modernity haunts all literature. It is revealed in numberless images and emblems that appear at all periods—in the obsession with a *tabula rasa*, with new beginnings—that finds recurrent expression in all forms of writing. No true account of literary language can bypass this persistent temptation of literature to fulfill itself in a single moment. The temptation of immediacy is constitutive of a literary consciousness and has to be included in a definition of the specificity of literature.

The manner in which this specificity asserts itself, however, the form of its actual manifestation, is curiously oblique and confusing. Often in the course of literary history writers openly assert their commitment to modernity thus conceived. Yet whenever this happens, a curious logic that seems almost uncontrolled, a necessity inherent in the nature of the problem rather than in the will of the writer, directs their utterance away from their avowed purpose. Assertions of literary modernity often end up by putting the possibility of being modern seriously into question. But precisely because this discovery goes against an original commitment that cannot simply be dismissed as erroneous, it never gets stated outright, but hides instead behind rhetorical devices of language that disguise and distort what the writer is actually saying, perhaps in contrast to what he meant to say. Hence the need for the interpreter of such texts to respond to levels of meaning not immediately obvious. The very presence of such complexities indicates the existence of a special problem: How is it that a specific and important feature of a literary consciousness, its desire for modernity, seems to lead outside literature into something that no longer shares this specificity, thus forcing the writer to undermine his own assertions in order to remain faithful to his vocation?

It is time to clarify what we are trying to convey with some examples taken from texts that openly plead the cause of modernity. Many, but by no means all, of these texts are written by people who stand outside literature from the start, either because they instinctively tend toward the interpretative distance of the historian, or because they incline toward a form of action no longer linked to language. During the quarrel between the Ancients and the Moderns, the debate between a traditional conception of literature and modernity that took place in France near the end of the seventeenth century and that is still considered by some[10] as the starting point of a "modern" sense of history, it is striking that the modern camp not only contained men of slighter literary talent, but that their arguments against classical literature were often simply against literature as such. The nature of the debate forced the participants to make comparative critical evaluations of ancient versus contemporary writing; it obliged them to offer something resembling readings of passages in Homer, Pindar, or Theocritus. Although no one covered himself with critical glory in the performance of this task—mainly because the powerful imperative of decorum (*bienséance*) tends to become a particularly opaque screen that stands between the antique text and the classical reading[11]—the partisans of the Ancients still performed a great deal better than the pro-moderns. If one compares the remarks of a "moderne" such as Charles Perrault on Homer or his application in 1688 of seventeenth-century *bienséance* to Hellenic texts in *Parallèle des anciens et des modernes* with Boileau's reply in *Réflexions*

[10] See, for example, Werner Krauss, "Cartaud de la Villate und die Entstehung des geschichtlichen Weltbildes in der Frühaufklärung," *Studien zur Deutschen und Französischen Aufklärung* (Berlin, 1963), and H. R. Jauss's substantial introduction to his facsimile edition of Charles Perrault, *Parallèle des anciens et des modernes* (Munich, 1964), pp. 12–13.

[11] Critical utterances concerning the Homeric question are particularly revealing in this respect, in a partisan of the Moderns like Charles Perrault as well as in a partisan of the Ancients like Boileau.

critiques sur quelques passages du rhéteur Longin of 1694,[12] it then becomes clear that the *"anciens"* had a notion of decorum that remained in much closer contact with literature, including its constitutive impulse toward literary modernity, than did the "modernes." This fact undoubtedly strengthens, in the long run, the cause of the moderns, despite their own critical shortcomings, but the point is precisely that a partisan and deliberately pro-modern stance is much more easily taken by someone devoid of literary sensitivity than by a genuine writer. Literature, which is inconceivable without a passion for modernity, also seems to oppose from the inside a subtle resistance to this passion.

Thus we find in the same period a detached and ironical mind like that of the early Fontenelle openly taking the side of the moderns in asserting that "nothing stands so firmly in the way of progress, nothing restricts the mind so effectively as an excessive admiration for the Ancients."[13] Having to demystify the merit of invention and origin on which the superiority of the Ancients is founded—and which, in fact, roots their merit in their genuine modernity—Fontenelle himself becomes entertainingly inventive in his assertion that the prestige of so-called origins is merely an illusion created by the distance separating us from a remote past. At the same time he expresses the mock-anxious fear that our own progressing rationality will prevent us from benefiting, in the eyes of future generations, from the favorable prejudice we were silly enough to bestow on the Greeks and the Romans.

[12] H. R. Jauss mentions as other convincing instances of critical insight among the defenders of the Ancients, la Bruyère's *Discours sur Théophraste* (1699) and Saint-Evremont's *Sur les poèmes des anciens* (1685).

[13] "Digression sur les anciens et les modernes," *Oeuvres,* IV (Paris, 1767), 170–200.

En vertu de ces compensations, nous pouvons espérer qu'on nous admirera avec excès dans les siècles à venir, pour nous payer du peu de cas que l'on fait aujourd'hui de nous dans le nôtre. On s'évertuera à trouver dans nos ouvrages des beautés que nous n'avons point prétendu y mettre; telle faute incontestable et dont l'auteur conviendrait lui-même aujourd'hui trouvera des défenseurs d'un courage invincible; et Dieu sait avec quel mépris on traitera en comparaison de nous, les beaux esprits de ces temps-là, qui pourront bien être des américains. C'est ainsi que le même préjugé nous abaisse dans un temps, pour nous élever dans un autre, c'est ainsi qu'on en est la victime et puis la divinité; jeu assez plaisant à considérer avec des yeux indifférents.

The same playful indifference prompts Fontenelle to add the remark:

Mais il y a toutes les apparences du monde que la raison se perfectionnera, et que l'on se désabusera généralement du préjugé grossier de l'Antiquité. Peut-être ne durera-t-il pas encore longtemps! peut-être à l'heure qu'il est admirons-nous les Anciens en pure perte, et sans devoir jamais être admiré en cette qualité-là. Ce serait un peu fâcheux.[14]

[14] "By virtue of these compensations, we can hope to be excessively admired in future centuries, to make up for the little consideration we are given in our own. Critics will vie to discover in our works hidden beauties that we never thought of putting there; obvious weaknesses, that the author would be the first to acknowledge if they were pointed out to him to-day, will find staunch defenders. God knows with what contempt the fashionable writers of these future days—which may well turn out to be Americans—will be treated in comparison with us. The same prejudice that degrades us at one time enhances our value at another; we are first the victims, then the gods of the same error in judgment—an amusing play to observe with detached eyes" (*ibid.*, pp. 195-196). "But, in all likelihood, reason will grow more perfect in time and the crude prejudice in favor of the Ancients is bound to vanish. It may well not be with us much longer. We may well be wasting our time admiring the Ancients in vain, without

Fontenelle's historical irony is far from being unliterary, but if taken at face value it stands at the very opposite pole of the impulse toward action without which literature would not be what it is. Nietzsche admired Fontenelle, but it must have been as an apollinian anti-self, for nothing is more remote from the spirit of modernity than Fontenelle's *perfectibilité*, a kind of statistical, quantitative balance between right and wrong, a process of trial-by-chance that may perhaps lead to certain rules by means of which aberrations could be prevented in the future. In the name of *perfectibilité*, he can reduce critical norms to a set of mechanical rules and assert, with only a trace of irony, that literature progressed faster than science because the imagination obeys a smaller number of easier rules than does reason. He can easily dismiss poetry and the arts as "unimportant," since he pretends to have moved so far away from their concerns. His stance is that of the objective, scientific historian. Even if taken seriously, this stance would engage him in a task of interpretation closer to literature than that of Charles Perrault, for example, who has to resort to the military and imperial achievements of his age to find instances of the superiority of the moderns. That such a type of modernism leads outside literature is clear enough. The *topos* of the antiliterary, technological man as an incarnation of modernity is recurrent among the *idées reçues* of the nineteenth century and symptomatic of the alacrity with which modernity welcomes the opportunity to abandon literature altogether. The opposite temptation toward a purely detached interpretation, of which we find an ironic version in Fontenelle, also reveals the inherent trend to draw away from the literary. Perrault's committed, as well as

expectations of ever being admired in the same capacity. What a pity!" (*ibid.*, p. 199).

255

Fontenelle's detached, modernism both lead away from literary understanding.

Our examples may have been one-sided, however, since we were dealing with nonliterary figures. More revealing is the case of writers whose proximity to literature is beyond dispute and who find themselves, in true accordance with their literary vocation, defenders of modernity—not just in the choice of their themes and settings, but as representative of a fundamental attitude of mind. The poetry of Charles Baudelaire, as well as his plea for modernity in several critical texts, would be a good case in point.

As seen in the famous essay on Constantin Guys, "Le peintre de la vie moderne," Baudelaire's conception of modernity is very close to that of Nietzsche in his second *Unzeitgemässe Betrachtung*. It stems from an acute sense of the present as a constitutive element of all esthetic experience:

Le plaisir que nous retirons de la représentation du présent tient non seulement à la beauté dont il peut être revêtu, mais aussi à sa qualité essentielle de présent.[15]

The paradox of the problem is potentially contained in the formula *"représentation du présent,"* which combines a repetitive with an instantaneous pattern without apparent awareness of the incompatibility. Yet this latent tension governs the development of the entire essay. Baudelaire remains faithful throughout to the seduction of the present; any temporal awareness is so closely tied for him to the present moment that memory comes to apply more naturally to the present than it does to the past:

[15] "The pleasure we derive from the *representation of the present* (la représentation du présent) is not merely due to the beauty it may display, but also to the essential 'present-ness' of the present." In F. F. Gautier, ed., *L'Art romantique, Oeuvres complètes*, IV (Paris, 1923), 208.

Malheur à celui qui étudie dans l'antique autre chose que l'art pur, la logique, la méthode générale! Pour s'y trop plonger, il perd *la mémoire du présent;* il abdique la valeur et les privilèges fournis par la circonstance; car presque toute notre originalité vient de l'estampille que le *temps* imprime à nos sensations.[16]

The same temporal ambivalence prompts Baudelaire to couple any evocation of the present with terms such as *"représenta-tion," "mémoire,"* or even *"temps,"* all opening perspectives of distance and difference within the apparent uniqueness of the instant. Yet his modernity too, like Nietzsche's, is a forgetting or a suppression of anteriority: The human figures that epitomize modernity are defined by experiences such as childhood or convalescence, a freshness of perception that results from a slate wiped clear, from the absence of a past that has not yet had time to tarnish the immediacy of perception (although what is thus freshly discovered prefigures the end of this very freshness), of a past that, in the case of convalescence, is so threatening that it has to be forgotten.

All these experiences of immediacy coupled with their implicit negation, strive to combine the openness and freedom of a present severed from all other temporal dimensions, the weight of the past as well as the concern with a future, with a sense of totality and completeness that could not be achieved if a more extended awareness of time were not also involved. Thus we find Constantin Guys, who is made to serve as a kind of emblem for the poetic mind, to be a curious synthesis of a man of action (that is, a man of the moment, severed from past and future) with an observer and recorder of moments that

---

[16] "Woe to him who, in Antiquity, studies anything besides pure art, logic and general method! By plunging into the past he may well lose the *memory of the present* (la mémoire du présent). He abdicates the values and privileges provided by actual circumstance, for almost all our originality stems from the stamp that time prints on our sensations" (*ibid.*, pp. 224–225). The italics are mine.

are necessarily combined within a larger totality. Like the photographer or reporter of today, he has to be present at the battles and the murders of the world, not to inform, but to freeze what is most transient and ephemeral into a recorded image. Constantin Guys, before being an artist, has to be *homme du monde*, driven by curiosity and "always, spiritually, in the state of mind of the convalescent." The description of his technique offers perhaps the best formulation of this ideal combination of the instantaneous with a completed whole, of pure fluid movement with form—a combination that would achieve a reconciliation between the impulse toward modernity and the demand of the work of art to achieve duration. The painting remains steadily in motion and exists in the open, improvised manner of a sketch that is like a constant new beginning. The final closing of the form, constantly postponed, occurs so swiftly and suddenly that it hides its dependence on previous moments in its own precipitous instantaneity: The entire process tries to outrun time, to achieve a swiftness that would transcend the latent opposition between action and form.

Ainsi, dans l'exécution de M. G. se montrent deux choses: l'une, une contention de mémoire résurrectioniste, évocatrice, une mémoire qui dit à chaque chose: "Lazare, lève-toi!"; l'autre, un feu, une ivresse de crayon, de pinceau, ressemblant presque à une fureur. C'est la peur de n'aller pas assez vite, de laisser échapper le fantôme avant que la synthèse n'en soit extraite et saisie . . . M. G. commence par de légères indications au crayon, qui ne marquent guère que la place que les objets doivent tenir dans l'espace. Les plans principaux sont indiqués ensuite . . . Au dernier moment, le contour des objets est définitivement cerné par de l'encre . . . Cette méthode si simple et presque élémentaire . . . a cet incomparable avantage qu'à n'importe quel point de son progrès, chaque dessin a l'air suffisamment fini; vous

nommerez cela une ébauche si vous voulez, mais ébauche par-
faite.[17]

That Baudelaire has to refer to this synthesis as a *"fantôme"*
is another instance of the rigor that forces him to double any
assertion by a qualifying use of language that puts it at once
into question. The Constantin Guys of the essay is himself a
phantom, bearing some resemblance to the actual painter, but
differing from him in being the fictional achievement of what
existed only potentially in the "real" man. Even if we consider
the character in the essay to be a mediator used to formulate
the prospective vision of Baudelaire's own work, we can still
witness in this vision a similar disincarnation and reducton of
meaning. At first, in the enumeration of the themes that the
painter (or writer) will select, we again find the temptation
of modernity to move outside art, its nostalgia for the immediacy, the facticity of entities that are in contact with the
present and illustrate the heroic ability to ignore or to forget
that this present contains the prospective self-knowledge of
its end. The figure chosen can be more or less close to being
aware of this: It can be the mere surface, the outer garment

---

[17] "In M(onsieur) G(uys)'s manner, two features can be observed;
in the first place, the contention of a highly suggestive, resurrecting
power of memory, a memory that addresses all things with: "Lazarus,
arise!"; on the other hand, a fiery, intoxicating vigor of pencil and
brushstroke that almost resembles fury. He seems to be in anguish
of not going fast enough, of letting the phantom escape before the
synthesis has been extracted from it and recorded . . . M. G. begins
by slight pencil-marks that merely designate the place assigned to
various objects in space. Then he indicates the main surfaces. . . . At
the last moment, the definitive contour of the objects is sealed with
ink. . . . This simple, almost elementary method . . . has the incomparable advantage that, at each point in the process of its elabora-
tion, each drawing seems sufficiently completed; you may call this a
sketch, if you like, but it is a perfect sketch" (*ibid.*, p. 228).

of the present, the unwitting defiance of death in the soldier's colorful coat, or it can be the philosophically conscious sense of time of the dandy. In each case, however, the "subject" Baudelaire chose for a theme is preferred because it exists in the facticity, in the modernity, of a present that is ruled by experiences that lie outside language and escape from the successive temporality, the duration involved in writing. Baudelaire states clearly that the attraction of a writer toward his theme—which is also the attraction toward an action, a modernity, and an autonomous *meaning* that would exist outside the realm of language—is primarily an attraction to what is not art. The statement occurs with reference to the most anonymous and shapeless "theme" of all, that of the crowd: "C'est un moi insatiable de non-moi."[18] If one remembers that this "*moi*" designates, in the metaphor of a subject, the specificity of literature, then this specificity is defined by its inability to remain constant to its own specificity.

This, at least, corresponds to the first moment of a certain mode of being, called literature. It soon appears that literature is an entity that exists not as a single moment of self-denial, but as plurality of moments that can, if one wishes, be represented—but this is a mere representation—as a succession of moments or a duration. In other words, literature can be represented as a movement and is, in essence, the fictional narration of this movement. After the initial moment of flight away from its own specificity, a moment of return follows that leads literature back to what it is—but we must bear in mind that terms such as "after" and "follows" do not designate actual moments in a diachrony, but are used purely as *metaphors* of duration. Baudelaire's text illustrates this return, this *reprise*, with striking clarity. The "*moi insatiable de non-moi*" has been moving toward a series of "themes" that reveal the

[18] "It is a self insatiable for non-selfhood" (*ibid.*, p. 219).

impatience with which it tries to move away from its own center. These themes become less and less concrete and substantial, however, although they are being evoked with increasing realism and mimetic rigor in the description of their surfaces. The more realistic and pictorial they become, the more abstract they are, the slighter the residue of meaning that would exist outside their specificity as mere language and mere *significant*. The last theme that Baudelaire evokes, that of the carriages, has nothing whatever to do with the facticity of the carriage—although Baudelaire insists that in the paintings by Constantin Guys "toute [la] carrosserie est parfaitement orthodoxe; chaque partie est à sa place et rien n'est à reprendre." (the entire structure of the carriage-body is perfectly orthodox: every part is in its place and nothing needs to be corrected.)[19] The substantial, thematic *meaning* of the carriage as such, however, has disappeared:

Dans quelque attitude qu'elle soit jetée, avec quelque allure qu'elle soit lancée, une voiture, comme un vaisseau, emprunte au mouvement une grâce mystérieuse et complexe très difficile à sténographier. Le plaisir que l'oeil de l'artiste en reçoit est tiré, ce semble, de la série de figures géométriques que cet objet, déjà si compliqué, engendre successivement et rapidement dans l'espace.[20]

What is here being stenographed is the movement by which, in apparent and metaphorical succession, literature first moves away from itself and then returns. All that remains of the

[19] *Ibid.*, p. 259.
[20] "Regardless of attitude and position, regardless of the speed at which it is launched, a carriage, like a ship, receives from its motion a mysteriously complex graceful air, very hard to capture in short-hand (très difficile à sténographier). The pleasure that the artist's eye derives from it is drawn, or so it seems, from the sequence of geometrical figures that this already so complicated object engenders successively and swiftly in space" (*ibid.*).

theme is a mere outline, less than a sketch, a time-arabesque rather than a figure. The carriage has been allegorized into nothingness and exists as the purely temporal vibration of a successive movement that has only linguistic existence—for nothing is more radically metaphorical than the expression "*figures géométriques*" that Baudelaire is compelled to use to make himself understood. But that he wants to be understood, and not misunderstood in the belief that this geometry would have recourse to anything that is not language, is clear from its implied identification with a mode of writing. The *stenos* in the word stenography, meaning narrow, could be used to designate the confinement of literature within its own boundaries, its dependence on duration and repetition that Baudelaire experienced as a curse. But the fact that the word designates a form of writing indicates the compulsion to return to a literary mode of being, as a form of language that knows itself to be mere repetition, mere fiction and allegory, forever unable to participate in the spontaneity of action or modernity.

The movement of this text—that could be shown to parallel the development of Baudelaire's poetry as it moves from the sensory richness of the earlier poems to their gradual allegorization in the prose versions of the *Spleen de Paris*—recurs with various degrees of explicitness in all writers and measures the legitimacy of their claim to be called writers. Modernity turns out to be indeed one of the concepts by means of which the distinctive nature of literature can be revealed in all its intricacy. No wonder it had to become a central issue in critical discussions and a source of torment to writers who have to confront it as a challenge to their vocation. They can neither accept nor reject it with good conscience. When they assert their own modernity, they are bound to discover their dependence on similar assertions made by their literary predecessors; their claim to being a new beginning turns out to be the repetition of a claim that has always already been made. As soon as Baudelaire has to replace the single instant of invention, conceived as an act, by a successive movement that involves at least two distinct moments, he enters into a world that assumes the depths and complications of an articulated time, an interdependence between past and future that prevents any present from ever coming into being.

The more radical the rejection of anything that came before, the greater the dependence on the past. Antonin Artaud can go to the extreme of rejecting all forms of theatrical art prior to his own; in his own work, he can demand the destruction of any form of written text—he nevertheless finally has to ground his own vision in examples such as the Balinese theater, the least modern, the most text-frozen type of theater conceivable. And he has to do so with full knowledge that he thus destroys his own project, with the hatred of the traitor for the camp that he has chosen to join. Quoting the lines in which Artaud attacks the very concept of the theater on which he has waged his entire undertaking ("Rien de plus impie que le système des Balinais . . ."), Jacques Derrida can rightly comment: "[Artaud] was unable to resign himself to a theater based on repetition, unable to renounce a theater that would do away with all forms of repetition."[21] The same fatal interplay governs the writer's attitude toward modernity: He cannot renounce the claim to being modern but also cannot resign himself to his dependence on predecessors— who, for that matter, were caught in the same situation. Never is Baudelaire so close to his predecessor Rousseau as in the extreme modernity of his latest prose poems, and never is Rousseau so tied to his literary ancestors as when he pretends to have nothing more to do with literature.

[21] "Le théâtre de la cruauté et la clôture de la représentation," *L'Écriture et la différence* (Paris, 1967), p. 367.

The distinctive character of literature thus becomes manifest as an inability to escape from a condition that is felt to be unbearable. It seems that there can be no end, no respite in the ceaseless pressure of this contradiction, at least as long as we consider it from the point of view of the writer as subject. The discovery of his inability to be modern leads him back to the fold, within the autonomous domain of literature, but never with genuine appeasement. As soon as he can feel appeased in this situation he ceases to be a writer. His language may be capable of a certain degree of tranquillity; it is, after all, the product of a renunciation that has allowed for the metaphorical thematization of the predicament. But this renunciation does not involve the subject. The continuous appeal of modernity, the desire to break out of literature toward the reality of the moment, prevails and, in its turn, folding back upon itself, engenders the repetition and the continuation of literature. Thus modernity, which is fundamentally a falling away from literature and a rejection of history, also acts as the principle that gives literature duration and historical existence.

The manner in which this inherent conflict determines the structure of literary language cannot be treated within the limits of this essay. We are more concerned, at this point, with the question of whether a history of an entity as self-contradictory as literature is conceivable. In the present state of literary studies this possibility is far from being clearly established. It is generally admitted that a positivistic history of literature, treating it as if it were a collection of empirical data, can only be a history of what literature is not. At best, it would be a preliminary classification opening the way for actual literary study and, at worst, an obstacle in the way of literary understanding. On the other hand, the intrinsic interpretation of literature claims to be anti- or a-historical, but often presupposes a notion of history of which the critic is not himself aware.

In describing literature, from the standpoint of the concept of modernity, as the steady fluctuation of an entity away from and toward its own mode of being, we have constantly stressed that this movement does not take place as an actual sequence in time; to represent it as such is merely a metaphor making a sequence out of what occurs in fact as a synchronic juxtaposition. The sequential, diachronic structure of the process stems from the nature of literary language as an entity, not as an event. Things do not happen as if a literary text (or a literary vocation) moved for a certain period of time away from its center, then turned around, folding back upon itself at one specific moment to travel back to its genuine point of origin. These imaginary motions between fictional points cannot be located, dated, and represented as if they were places in a geography or events in a genetic history. Even in the discursive texts we have used—in Baudelaire, in Nietzsche, or even in Fontenelle—the three moments of flight, return, and the turning point at which flight changes into return or vice-versa exist simultaneously on levels of meaning that are so intimately intertwined that they cannot be separated. When Baudelaire, for example, speaks of *"représentation du présent,"* of *"mémoire du présent,"* of *"synthèse du fantôme,"* or of *"ébauche finie,"* his language names, at the same time, the flight, the turning point, and the return. Our entire argument lies compressed in such formulations. This would even be more obvious if we had used poetic instead of discursive texts. It follows that it would be a mistake to think of literary history as the diachronic narrative of the fluctuating motion we have tried to describe. Such a narrative can be only metaphorical, and history is not fiction.

With respect to its own specificity (that is, as an existing entity susceptible to historical description), literature exists at the same time in the modes of error and truth; it both betrays and obeys its own mode of being. A positivistic history that sees literature only as what it is not (as an objective fact, an empirical psyche, or a communication that transcends the literary text as text) is, therefore, necessarily inadequate. The same is true of approaches to literature that take for granted the specificity of literature—what the French structuralists, echoing the Russian formalists, call literary (*littérarité*) of literature. If literature rested at ease within its own self-definition, it could be studied according to methods that are scientific rather than historical. We are obliged to confine ourselves to history when this is no longer the case, when the entity steadily puts its own ontological status into question. The structuralist goal of a science of literary forms assumes this stability and treats literature as if the fluctuating movement of aborted self-definition were not a constitutive part of its language. Structuralist formalism, therefore, systematically bypasses the necessary component of literature for which the term "modernity" is not such a bad name after all, despite its ideological and polemical overtones. It is a very revealing paradox, confirming again that anything touching upon literature becomes at once a Pandora's box, that the critical method which denies literary modernity would appear—and even, in certain respects, would be—the most modern of critical movements.

Could we conceive of a literary history that would not truncate literature by putting us misleadingly *into* or *outside* it, that would be able to maintain the literary aporia throughout, account at the same time for the truth and the falsehood of the knowledge literature conveys about itself, distinguish rigorously between metaphorical and historical language, and account for literary modernity as well as for its historicity?

Clearly, such a conception would imply a revision of the notion of history and, beyond that, of the notion of time on which our idea of history is based. It would imply, for instance, abandoning the preassumed concept of history as a generative process that we found operative in Nietzsche's text—although this text also began to rebel against it—of history as a temporal hierarchy that resembles a parental structure in which the past is like an ancestor begetting, in a moment of unmediated presence, a future capable of repeating in its turn the same generative process. The relationship between truth and error that prevails in literature cannot be represented genetically, since truth and error exist simultaneously, thus preventing the favoring of the one over the other. The need to revise the foundations of literary history may seem like a desperately vast undertaking; the task appears even more disquieting if we contend that literary history could in fact be paradigmatic for history in general, since man himself, like literature, can be defined as an entity capable of putting his own mode of being into question. The task may well be less sizable, however, than it seems at first. All the directives we have formulated as guidelines for a literary history are more or less taken for granted when we are engaged in the much more humble task of reading and understanding a literary text. To become good literary historians, we must remember that what we usually call literary history has little or nothing to do with literature and that what we call literary interpretation—provided only it is good interpretation—is in fact literary history. If we extend this notion beyond literature, it merely confirms that the bases for historical knowledge are not empirical facts but written texts, even if these texts masquerade in the guise of wars or evolutions.

The Authors

M. H. Abrams, born in 1912, is Frederic J. Whiton Professor of English at Cornell University. Mr. Abrams is the author of *The Milk of Paradise* (1934, 2d ed. 1970), *The Mirror and the Lamp* (1953), *A Glossary of Literary Terms* (1957, 2d ed. 1970), and *Natural Supernaturalism* (1971); he is the general editor of *The Norton Anthology of English Literature* (1962, 2d ed. 1968).

Morton W. Bloomfield, born in 1913, is chairman of the English Department at Harvard University. Mr. Bloomfield is the author of *Seven Deadly Sins* (1952), *"Piers Plowman" as a Fourteenth Century Apocalypse* (1962), and *Essays and Explorations* (1970); he is the coauthor of *A Linguistic Introduction to the History of English* (1963).

Paul de Man, born in 1920, is professor of French and comparative literature at Yale University. He is the author of *Blindness and Insight: Studies in the Rhetoric of Contemporary Criticism* (1971) and of numerous articles on literary theory and on Romantic and post-Romantic literature.

Northrop Frye, born in 1912, is University Professor at the University of Toronto and has been a Fellow of the Royal

269

Society of Canada since 1951. Mr. Frye was the recipient of the Royal Society's Lorne Pierce Medal in 1958 and the Canada Council Medal in 1967 and presently serves as advisory member of the Canadian Radio Television Commission. He is the author of *Fearful Symmetry: A Study of William Blake* (1947), *Anatomy of Criticism* (1957), *The Educated Imagination* (1963), *Fables of Identity* (1963), *The Modern Century* (1967), and nine other books.

GEOFFREY HARTMAN, born in 1929, is professor of English and comparative literature at Yale University. Mr. Hartman is the author of *The Unmediated Vision* (1954), *André Malraux* (1960), *Wordsworth's Poetry* (1964), for which he received the Christian Gauss Prize in 1965, and *Beyond Formalism: Literary Essays* (1970).

E. D. HIRSCH, JR., born in 1928, is professor of English at the University of Virginia. Mr. Hirsch is the author of *Wordsworth and Schelling* (1960), *Innocence and Experience* (1964), and *Validity in Interpretation* (1967).

Index

Adam, 144, 171, 217
Adams, John, 156
Addison, Joseph, 43, 44
Adelard of Bath, 80
Adler, Alfred, 169
Ahab, 85–86, 88
Alcott, Bronson, 222
Antonioni, Michelangelo, 201–202
Apollo, 213–214, 216, 217, 219, 223
Aquinas, Thomas, 75, 86, 97, 172
Arendt, Hannah, 77
Ariosto, Lodovico, 222
Aristotle, 12, 18–23, 25, 26, 34, 39, 47, 107, 119, 172, 207
Arnold, Matthew, 16, 37–39, 48, 83n, 96, 112, 137–139, 147, 184, 230
Artaud, Antonin, 245, 250, 263
Auden, W. H., 160
Auerbach, Erich, 234
Augustine, Saint, 79
Austin, J. L., 54

Bacon, Francis, 118
Bakhtin, M. M., 223
Ballanche, Pierre, 206
Baudelaire, Charles, 142, 256–263, 265
Baumgarten, Alexander, 43, 44
Beatles, 221
Bell, Clive, 13–14, 15, 18, 24, 25
Bernhardt, Sarah, 95
Blake, William, 34, 93–94, 98, 100, 141, 168, 186, 204, 206, 207–208, 220, 221

Boccaccio, Giovanni, 162
Bodkin, Maud, 95
Boileau-Despreaux, Nicolas, 124, 252–253
Bridges, Robert Seymour, 200–201
Brooks, Cleanth, 34, 209
Browne, Sir Thomas, 143, 146
Buber, Martin, 82
Bunuel, Luis, 201–202
Burke, Edmund, 140, 175, 183
Burke, Kenneth, 209
Burkhardt, Sigurd, 209
Butler, Samuel, 192
Byron, George Gordon Noel, Lord, 96

Caedmon, 235
Caesar, Julius, 143, 147, 164
Calderón de la Barca, Pedro, 130
Carlyle, Thomas, 95, 153
Céline, Louis-Ferdinand, 170
Cervantes Saavedra, Miguel de, 205, 223
Chapman, George, 116
Charles II, 102
Chatterton, Thomas, 221
Chaucer, Geoffrey, 38, 39, 224
Chesterton, G. K., 176
Chomsky, Noam, 232
Cicero, 119
Claudel, Paul Louis Charles, 169–170
Clout, Colin, 227, 228, 235

271

Index

Coleridge, Samuel Taylor, 25, 26–30, 33, 38, 94, 124, 125, 140
Copernicus, Nicolaus, 113
Cournot, Antoine, 230, 234
Cromwell, Thomas, 228–229
Curtius, E. R., 231

Dante Alighieri, 38, 42, 126, 130, 137, 205, 222
Darwin, Charles, 175
Degas, Hilaire Germain Edgar, 178
Della Mirandola, Pico, 123
de Man, Paul, 219n
Derby, Countess Dowager of, 226, 227, 228, 229
Derrida, Jacques, 263
Dickinson, Emily, 192
Dilthey, Wilhelm, 62–64, 80
Don Juan, 75, 78, 89
Donne, John, 34
Don Quixote, 143, 224
Dylan, Bob, 193

Eliot, T. S., 25, 96, 97, 102, 111, 121, 140, 200–201, 205, 208
Elizabeth II, 163
Emerson, Ralph Waldo, 234
Empson, William, 208
Engels, Friedrich, 81, 177
Erasmus, Desiderius, 111, 173

Fellini, Federico, 201–202
Flaubert, Gustave, 140
Fontenelle, Bernard Le Bovier de, 253–256, 265
France, Anatole, 16
Freud, Sigmund, 100, 142, 169
Frye, Northrop, 201, 203–206, 207

Gibbon, Edward, 193
Gloriana, 227, 235
Godard, Jean-Luc, 201–203, 225
Goethe, Johann Wolfgang, 95, 126, 245
Goldmann, Lucien, 199
Gosson, Stephen, 114–115, 118–119
Graves, Robert, 125
Guevara, Che, 156
Gurdjieff, 160
Guys, Constantin, 256–261

Hampshire, Stuart, 35, 37, 40–41

Harvey, Gabriel, 122, 223
Hassan, Ihab, 204
Hayley, William, 98
Hegel, Georg Wilhelm Friedrich von, 80, 171, 210, 219
Heidegger, Martin, 191
Heilman, Robert, 34
Heraclitus, 118
Herder, Johann Gottfried von, 224, 231
Hirsch, E. D., 50–52
Homer, 38, 103, 115, 116, 117, 125, 147, 252
Hopkins, Gerard Manley, 120, 169–170
Horace, 25
Housman, A. E., 77, 85, 210
Hulme, T. E., 41–42, 140
Husserl, Edmund, 219
Huxley, Aldous, 54
Hythlodaye, 181

Ishmael, 85–86, 88

James, Henry, 204
Jauss, Hans Robert, 198
Jefferson, Thomas, 126, 155, 156
Jesus, 110, 137, 145, 146, 163, 167
Johnson, Samuel, 48
Julian the Apostate, 164
Jung, Carl, 169, 220

Kant, Immanuel, 25, 45–46, 93, 181
Keats, John, 140, 211, 213–217, 219, 221, 224, 247
Kennick, William E., 8, 10, 11, 35, 40–41
Kierkegaard, Sören, 75, 110, 139–140, 156, 161, 170–171, 190
King, Edward, 98
Kipling, Rudyard, 126
Knight, G. Wilson, 34
Krauss, Werner, 197–198, 199, 202, 205

Lawrence, D. H., 96, 124, 125
Leibnitz, Gottfried Wilhelm von, 44, 232
Lenin, 126, 163
Leporello, 75, 78, 89, 161
Lévi-Strauss, Claude, 201, 206–207, 208

Lewis, Wyndham, 125, 140, 159
Lincoln, Abraham, 126, 155
Liu Shao-Chi, 111
Locke, John, 180, 182
Longinus, 25, 39
Lucretius, 192
Luther, Martin, 173

McLuhan, Marshall, 99–100, 101, 118, 161
Malinowski, Bronislaw, 208
Mallarmé, Stéphane, 140, 212, 213
Malraux, André, 234
Mann, Thomas, 224
Mannheim, Karl, 59, 60
Mao Tse-tung, 126, 159
Marcel, Gabriel, 77
Marcus Aurelius, 111–112
Marvell, Andrew, 228
Marx, Karl, 80, 81, 111, 115, 126, 142, 210
Melville, Herman, 86n
Merleau-Ponty, Maurice, 87
Michelet, Jules, 222
Mill, John Stuart, 63, 64, 184
Miller, Arthur, 22–23
Miller, J. Hillis, 86n
Milton, John, 42, 60, 98, 137, 144, 149, 167, 168, 171, 210, 211, 215, 216, 217, 221, 222, 225–229
Mnemosyne, 214, 216, 221
Moore, G. E., 3
More, Sir Thomas, 180, 181, 182
Moritz, Karl Philipp, 44
Morris, William, 141
Mozart, 140, 202; see also Leporello

Newman, John Henry, 138, 184
Newmann, Erich, 220
Newton, Sir Isaac, 126
Nietzsche, Friedrich, 137, 242–250, 255, 256, 257, 265, 267
Novalis, 242

Odysseus, 86n
Ong, Reverend Walter, 82n
Origen, 111
Orpheus, 115, 123, 202
Orwell, George, 54
Ovid, 106, 113
Owen, Robert, 111

Pascal, Blaise, 113
Paul, 147, 163
Peacock, Thomas Love, 115, 123–124, 125, 127–128, 132
Pearce, Roy Harvey, 89n
Perrault, Charles, 252, 255–256
Picon, Gaetan, 78
Pindar, 252
Plato, 19, 48, 118, 123, 131, 139, 180, 181, 182, 207, 209–210, 216, 219
Plotinus, 220
Pope, Alexander, 117, 124
Popper, Karl, 51
Pound, Ezra, 124, 125, 140, 155–156, 200–201
Pythagoras, 164

Quintillian, 119

Rabelais, François, 205, 222–223
Racine, Jean Baptiste, 199
Raleigh, Sir Walter, 95
Raphael, 167
Renan, Ernest, 145
Resnais, Alain, 201–202
Richard II, 102
Richards, I. A., 201, 208–210
Rickert, Heinrich, 63
Rilke, Rainer Maria, 140
Rimbaud, Arthur, 103, 142, 245, 250
Rivarol, Comte de, 232
Rousseau, Jean Jacques, 180, 182, 191, 243, 263
Russell, Bertrand, 3

Saint-Simon, Claude Henri, 111, 206
Schlegel, Friedrich, 242
Scot, Reverend David, 78
Seneca, 234
Shaftesbury, Anthony Ashley Cooper, Earl of, 44, 45
Shakespeare, William, 22, 28–29, 34, 38, 60, 70–71, 96, 121, 165–166, 212, 223, 224
Shelley, Percy Bysshe, 34, 100, 114–115, 124, 126, 127–133, 137, 191
Sidney, Sir Philip, 114–115, 116, 118–122, 124, 127, 128, 131–133, 147, 158, 191
Simmel, Georg, 76
Snow, C. P., 132, 179

Index

Socrates, 40, 131, 139, 181, 182, 210
Sorel, Georges, 114
Spenser, Edmund, 122, 216, 223, 224, 227, 228
Spitzer, Leo, 100
Staiger, Emil, 242
Stendhal, 87
Stevens, Wallace, 160, 166
Stevenson, C. L., 6, 10

Tennyson, Alfred, Lord, 34
Thoreau, Henry David, 155, 156, 222
Tillich, Paul, 105–106
Trilling, Lionel, 48
Trotsky, Leon, 111
Truffaut, François, 201–202

Van Gennep, Arnold, 212
Van Gogh, Vincent, 178
Velikowski, 160
Vico, Giambattista, 104, 106, 123
Virgil, 228
Vivaldi, Antonio, 116
Voltaire, 205

Warren, Austin, 197
Warren, Robert Penn, 75
Weber, Max, 65
Weil, Eric, 86n
Weitz, Morris, 4, 5–11, 15–17, 26, 28, 30–32, 35, 41–42
Wellek, René, 197
Wells, H. G., 175–176
Wheelwright, Philip, 34
Whewell, William, 62–63, 64
Whitehead, Alfred North, 52
Whitman, Walt, 155
Windelband, Wilhelm, 63, 64
Wittgenstein, Ludwig, 3–5, 8, 12–13, 16, 24, 26, 30–31, 46, 53, 54, 164
Woolf, Virginia, 204
Wordsworth, William, 34, 42, 96, 124, 210, 215, 216, 217, 219, 220

Yeats, William Butler, 100, 125, 127, 160, 161, 200–201, 213, 221–222
Yu, Beongcheon, 85

Ziff, Paul, 41

Library of Congress Cataloging in Publication Data
(For library cataloging purposes only)
Main entry under title:

In search of literary theory.

  (Studies in the humanities)
  Five of the essays originally appeared in the Spring 1970 issue of Daedalus.
  Includes bibliographical references.
    1. Criticism—Addresses, essays, lectures. 2. Literature—History and criti-
cism—Theory, etc.—Addresses, essays, lectures. I. Abrams, Meyer Howard.
  II. Bloomfield, Morton Wilfred, date.   ed. III. Daedalus. IV. Series.
PN85.15   801'95   70-38119
ISBN 0-8014-0714-1